XENOPHON'S

The Expedition of Cyrus

OXFORD APPROACHES TO

CLASSICAL LITERATURE

SERIES EDITORS
Kathleen Coleman and Richard Rutherford

OVID's *Metamorphoses*
ELAINE FANTHAM

PLATO's *Symposium*
RICHARD HUNTER

CAESAR's *Civil War*
WILLIAM W. BATSTONE
CYNTHIA DAMON

POLYBIUS' *Histories*
BRIAN C. McGING

TACITUS' *Annals*
RONALD MELLOR

XENOPHON's *Anabasis,* OR *The Expedition of Cyrus*
MICHAEL A. FLOWER

XENOPHON'S
Anabasis, OR
The Expedition
of Cyrus

MICHAEL A. FLOWER

OXFORD
UNIVERSITY PRESS

OXFORD

UNIVERSITY PRESS

Oxford University Press, Inc., publishes works that further
Oxford University's objective of excellence
in research, scholarship, and education.

Oxford   New York
Auckland   Cape Town   Dar es Salaam   Hong Kong   Karachi
Kuala Lumpur   Madrid   Melbourne   Mexico City   Nairobi
New Delhi   Shanghai   Taipei   Toronto

With offices in
Argentina   Austria   Brazil   Chile   Czech Republic   France   Greece
Guatemala   Hungary   Italy   Japan   Poland   Portugal   Singapore
South Korea   Switzerland   Thailand   Turkey   Ukraine   Vietnam

Copyright © 2012 by Oxford University Press, Inc.

Published by Oxford University Press, Inc.
198 Madison Avenue, New York, NY 10016

www.oup.com

Oxford is a registered trademark of Oxford University Press in the
UK and in certain other countries

Library of Congress Cataloging-in-Publication Data
Flower, Michael A.
Xenophon's Anabasis, or, the Expedition of Cyrus / Michael Flower.
p.   cm.
Includes bibliographical references and index.
ISBN 978-0-19-518867-7 (hardcover); ISBN 978-0-19-518868-4 (paperback)
1. Xenophon. Anabasis.
2. Greece—History—Expedition of Cyrus, 401 B.C.—Historiography.
3. Iran—History—To 640—Historiography.
4. Cyrus, the Younger, d. 401 B.C. I. Title.
PA4494.A7F56   2012
935'.05092—dc23   2011041403

1 3 5 7 9 8 6 4 2

Printed in the United States of America
on acid-free paper

For Isabel and Rosalind Flower

Editors' Foreword

The late twentieth and early twenty-first centuries have seen a massive expansion in courses dealing with ancient civilization and, in particular, the culture and literature of the Greek and Roman world. Never has there been such a flood of good translations available: Oxford's own World Classics, the Penguin Classics, the Hackett Library, and other series offer the English-speaking reader access to the masterpieces of classical literature from Homer to Augustine. The reader may, however, need more guidance in the interpretation and understanding of these works than can usually be provided in the relatively short introduction that prefaces a work in translation. There is a need for studies of individual works that will provide a clear, lively, and reliable account based on the most up-to-date scholarship without dwelling on the minutiae that are likely to distract or confuse the reader.

It is to meet this need that the present series has been devised. The title *Oxford Approaches to Classical Literature* deliberately puts the emphasis on the literary works themselves. The volumes in this series will each be concerned with a single work (with the exception of cases where a "book" or larger collection of poems is treated as one work). These are neither biographies nor accounts of literary movements or schools. Nor are they books devoted to the total oeuvre of one author: our first volumes consider Ovid's *Metamorphoses* and Plato's *Symposium*, not the works of Ovid or Plato as a whole. This is, however, a question of emphasis, and not a straitjacket: biographical issues, literary and cultural background, and related works by the same author are discussed where they are obviously relevant. Authors have also been encouraged to consider the influence and legacy of the works in question.

As the editors of this series, we intend these volumes to be accessible to the reader who is encountering the relevant work for the first time; but we also intend that each volume should do more than simply provide the basic facts, dates, and summaries that handbooks generally supply. We would like these books to be essays in criticism and interpretation that will do justice to the subtlety and complexity of the works under discussion. With this in mind, we have invited leading scholars to offer personal assessments and appreciations of their chosen works, anchored within the mainstream of classical scholarship. We have thought it particularly important that our authors be allowed to set their own agendas and to speak in their own voices rather than repeating the *idées reçues* of conventional wisdom in neutral tones.

The title *Oxford Approaches to Classical Literature* has been chosen simply because the series is published by Oxford University Press, USA; it in no way implies a party line, either Oxonian or any other. We believe that different approaches are suited to different texts, and we expect each volume to have its own distinctive character. Advanced critical theory is neither compulsory nor excluded; what matters is whether it can be made to illuminate the text in question. The authors have been encouraged to avoid obscurity and jargon, bearing in mind the needs of the general reader; but, when important critical or narratological issues arise, they are presented to the reader as lucidly as possible.

This series was originally conceived by Professor Charles Segal, an inspiring scholar and teacher whose intellectual energy and range of interests were matched by a corresponding humility and generosity of spirit. Although he was involved in the commissioning of a number of volumes, he did not—alas—live to see any of them published. The series is intended to convey something of the excitement and pleasure to be derived from reading the extraordinarily rich and varied literature of Greco-Roman antiquity. We hope that these volumes will form a worthy monument to a dedicated classical scholar who was committed to enabling the ancient texts to speak to the widest possible audience in the contemporary world.

Kathleen Coleman, Harvard University
Richard Rutherford, Christ Church, Oxford

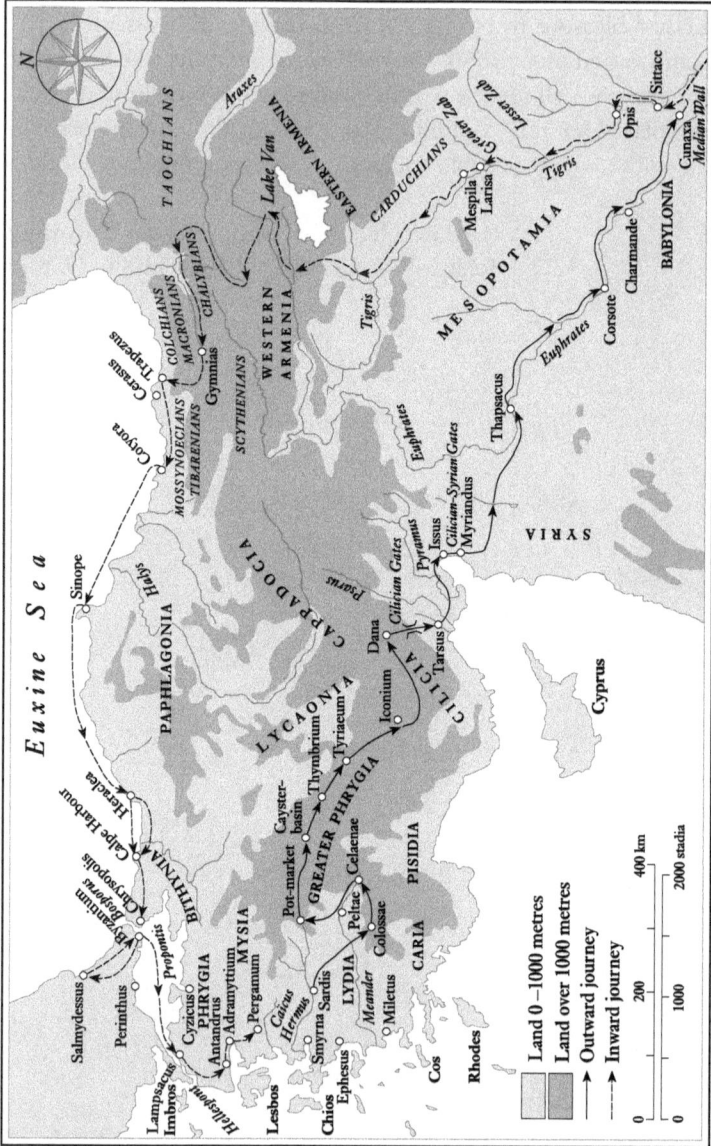

THE MARCH OF THE TEN THOUSAND

Land 0–1000 metres
Land over 1000 metres
Outward journey
Inward journey

Preface

The *Expedition of Cyrus* is an English version of the ancient Greek title *Anabasis* (which means "a march inland"). Although the subject matter is indeed the expedition of Cyrus, a Persian prince, I will use the Greek title throughout this book, since that is the one by which it is most commonly known. I first heard the name of Xenophon and was introduced to his *Anabasis* in the fall of my sophomore year at the University of California at Berkeley. Xenophon famously brought back his fellow Greeks to safety from the brink of total disaster; comparing great things to small, I am not ashamed to admit that he did the same for me. I had a very rough introduction to classical Greek during my freshman year. At the start of my sophomore year, I was simultaneously introduced to the best teacher of the ancient Greek language I have ever had, the late W. K. Pritchett, and to the Greek writer who would always remain my favorite author. When I was invited to contribute a book on the *Anabasis* to this series, I saw it as an opportunity both to fulfill an ambition of my youth and, in a sense, to discharge a debt.

There are many good translations of the *Anabasis*, and an especially readable one is the brilliantly evocative rendition by Robin Waterfield (2005) in the series Oxford World's Classics. Nonetheless,

I have provided my own translations throughout this book, for every act of translation is also an act of interpretation. I have also attempted to attain a proper balance between readability and accuracy, a thing that can be immensely difficult to achieve, even for experienced translators.

Since pagination differs between translations, I have cited the *Anabasis* throughout by book, chapter, and section numbers. The Greek text is divided into seven books, each of which corresponds to one ancient papyrus roll. This system of tripartite division by book, chapter, and section is universal to all Greek editions of the *Anabasis* and to almost all translations (the Penguin translation omits section numbers). But the reader should also be forewarned that differences between translations reflect not only the tastes and skill of translators, but also differences in the Greek texts of various scholarly editions of the *Anabasis*. The problem is that our medieval manuscripts of the *Anabasis* do not always agree, and thus translations can differ accordingly. Even a minor discrepancy, say in the spelling of a verb (since tense is indicated by verb forms), can affect the meaning of a sentence. In one place, moreover, the manuscripts differ as to whether a short speech is given by "Theopompus" or by "Xenophon" (2.1.12), and the choice between them has significant implications for the interpretation of a range of issues. I have consulted both the Oxford Classical Text (Marchant 1904, which is still in print), and the more recent, and more reliable, revised Teubner text (Hude 1972; not in print). The Loeb Classical Library edition by John Dillery (2001) is mainly based on the revised Teubner text, and has a very accurate facing English translation. These various editions and translations are listed in the bibliography.

Despite the ready availability of affordable translations, I would urge anyone who has a passion for Xenophon to read his works in the original ancient Greek. Xenophon is the easiest of the classical Greek prose writers for the beginning student of the language: his style is clear and crisp, as well as being vivid and eloquent. After a few months to a year of study of classical Greek, it is possible to read the *Anabasis* in an annotated edition (that is, one with notes and vocabulary). I highly recommend the edition of books 1–4 that served me extremely well as an undergraduate and that I have taught from many times: *Xenophon's Anabasis: Books I–IV*, edited by Maurice W. Mather and Joseph William Hewitt (University of Oklahoma Press, 1979).

As an aide to the general reader, I have explained unfamiliar terms on their first occurrence, and there is a glossary of frequently mentioned individuals at the back of the book. A particular point of confusion might be my use of the name Lacedaemonian(s), where, less accurately, most translators might simply write Spartan(s). Although these terms are often used synonymously in modern works, the technical difference is that a Spartan (or, more correctly, Spartiate) was a full citizen with voting rights who had passed through a very rigid system of state education, whereas the term Lacedaemonian included both the Spartiates themselves and the second-class members of their society called *perioeci* (who were freeborn but lacked voting rights: the word literally means "those who dwell nearby"). These two groups together formed the "Spartan" army and were collectively known as "Lacedaemonians." In the *Anabasis,* it is not always clear to which category someone belongs, since Xenophon, like other classical authors, mostly used the term Lacedaemonian. Dractonius is the only character explicitly called a Spartiate, although Clearchus and Cheirisophus must have been full citizens, too; and Dexippus is the only one called a *perioecus* (although Neon was also assuredly in that category).

I was able to complete this book thanks to a sabbatical leave from Princeton University followed by a Fellowship from the Loeb Classical Library Foundation. This support came at a critical time. I am grateful to my editors, Kathleen Coleman and Richard Rutherford, for the invitation to contribute to this series and for their numerous improvements to my manuscript. My former teacher George Cawkwell was always ready to answer all sorts of random questions. Christopher Pelling, as always, pushed me in new directions. John Marincola shared his insights and discussed my ideas with me whenever asked, and I am in his debt for encouraging me to undertake this project. My copy editor, Martha Ramsey, applied her considerable talents to improving my prose. Harriet Flower read and commented on the entire manuscript, as did my daughter Isabel Flower (who, along with her sister Rosalind, also assisted me in other ways too numerous to mention). Needless to say, all errors that remain are my own.

Contents

Xenophon's *Anabasis*, or *The Expedition of Cyrus*

Introduction

In Walter Hill's controversial 1979 movie *The Warriors* (which was adapted from the 1965 novel of the same name by Sol Yurick), a gang from Coney Island called the Warriors is invited to attend a massive rally twenty-seven miles away. All the big gangs in the city will be there, and Cyrus, the leader of one of them, plans to consolidate the various bands of street criminals under his benevolent rule. Unfortunately, Cyrus is assassinated, and in the resulting chaos the Warriors are blamed for the murder. The leader of the Warriors is also killed, and under a new untested leader they must make it back home with both the police and every gang in the city looking for them.

Any correspondence between this synopsis and Xenophon's *Anabasis* is strictly *not* coincidental. In 401 BC, Cyrus, a young and charismatic Persian prince, enlisted more than ten thousand Greek mercenaries in his quest to secure the vast Persian empire for himself by overthrowing his brother, the reigning king. The Athenian aristocrat Xenophon was among those Greeks. Cyrus was killed in a great battle. Most of the Greek commanders subsequently fell victim to treachery and were executed. Xenophon found himself in the position of taking charge and leading the band of mercenaries all the way from the vicinity of Babylon back to the Greek cities in Turkey. Their attempt to reach the sea turned into a desperate but also heroic journey, as they struggled to cross mountains, rivers, and plains in the face of numerous enemies.

One wonders how many viewers of Walter Hill's "cult" film realize his artistic debt to a book written in the fourth century BC. A hundred years ago, it would not have been difficult for many, perhaps most, educated English speakers to recognize the allusions. Such is no longer the case. Appreciation of the *Anabasis* both as literature and as history has suffered greatly from its use as a school text in the nineteenth century and the beginning and the middle of the twentieth. In Princeton University's Firestone Library, in the section reserved for "old" texts, the passerby is suddenly confronted by an entire wall of shelves devoted to school commentaries on Xenophon's *Anabasis*. The same experience could be repeated in academic libraries throughout the world. Between 1820 and 1980, approximately 120 different school editions were published with text in ancient Greek and modern commentary in various languages, although primarily in English (fifty-four) and German (forty-three). The *Anabasis* was *the* basic text for beginners in the study of Attic Greek from the early nineteenth century through the middle of the twentieth (see Rijksbaron 2002). When the coeducational Institute for Colored Youth was established in Philadelphia in 1837, one of its purposes was to provide a classical education to African-American students; the two Greek texts selected for study were the New Testament and Xenophon's *Anabasis*.

It was only relatively recently, in fact, that Xenophon was mostly dropped from the college curriculum, replaced by authors (primarily Plato) who, quite wrongly, were deemed to be more in accord with the interests of today's students. Nonetheless, the cultural biases that have marginalized the text as an adventure story for adolescent boys can be dispelled by innovative methods of literary criticism that pose new questions and reconfigure traditional ones. The *Anabasis* deserves to be read more widely, not only because it is the most important autobiographical narrative to have survived from ancient Greece but also because the narratological and rhetorical strategies that shape the text are as sophisticated as those employed by any other classical prose writer.

There are indeed themes in the *Anabasis* that may seem all too relevant for a modern reader. In Herodotus's *Histories*, the tyrannical Xerxes crosses boundaries, literal and figurative, and is defeated by the freedom-loving Greeks, but in the *Anabasis* it is the Greeks who transgress. They are misled by a charismatic foreigner (Cyrus) who conceals the true purpose of the expedition and then plays down the level of resistance to be expected. Cyrus wishes to depose his brother, King Artaxerxes, and in order to convince the Greeks to follow him, he must mislead them. But when Cyrus is killed and the Greeks find themselves leaderless—near Babylon, in modern Iraq—their encounter with "the other" turns into a long, grueling march back to the Greek cities of Asia Minor. Themes of central importance to Xenophon's contemporary audience are explored along the way: the qualities of good leadership, the relationships between Greeks and barbarians and among the Greeks themselves, and the ways the gods communicate with humans and intervene in their affairs. Moreover, these themes are expressed no less profoundly than in the works of other classical authors who are currently more widely read. That judgment, though it might seem hyperbolic, would not have surprised Renaissance readers, some of whom (such as Edmund Spenser in his introduction to *The Faerie Queene*) ranked Xenophon even above Plato.

Xenophon's other writings share some of the same thematic concerns. Since he was a philosopher and a historian as well as a professional soldier, all too often his many works are examined in isolation because they fall into different genres that now come under the purview of different academic specializations. In what follows, I shall stress the connections with these other writings, and especially with another highly influential work, the *Cyropaedia* (or "The education of Cyrus"), a philosophical romance about an earlier Cyrus, the founder of the Persian empire.

Since this book is primarily a literary study, it is important to say something about theory. Here my methodological approach is eclectic, consisting of a historically informed close reading that pays particular attention to rhetorical and narrative strategies. As a critic of literature, I strongly believe in the necessity of "fluid and flexible modes of literary interpretation" (Davis and Womack 2002: 156) that, in particular, combine formalist criticism with reader response theory. By formalism I mean the study of the specific formal structures that will determine, at least in part, a given reader's response to a text. Reader-response theory, on the other hand, recognizes that every reader has preconceived notions and particular life experiences that will determine how he or she interprets a text's formal structures and assigns them meaning. At the same time, as a historian, I believe equally strongly in the value of situating a text within its unique historical and cultural context (a method sometimes called "new historicism"). Cultural context is indeed important. Even though modern readers will approach the *Anabasis* with their own "horizon of expectations" (that is, they will interpret it in light of their own experiences), those horizons can be enlarged. At the same time, the *Anabasis* has its own independent integrity as a self-contained work of literature. Although we cannot be sure of Xenophon's personal intentions and motivations, the story is told in a certain way and from a particular point of view. My goal is to provide as multifaceted an exploration of the *Anabasis* as I am able.

There are several different levels of meaning in the *Anabasis*. Some of those levels are surely a result of authorial intent, and it would be perverse to claim otherwise; but other levels are suggested by events that have transpired since the time of writing and are a function of readers' experiences, both individual and collective. The *Anabasis* reflects cultural values and ideologies, but it also played a role in shaping, perpetuating, and altering them. So while close readings are valuable in order to appreciate the *Anabasis* as a work of literature with its own internal coherence, it is essential to bear in mind that it is not an autonomous or self-sufficient verbal artifact. It is implicated not only in Xenophon's other writings but also in the entire political, social, cultural, and ideological world of which he was a part. In other words, the *Anabasis* is both a unique work of creative art and a text that is part of a much larger network of cultural productions. Other texts are tied to the *Anabasis* by an intricate web of influence and allusion. While a literary text may *seem* to inhabit its own self-sufficient and autonomous world, it actually is part of a textual neighborhood. In the case of the *Anabasis*, the closest neighbors will be Xenophon's various other writings. The *Iliad* and *Odyssey* inhabit one of the outer edges of this textual community. At another edge lie the cultural productions of the twentieth century and beyond (such as the film *The Warriors* and a forthcoming remake) that have been influenced by the *Anabasis* and that may in turn influence how we read it in the future.

Whatever else it may be or may mean, the *Anabasis* is an attempt to influence the social memory, or collective memory, of Xenophon's expedition both among his contemporaries and in future generations. It did not take long for the exploit of the Ten Thousand to make an impression on the Greek world. But were the Ten Thousand undisciplined brigands and was Xenophon a self-serving, profit-seeking, backstabbing mercenary commander? Or were they a well-disciplined and cohesive force of the better sort of people (6.4.8), led by an unwilling commander whom Zeus himself had selected to bring them to safety? The truth is probably irrecoverable. Attempts to get at the "true story" of what actually happened by reading between the lines of the *Anabasis* and by rationalizing its narrative are likely to tell us more about the cleverness of modern scholars than about the events of 401–399 BC.

What we can do with some hope of success is to analyze the way Xenophon tells the story and how he constructs his own role and self-image within the narrative. Whether he is telling the whole truth, some of the truth, or none of the truth is for each reader of the *Anabasis* to decide for herself or himself. The most important thing is that the reader enjoy the story and appreciate the literary art that has created it, and perhaps learn something of value from the lessons that Xenophon is attempting to teach by example. There are of course actions that lie behind Xenophon's representation of them. But it is an illusion that one can move from the representation back to the reality, even if one's imagination can conjure up the scenes that Xenophon relates as if they were taking place just as he describes them. Ultimately, what we have is the representation, and the mark of a great work of literature is that it can stand alone as something timeless, even when divorced from its historical context and contemporary audience. It is the representation of the story, rather than a positivist reconstruction of the facts that lie behind it, that will be of primary concern to me.

Yet it is only natural for most of us to wonder about the truth of Xenophon's story, and surely its perceived veracity influences our appreciation of the *Anabasis* as a work of literature. So to dismiss the question of historicity *tout court* both runs counter to our curiosity about what really happened in the past—even if we can only hope to retrieve it in a very partial way—and diminishes our literary appreciation of the text. In other words, in order to fully appreciate what Xenophon is doing with the narrative and how he is interacting with the expectations of his intended audiences, we need to know what his contemporaries thought and said about the same events. That leads to the further question how and why Xenophon's account differs from other accounts; and, as soon as that issue is raised, we are already pondering whose account was the truer one. It is not sufficient simply to conclude that Xenophon's version differed from other versions and that he sought to impose his version of events on posterity. We must also consider whether, and to what extent, his account attempts self-consciously either to falsify or to correct what he believed had taken place according to his recollection of his own experiences. The question of historical veracity cannot be completely neglected. It is only in the academic's study that all versions of an event are equally true. In real life, we demand an accounting.

The conventions of historical writing, whether modern or ancient, are not as transparent as they may seem. It would surely be an exaggeration to say that ancient historians were *more* concerned with verisimilitude (resemblance or likeness to reality) than with attempting to portray events as they actually happened. But it would be perfectly fair to say that they were as interested in making the story seem true as they were in making it factually accurate. In fact, all historians, or at least those who have any pretensions to literary merit, strive to make the storyline clear, crisp, tight, convincing, and engaging. To do so might entail rearranging the order of events, omitting some details while embellishing others, and adding speeches in direct quotation even when the precise words that were spoken cannot actually be known or remembered.

Although such artistic license may be employed simply for the sake of making the story more appealing, it is never morally neutral. For artistic license can simultaneously serve the purpose of giving greater emphasis to particular themes or putting the actions of certain characters, including the author, in a better light. Thucydides, whom many consider the most exacting of the Greek historians in the pursuit of factual accuracy, certainly engages in various kinds of distortions for a variety of purposes, some literary and thematic, others as a type of disinformation. Once, when writing up a certain incident in my life, I found myself *almost* unconsciously changing the chronological order of two events, both because it made for a crisper storyline and because it made me look better. We cannot expect either Xenophon or any other historian to give us a fully transparent and unmediated window into the past.

Rather than offering a definitive, hegemonic reading of the *Anabasis*, my intention is to open up different possible readings. I would like to signpost for readers various interpretative pathways that they can explore on their own as they read and think about the text. I have read the *Anabasis* many times in Greek and a few times in English, and with each reading I see something new in the text, a different nuance, message, connection, or meaning. No single reading, not even a personal one, can ever really be definitive.

I am not advocating, however, a parity of readings. It is necessary to persuade others of the pertinence of a particular interpretation by pointing to passages, sentences, and even individual words that support it (Culler 1997: 65). Moreover, a literary work itself imposes some logical constraints on how we interpret it and exercises a degree of determinacy over how we respond to it (Eagleton 1996: 72–78). So, even though a text may mean different things to different readers and those "meanings" may be quite independent of what the original author intended to convey, all readings are not equally valid. I hope that this book will benefit present and future readers of the *Anabasis* by expanding their "horizon of expectations" (Culler 1997: 63) and thus helping them to see and understand dimensions of the story they otherwise might have missed. For even if interpretation is ultimately subjective, it is still the case that knowledge of the historical and cultural background, as well as of Xenophon's life and other writings, will enhance the way one approaches, appreciates, and interprets this particular work.

The reception of the *Anabasis* (from antiquity until the present) is an immense topic in itself and the subject of two superbly detailed studies (Rood 2004a, 2010b). This vast subject can only be touched on in this book, and it is treated throughout rather than in a single chapter at the end. Nonetheless, one of the most interesting things about the *Anabasis* is the way its meaning, as well as the use to which the text has been put, has changed over time in relation to changing circumstances. It is important to stress that different communities of readers have seen very different things in the text. In an article in a 1935 issue of *Classical Weekly*, the scholar R. C. Horn complained, "Many in these latter days, when pacifism is fashionable, belittle Xenophon and the *Anabasis* as a war book which will rouse war feeling among the young." Twenty years later, in the same journal, another scholar (Anne Kingsbury) wrote, "One thought especially permeates the work, in every speech and action—the cruelty and suffering brought by war to the army, to the civilians, and to able leaders. It is a subsidiary thought, perhaps, but always present—as it is in [Euripides's] *Troades* and *Phoenissae*." Is the *Anabasis* antiwar or prowar, a book that will rouse the young to fight wars or to seek peace? Surely the answer, to a greater or lesser degree, depends on the personal experience and ideological orientation of the interpreter. In our current historical moment, the antiwar interpretation seems to have special resonance. In the *New York Times* of February 4, 2007, the journalist Nicholas D. Kristof, in an op-ed article entitled "Under Bush's Pillow," claimed that he had received "400 comments from readers offering literary or historical parallels to the Bush administration and Iraq. One of the most commonly cited was Xenophon's ancient warning, in *Anabasis*, of how much easier it is to get into a Middle Eastern war than out. . . . Xenophon's subtext is how the slog of war corrodes soldiers and allows them to do terrible things." If the *Anabasis*, however, were merely a text that could teach us a lesson about war and peace, it would be one of countless such books. There must be some other quality that explains its enduring popularity from antiquity to the present.

After Leo Tolstoy finished his monumental novel *War and Peace* in 1870, he taught himself ancient Greek, apparently looking for a diversion, and within a few months had read all of the *Anabasis*. He later claimed that this work, together with Homer's *Odyssey* and *Iliad*, had made a very great impact on him (Lane Fox 2004a: 2–3). What might this impact have been, which has made itself felt by so many individuals from Xenophon's time till our own? As a schoolboy at Eton, the future theologian E. B. Pusey read the whole of the *Anabasis* in less than a week when confined to bed with a bad foot (Rood 2004a: 43). A few years later, in a letter dated January 5, 1821, Lord Byron read it while visiting Italy and when not in bed: "Read Mitford's History of Greece—Xenophon's Retreat of the Ten Thousand. . . . Clock strikes—going out to make love. Somewhat perilous, but not Disagreeable." Tolstoy, Pusey, Byron—why did they (and so many others before and after them) decide to spend their time with this particular book when so many others, both ancient and modern, were at hand? Simply put, the *Anabasis* has had a lasting appeal because it speaks across time and space to the interests and imaginations of successive generations of readers, and can sustain various different readings, despite its apparently simple narrative surface.

Xenophon was a favorite with the Romans because they found him both easy to read and full of practical advice on issues ranging from warfare to hunting to household management. So when Mark Antony, during his disastrous Parthian campaign, kept exclaiming "O the Ten Thousand!" his fellow soldiers would immediately have caught the allusion (Plutarch, *Antony* 45). Nonetheless, the *Anabasis* did not become Xenophon's most famous book until fairly recently. Among the Romans and during the Renaissance as well, pride of place was given to the *Cyropaedia*, since it seemed to offer such useful paradigms of behavior for statesmen and monarchs. Scipio Africanus the Younger is reported by Cicero to have kept a copy of it with him at all times (*Letter to His Brother Quintus* 1.1.23; *Tusculan*

Disputations 2.62). During the eighteenth century, Xenophon's most popular work was the *Memorabilia* (or "Conversations with Socrates"). The *Anabasis*, by contrast, although highly esteemed in the eighteenth century, only came to be generally regarded as Xenophon's "masterpiece" in the nineteenth.

In the twentieth century, Xenophon's reputation as a historian declined as the accuracy of his *Hellenica* (a history of Greece from 411 to 362 BC) was increasingly questioned. Even if some have also questioned the truthfulness of the *Anabasis*, its graphic and stirring narrative and its status as a memoir of lived experience place it in a class of its own among the surviving examples of classical Greek prose literature. The judgment of Edward Gibbon, that luminous historian, well expresses the sentiment of modern times. In volume 2 of his *Decline and Fall of the Roman Empire* (1781, n. 115), Gibbon made his preference clear: "The *Cyropaedia* is vague and languid, the *Anabasis* circumstantial and animated. Such is the eternal difference between fiction and truth." Another illustrious historian, Lord Macaulay, also thought little of the *Cyropaedia* but came to have an extremely high opinion of the *Anabasis*. After reading it for the third time, he wrote at the end of his personal copy: "One of the very first works that antiquity has left us. Perfect in its kind.—October 9, 1837" (Trevelyan 1876: 475). Though I would not wish to slight the historical and philosophical importance of Xenophon's more purely didactic works, it is in the *Anabasis* that his life and ideas find their most perfect expression.

·1·

The *Anabasis* in Context

Anybody can make history. Only a great man can write it.
—*Oscar Wilde*, The Critic as Artist

Xenophon was taking a tremendous personal risk when he left his native city to follow a Persian prince on an adventure in a faraway land. Xenophon's Boeotian guest-friend (*xenos* in Greek), aptly named Proxenus ("patron"), invited Xenophon to join him on Cyrus's expedition (guest-friendship, *xenia*, was a ritualized relationship, involving reciprocal obligations, between elites from different communities). Proxenus made the striking assertion that "he considered Cyrus to be of greater importance to himself than his own homeland" (3.1.4). That is a truly extraordinary thing for a Greek to say about a non-Greek, or, in their parlance, about a "barbarian." Proxenus's enthusiasm partly reflects the mindset of an era in which mercenary service was becoming increasingly common, and partly too the remarkable charms of Cyrus the Younger (who had become a guest-friend both of Proxenus and of other elite Greeks: 1.1.10–11; 1.3.3). In Proxenus's obituary notice we are told that he undertook service with Cyrus "expecting that he would thus acquire considerable fame, great power, and a lot of money" (2.6.17).

Who was this Cyrus that he could inspire such hopes and such loyalty? His namesake Cyrus the Great (also referred to as Cyrus the Elder) had created the Persian Empire in the middle of the sixth century BC and was the subject of Xenophon's historical romance,

13

the *Cyropaedia* ("The Education of Cyrus"). Cyrus the Younger desired to become the second Persian king of that name. In 407 BC, when he was a mere seventeen, his father, King Darius II, had given him a huge satrapy (province) in Asia Minor (modern-day Turkey). Cyrus's mandate was to aid the Spartans in their long-drawn-out war with Athens (the Peloponnesian War of 431–404 BC). His successful intervention on Sparta's behalf culminated in the naval battle of Aegospotami in the autumn of 405, in which the Athenian navy was destroyed by a Peloponnesian fleet financed by Persian money.

Those events are narrated in the first two books of Xenophon's continuation of Thucydides, his *Hellenica*. The *Anabasis* tells the story of Cyrus's attempt in 401 BC, when he was twenty-three, to usurp the kingship from his brother Artaxerxes, who had become king after their father's death in the autumn of 405. Xenophon's account implies that Cyrus started his rebellion, and his quest for kingship, because King Artaxerxes had arrested him on a false charge of treason and would have put him to death, had not their mother, Parysatis, intervened (1.1.3). The biographer Plutarch, however, writing in the first century AD (but using earlier sources now lost to us), offers a different chronology and motive. Plutarch claims that Cyrus, with his mother's support, had hoped to be named Darius's successor and began to plot when he was passed over in favor of his older brother (*Artaxerxes* 2–3). Whatever the truth was, since Cyrus's satrapy included the coastal Greek cities of Ionia, it was possible for him to raise in secret a large force of Greek mercenaries, who are conventionally known as the "Ten Thousand." In actuality, they comprised some thirteen thousand fighting men, of whom about 10,600 were hoplites (heavy infantry armed with breastplate, greaves, sword, spear, and shield). Xenophon himself never calls them the Ten Thousand, a form of reference that is first attested centuries later. In the *Anabasis*, they are merely "the Greeks" or "the Greek army." In his *Hellenica* (3.2.7; 3.4.20) he twice refers to them as the "Cyreans" (that is, the soldiers employed by Cyrus).

If Cyrus had prevailed over Artaxerxes at the climax of his campaign against him, the famous battle of Cunaxa, and become king in his stead, the subsequent history of Greece, as well as of Persia, might have been very different. He might even now be as famous as Cyrus the Great. At the very least, the Spartans would have had a valuable ally, one personally indebted to their assistance, who undoubtedly would have supported their hegemony in mainland Greece. Cyrus had appealed to the Spartans to requite his aid to them during the war with Athens. The Spartans accordingly sent a fleet of warships to enable Cyrus's entry into Cilicia, as well as one of their own citizens, Cheirisophus, with seven hundred hoplites under his command (*Hellenica* 1.1.1–2; *Anabasis* 1.2.21–22; 1.4.2–3).

As it turned out, King Artaxerxes II (reigned 405–358) was long in forgiving Sparta for interfering in what was essentially a dynastic civil war. Not until 386 did he finally consent to a peace agreement (the so-called King's Peace), making a deal whereby he guaranteed Sparta control over mainland Greece in exchange for an acknowledgement of his possession of the Greek cities of Asia. Seen in this light, the battle of Cunaxa was an epoch-making confrontation. Its significance rivals that of Salamis and Plataea, the Greeks' decisive victories over the Persians during their invasion of Greece in 480–479 BC. Furthermore, Cunaxa was a fight Cyrus might have won, if Clearchus, the Greek general Cyrus most favored, had obeyed his orders, and if Cyrus, in the heat of battle, had not rashly charged straight for his brother, throwing his life away in the process.

The seven books (equivalent to seven ancient papyrus rolls) of the *Anabasis* may be loosely summarized as follows. In book 1 Cyrus, dishonored by his brother and desiring to become king in his stead, secretly gathers an army of mercenaries through the agency of a number of professional Greek soldiers who serve as the generals of his Greek contingents. Only one of them, the Spartan exile Clearchus, knows that Cyrus intends to attack the Persian king. When the rank and file learn the true purpose of the expedition, they are angry, but they decide nonetheless to follow Cyrus. His itinerary takes them from his provincial capital of Sardis in Lydia all the way to the vicinity of Babylon in modern Iraq, where his brother meets him in battle. (Xenophon himself does not mention the name of the place where the battle was fought; "Cunaxa" first appears in Plutarch's life of *Artaxerxes* at 8.2.) Although the

Greeks, who are stationed on the right wing of the army, rout the barbarians posted opposite them without suffering a single fatality, Cyrus himself, who commands the center, is killed. The narrative of the battle is interrupted by a lengthy obituary of Cyrus, which stresses his qualities as a leader.

After Cyrus's death, the Greek mercenaries find themselves stranded in the heart of the Persian Empire without much hope of escape (book 2). Refusing to surrender their arms, they conclude a treaty with the king. By the terms of the treaty, the Persian satrap Tissaphernes is supposed to escort them home, but this duplicitous satrap is able to take advantage of rivalries among the Greek generals, principally between Clearchus and the Thessalian Menon. After deceiving Clearchus with feigned overtures of friendship, Tissaphernes lures five of the Greeks' seven generals and twenty of their captains to a parley inside his tent. The captains are cut down while waiting outside; the generals are seized and sent to Artaxerxes, who has them beheaded. All of this is carried out on the assumption that leaderless men will quickly surrender.

Book 3 opens with the Greeks in a state of total despair. Tissaphernes, however, has not counted on the appearance of a young Athenian, a pupil of Socrates with innate qualities of leadership whose name is Xenophon. Xenophon is here given a formal introduction (although he has made cameo appearances in books 1 and 2), and the narrator explains that he had been invited to join the expedition by his guest-friend Proxenus, a Boeotian. Xenophon now rouses himself from a sleepless night and rallies the Greek army. The Greeks elect a new set of generals (to replace those who were seized), including him, despite the fact that he claims to have followed the expedition in a nonmilitary capacity. Making a heroic escape, the Greeks move up the Tigris River, where they are harassed by Tissaphernes and his Persian cavalry, and then (in book 4) into the mountains of Kurdistan and the snow-covered highlands of western Armenia.

Book 4 narrates the march of the Ten Thousand across central Anatolia. They catch their first glimpse of the sea from the top of Mount Theches (where they famously shout "The sea! The sea!")

and finally reach the Greek city Trapezus on the Black Sea. In fulfillment of a vow, the Greeks offer sacrifice to the gods and hold athletic contests. But their problems are far from over, and books 5–7 are hardly less exciting or fraught with danger than what precedes them.

In book 5 the army proceeds from Trapezus to Cotyora, where Xenophon gets into considerable trouble with the soldiers for planning to settle them in a colony on the coast of the Black Sea. The book ends with Xenophon addressing the problem of growing indiscipline in the army and defending himself on a charge of having hit some soldiers during the march through Armenia. Near the beginning of book 6, the soldiers decide that they would fare better under one supreme commander and offer the position to Xenophon, who turns it down in favor of the Spartan Cheirisophus. This proves to be a fortuitous decision on his part, since within a few days the army breaks up into three separate units as a result of ethnic tensions. Xenophon saves the Arcadian and Achaean contingent from annihilation, and the three units are reunited at Calpe Harbor. While at Calpe they get into a serious dispute with Cleander, the Spartan governor of Byzantium, who has sailed there to meet them, but Xenophon manages to negotiate an amicable settlement.

At the beginning of book 7, the Greeks arrive at Byzantium (modern Istanbul) on the Bosporus, only to find themselves distrusted by the Spartan admiral Anaxibius, who forces them out of Byzantium and attempts to coerce them into serving under Spartan command in the Chersonese (the Gallipoli peninsula). The Ten Thousand, outraged by this high-handed treatment, break into Byzantium and offer to make Xenophon "a great man," but he restrains them from plundering the city. On Xenophon's recommendation, the remnants of the Ten Thousand, some five to six thousand men (those who have survived war and disease and have not dispersed), undertake mercenary service with prince Seuthes of Thrace during the winter of 399. They help Seuthes regain his ancestral kingdom under harsh winter conditions. This almost proves Xenophon's undoing, since Seuthes fails to give the troops the pay he promised, and the soldiers in turn suspect that Xenophon has pocketed it, as well as bribes, for himself. Two long speeches, one before the assembled troops who are on the verge of stoning him to death and the other to Seuthes in private, provide a detailed defense of Xenophon's actions. These speeches convince the internal audience (although not always the external one) of Xenophon's innocence and good intentions.

Finally, the Spartans decide to hire the Cyreans for a war they have declared against the Persian satrap Tissaphernes (who has now taken control of the Greek cities of Ionia), offering the soldiers regular pay and the opportunity to punish their former enemy. The Ten Thousand decide to accept this offer. Xenophon, for his part, declines repeated offers to remain with Seuthes, despite warnings that the Spartans intend to execute him, and he puts off for the fifth time the opportunity to sail home to Athens. At the request of his friends in the army, Xenophon leads the Ten Thousand to their new commander, the Spartan general Thibron, in western Asia Minor. The *Anabasis* then ends with a short episode in which Xenophon finally escapes poverty by capturing a rich Persian grandee along with his family and possessions. Two years after setting out with Cyrus from Sardis in February or early March 401 BC, having traversed two thousand miles, the Greek mercenaries find themselves back in the region where they had started out and once again at war with the Persian king and his agent the satrap Tissaphernes.

We do not know if Xenophon himself called his book the "Anabasis" or if he gave it any title at all. I suspect he did not. The title *Anabasis* first appears in a list of Xenophon's writings given by Diogenes Laertius (2.57), a writer of the third century AD who composed a set of short biographies of famous philosophers. At some point someone (perhaps a librarian at Alexandria) needed to provide a label for the papyrus rolls containing this work, and I suspect that the title was taken from the reference to "the *anabasis*" (march inland) of the Greek mercenaries at 1.4.9. In any case, book I alone technically deserves to be called an *anabasis* (which literally means "a march upcountry"), since books 2–4 relate the *katabasis* ("the march down country") of the Ten Thousand to the Black Sea, and books 5–6 their *parabasis* (or "march along the seacoast") to Byzantium on the Bosporus.

A Life in Arms and Books

Xenophon was most unfortunate in the timing of his birth, somewhere between 430 and 425 BC, since it fell during the opening years of the twenty-seven-year Peloponnesian War between Athens and Sparta (431–404). If this was a tale of two cities, it was the worst of times for both of them. Athens lost the war and her empire; but the drain on Spartan manpower, as well as the strains on Sparta's network of alliances with other cities, led ultimately to the Thebans' catastrophic defeat of Sparta at the battle of Leuctra in 371 BC. Xenophon, who came from an aristocratic family and was born a citizen of the cultural center of the Greek world, was no more immune to the afflictions of war than any other citizen. The one consolation of those years may have been his friendship with Socrates, whose follower he became. The story of their first meeting is dramatically, if perhaps not accurately, captured in a story related by Diogenes Laertius in his brief biography of Xenophon (2.48). He recounts that one day Socrates blocked Xenophon's path in a narrow alley and asked him where various items could be purchased, ending with the query "Where do men become good and honorable?" When the young Xenophon was at a loss for an answer, Socrates responded, "Then follow me, and learn."

Although Diogenes provides colorful anecdotes and intriguing tidbits of information about Xenophon's life, he was using sources that are now lost and whose reliability is questionable. The Hellenistic biographers on whom he drew had an unfortunate habit of inferring biographical "facts" from the works of the authors they were writing about (e.g., if Xenophon wrote an essay in which he praises Spartan education, then he *must* have sent his sons to be educated in Sparta, and so on). Yet such is our desire to know the facts of Xenophon's life that even unverifiable information seems better than none at all. And Diogenes's characterization of Xenophon, even if based only on a reading of his works, rings true: that he was a good man, modest and exceptionally handsome, fond of horses and of hunting, a good tactician, pious, fond of sacrificing, knowledgeable in matters of divination, and an emulator of Socrates (2.48, 56).

Ironically, the best evidence for Xenophon's life comes by way of asides in the *Anabasis* itself. It is a safe inference that he was no older than thirty when he set out with Cyrus, since Xenophon says (3.1.25) in his dawn speech to Proxenus's captains, "If you assign me the leadership, I do not plead my age as an excuse, but I believe that I am at the peak of my ability to defend myself from dangers." Since Proxenus was "about thirty" when he died (2.6.20), these would have been odd words if Xenophon had been older than this friend. When Xenophon was elected, he was one of the two youngest generals (3.2.37). We later learn from Xenophon's speech of self-defense before the army that he has not yet had any children (7.6.34). He never mentions in any of his works the family that he eventually did have, but Diogenes tells us (2.54) that he married a woman named Philesia and had two sons by her, Gryllus and Diodorus (who may have been twins, since they were nicknamed "the Dioscuri"). So when he undertook to join Proxenus in the spring of 401 BC, Xenophon was a young unmarried man between twenty-five and thirty, someone just old enough to replace Proxenus as a general.

Xenophon does not fully explain his motives for ignoring Socrates's advice not to get involved with Cyrus and for joining his friend Proxenus in Sardis (3.1.5: see also chapter 5). The reason for his reticence is not far to seek. It is highly likely that he served with the Athenian cavalry both during the Peloponnesian War and then afterward when the cavalry supported the so-called Thirty Tyrants, the junta who ruled Athens for eight months in Sparta's interests. When the junta fell from power and democracy was reestablished, the Athenians put into effect a general amnesty in 403 BC. Nonetheless, life in democratic Athens may not have been very comfortable for someone with Xenophon's record and acquaintances. When in 399 the Spartan Thibron requested that the Athenians send him a cavalry force for his war against Tissaphernes, we are told, "They sent him some of the cavalry who had served under the Thirty, believing it would be a gain for the people if they should live abroad and perish there" (*Hellenica* 3.1.4). To make matters worse, in 399 Socrates was executed on a charge of corrupting the youth and of not believing in the gods the city believed in. No wonder Xenophon was eager to leave Athens in 401 and not particularly insistent on returning before a decree of exile made that impossible.

Socrates was right to be worried about the consequences of associating with Cyrus, since Cyrus had played the pivotal role in helping the Spartans defeat Athens during the Peloponnesian War. He had done this by providing the Spartans with sufficient money, some from the Persian king and some from his own resources, for them to equip a fleet with which to defeat the Athenian navy and thus bring the war to a successful close. Cyrus's personal friendship with the Spartan admiral Lysander, the mastermind behind the decisive naval victory at Aegospotami in 405 BC in which almost the entire Athenian navy was captured, would have been well known at Athens. So it was perfectly reasonable that Socrates should have advised Xenophon to consult the oracle of Apollo about his journey, "suspecting that becoming Cyrus's friend would in some way be a cause for blame from the city's point of view, because Cyrus seemed to have fought with zeal on the side of the Lacedaemonians against Athens" (3.1.5).

What Xenophon does not mention in this passage, however, is that a significant number of his fellow mercenaries (probably more than half) were from cities in the Peloponnese and central Greece that had fought on the Spartan side. This even included his friend Proxenus. Xenophon always refers to Proxenus as a Boeotian (someone from the district of Boeotia in central Greece), yet Diodorus Siculus (14.19.8) calls him more specifically a Theban from Boeotia. Considering that Thebes was one of Athens's most bitter enemies during the Peloponnesian War, perhaps we should see Xenophon as attempting to gloss over his friend's background.

In any case, Xenophon was not only joining up with a foreign prince who had been instrumental in funding Athens's defeat; he was also about to join a mercenary army that contained many Greeks who had been enemies of Athens. Either Xenophon felt that the expedition would be of such short duration that none of his fellow citizens would notice his participation, or, unhappy at home, he hoped to win land and cities by serving Cyrus the Younger, much as in an earlier generation Gongylus of Eretria and Demaratus of Sparta had acquired cities by serving Xerxes, and Themistocles by serving the first Artaxerxes. When those hopes were dashed at the battle of Cunaxa, Xenophon's second choice was to found a colony on the Black Sea. When the Ten Thousand refused to participate in this, he hoped to be given fortified positions on the coast of the Propontis by Seuthes (7.6.34). When even that watered-down version of his previous plans did not work out, he followed King Agesilaus to Sparta. If he ever returned to Athens, and we do not know if he did, it would have been when he was a very old man. This essentially puts paid to the assertion of many modern scholars that Xenophon was always a loyal Athenian patriot at heart. Rather, he was an opportunist with a moral compass that was shaped by aristocratic values and modified by the instruction of Socrates. He saw that in the wake of the defeat of Athens in the Peloponnesian War he could make a better life for himself abroad. That also explains the tension in his writings between the allure of Persia and that of Sparta. If things had turned out differently at the battle of Cunaxa, had Cyrus lived to become the king of Persia, then Xenophon undoubtedly would have been content to live out his days as a wealthy landowning Persian vassal, a man not unlike Asidates, whose castle he plunders at the end of the *Anabasis*.

The *Anabasis* ends with the Spartan general Thibron taking over the remnants of the Ten Thousand (by then only five thousand men, according to Diodorus 14.37.1). It is a fair inference that Xenophon remained with them as their immediate commander and campaigned in Asia Minor under both Thibron and his replacement, Dercylidas. Xenophon is surely the unnamed "leader of the Cyreans" who delivers a short speech in the *Hellenica* (3.2.7). When the Spartan king, Agesilaus, appeared on the scene in 396 BC, Xenophon seems to have lost his command over the Cyreans but to have gained the most influential Greek patron that anyone at that time could have hoped for. The intimacy of their association comes out very clearly in the eulogy Xenophon wrote for Agesilaus (who lived to be eighty-four) in 360 BC, in which he calls him "a perfectly good man" (*Agesilaus* 1.1).

Agesilaus had arrived in Asia with the rather grand pretension of enacting a second Trojan War and contending with the Great King for the possession of Asia, an intention he advertised by sacrificing at Aulis in imitation of Agamemnon before him. Such at least was the propaganda. His practical objectives may have been limited to keeping the Greek cities situated along the coast of Turkey free of Persian control. Whatever his real aspirations and hopes may have been, in 394 Agesilaus was recalled to help defend Sparta against a powerful coalition of Greek states (Athens, Argos, Corinth, and Thebes) that had formed to challenge Spartan hegemony in Greece. Xenophon then returned with Agesilaus to mainland Greece, seven long years after he had departed from Athens. The trip back was not uneventful. Plutarch claims (*Agesilaus* 18.2) that Xenophon then fought against his fellow Athenians at the battle of Coronea in 394. Plutarch may be assuming this, but it is a fair enough inference from Xenophon's careful language in the *Anabasis*, where he gives a flash-forward to the time when "he was returning with Agesilaus from Asia on the expedition against the Boeotians" and "he thought that he himself would be heading into danger" (5.3.6).

Xenophon also refers three times in the *Anabasis* to his future exile from Athens. Scholars have endlessly debated whether he was exiled for participating in Cyrus's expedition against the king of Persia (who by 394 BC was once again on friendly terms with Athens) or for fighting against his native city at Coronea, or indeed for some other reason. This debate will never be settled, for the simple reason that Xenophon does not tell us either why or precisely when he was exiled. That information was either too well known to his contemporary readers to warrant mention or too embarrassing to communicate to posterity. Near the very end of book 7, we learn of Xenophon's fifth postponed attempt to sail back to Athens, "for the decree concerning exile had not yet been passed against him at Athens" (7.7.57). This concise statement does not necessarily imply that the decree was imminent—it says only as much as it does, that Xenophon had not yet been exiled in March 399. Although Xenophon himself leaves the circumstances of his exile hopelessly vague, later writers were ready enough to make their own guesses, which are not really more valid than ours (Pausanias 5.6.5; Diogenes Laertius 2.51; Dio Chrysostom, *Oration* 8.1). My own guess is that he stayed with Agesilaus in Asia because the decree of exile was passed in 399. One thing, however, is clear. After the battle of Coronea, if not before, Xenophon could not return home to Athens.

There was, however, another way for Xenophon's wanderings to come to an end. Sparta had recently concluded a war with one of her former allies, the city of Elis, which controlled the site of the Olympic games. One consequence of this war was that the Spartans appropriated the town of Scillus, which was strategically positioned on the border with Elean territory, and settled it with colonists of their own choosing. One of them was Xenophon, as he himself tells us in the most important autobiographical passage of the *Anabasis* (5.3.4–13).

The flash-forward to Xenophon's future life was prompted by the distribution of monies from the sale of prisoners at the Greek town of Cerasus on the Black Sea (5.3.4–13). A tenth of the profits were distributed to the generals, who were to use the money to make dedications to Apollo and Artemis of Ephesus (5.3). The narrator tells us that Xenophon placed a dedication in the treasury of the Athenians at Delphi that he inscribed with his own name and the name of Proxenus. But then the story gets rather more complex (5.3.6–7):

> As for the portion belonging to Artemis of Ephesus, at the time when Xenophon was returning with Agesilaus from Asia on the expedition against the Boeotians, he left it behind with Megabyzus, the warden of the temple of Artemis, since he thought that he himself would be heading into danger, and he instructed him, if he should survive, to give it back to him. But if he should come to any grief, Megabyzus was to have a dedication made and to dedicate to Artemis whatever he believed would be pleasing to the goddess. When Xenophon was in exile [or "had escaped danger," if we read the Greek aorist tense *ephugen* instead of the imperfect *epheugen*], and

was already residing in Scillus where he had been settled as a colonist by the Spartans, Megabyzus came to Olympia for the purpose of watching the games and gave him back his deposit.

The rest of the passage describes in loving detail the estate Xenophon purchased for the goddess, with its varied agricultural products and game for hunting, the temple he built, and the yearly festival he put on for the neighboring population from the tenth of the produce of the sacred land. But despite the detail of his description, the financial arrangements are left rather vague. Did the Spartans give Xenophon a house at Scillus as a present? Did he make a personal profit from the agricultural revenues of the precinct that he purchased for the goddess? In any case, this residence, so close to the site of the Olympic games, undoubtedly gave him the enviable opportunity to entertain guests from throughout the Greek world. And it was probably during his years at Scillus that he began his literary career. According to Diogenes (2.52) he arrived at Scillus with his wife and sons. He reputedly sent his sons to Sparta to undergo the famous Spartan education (Plutarch, *Agesilaus* 20.2 and *Moralia* 212b; Diogenes Laertius 2.54).

This idyllic period of Xenophon's life (when we can easily imagine that he spent his time managing his private estates and the sanctuary to Artemis, entertaining guest-friends, hunting, reading and writing, and venturing to Olympia for the games) came to a crashing close when the Spartans lost the battle of Leuctra in 371 BC. Spartan control over the Peloponnese then quickly began to unravel: the Eleans seized Scillus, and Xenophon had to flee to Corinth with his sons. In his *Guide to Greece* (written in the late second century AD), Pausanias records (5.6.6) a local Elean tradition that Xenophon was subsequently tried by the Olympic Council and allowed to live freely in Scillus, where his grave could still be seen. This certainly smacks of a much later tradition, perhaps invented during Roman times, to cover up the expulsion of one of the most famous writers of classical Greece.

At some point, the decree of exile against Xenophon was probably rescinded (or so claimed the third-century BC antiquarian Ister, as cited by Diogenes Laertius 2.59); but there is no evidence at all that he ever returned to Athens, even for a visit. However that may be, he did send his sons to Athens so that they might fight in the Athenian cavalry at the battle of Mantinea in 362 BC. If nothing else, this shows that he had not lost affection for his native city, and probably that his wife Philesia and his sons were Athenian citizens. Athens and Sparta were now in alliance against Thebes, and this was Xenophon's way of both contributing to the defense of Sparta and perhaps reintegrating his sons into Athenian society.

Gryllus distinguished himself in a cavalry skirmish that preceded the main battle, and received some extraordinary honors as a result. The Mantineans gave him a public burial and erected a monument to him on the spot where he fell; and at Athens a painting in the Stoa of Zeus Eleutherios depicted him in the act of wounding the illustrious Theban general Epaminondas (Pausanias 1.3.4; 8.11.6; 9.15.5). Diogenes Laertius, moreover, tells us something extremely important for gauging the reputation of Xenophon during his lifetime: "Aristotle says that there were innumerable writers of epitaphs and eulogies of Gryllus, who wrote in part to gratify his father. And also Hermippus, in his Life of Theophrastus, says that even Isocrates wrote a eulogy of Gryllus" (2.55). Aristotle's testimony we can trust, not least because he wrote a treatise on rhetoric with the title *Gryllus* (Diogenes Laertius 5.22); Hermippus's less so. But if Isocrates, the preeminent teacher of rhetoric and pamphleteer of the fourth century, deigned to write such a work, it proves that by 362 BC Xenophon was a major player in the literary culture of classical Greece. If Xenophon, in his old age, was a man worth flattering, it was not because of his wealth or political influence but because of his reputation as a writer. That conclusion should have important consequences for our interpretation of the *Anabasis*.

The last datable reference in Xenophon's works is to 355 BC (*Ways and Means* 5.9). If he was born in, say, 430, then he lived to be at least seventy-five. One should not assume, however, that an author publishes his last work and then immediately drops dead. If he lost his estates and most of his possessions in 371, he probably did not die rich; but he did, at least, die famous. Ironically, Xenophon's role in the *Anabasis* was his moment of military glory, just as the *Anabasis* itself is now generally considered his most important literary creation. A recurrent pattern in books 3–7 is that the Greeks are in trouble and then Xenophon saves the day by offering a clever, even if sometimes rather obvious, solution. Yet Xenophon seems to have had a completely undistinguished military career in subsequent years. Partly, perhaps, this was a function of his serving under Spartans and never again being given the opportunity to exercise high command. As an exile from his native city, he was denied access to the generalship at Athens, and as a non-Spartan he could never hold a command that gave scope for his own strategic initiative. But it may also be that Xenophon was the leader created by the moment; that he was the right person at the right time; and that, having once performed brilliantly, he then retired to the sidelines and eventually to the life of a country squire and prodigious writer. Even in the context of the *Anabasis*, he distinguishes himself as a shrewd tactician, able to get the army out of difficult situations, storm a fortress, or force a crossing, rather than as a strategist.

Related Works

Xenophon was a highly versatile and inventive writer. He composed in several different genres, and invented new ones. His works can be divided into roughly three categories: historical works, philosophical writings, and short treatises. The historical works are the *Anabasis* and *Hellenica*. The *Hellenica* narrates events from where Thucydides left off in 411 BC until the anticlimactic battle of Mantinea in 362. Differences in style and content suggest that the *Hellenica* was written at different times. The first part, which ends with the defeat of Athens in the Peloponnesian War, was probably written in the 380s or 370s. The bulk of the *Hellenica*, from book 2.3.10 to the end, seems fairly certain to have been composed in the 350s. This means that the parts of the *Hellenica* that mention Cyrus's expedition and narrate the subsequent military operations of the Spartans in Asia Minor (books 3 and 4) were written later than the *Anabasis*.

Notwithstanding the importance of his historical writings to the modern study of Greek history, Xenophon was best known in antiquity as a philosopher. His Socratic works should be read alongside those of Plato, who was his exact contemporary and seemingly his rival (Aulus Gellius 14.3; Diogenes Laertius 2.57; 3.34). These include two works that have the same titles as two of Plato's writings: an *Apology* of Socrates and a *Symposium*. His longest Socratic work is the *Memorabilia* (or "Conversations of Socrates"), a loosely organized collection of vignettes in which Socrates converses with individuals from all walks of life. There is also one non-Socratic philosophical work, the *Hiero*, a dialogue between a Syracusan tyrant of that name and the famous poet Simonides of Ceos. To the third category belongs a range of short didactic and technical treatises: *On Hunting, Cavalry Commander, Constitution of the Lacedaemonians*, and *Ways and Means* (an essay on how to improve the Athenian economy, probably Xenophon's final work). The *Agesilaus*, his eulogy of the Spartan king of that name, is difficult to place. It is a short work that contains the same historical material to be found in his *Hellenica*, but with a strongly biographical and moralizing slant that emphasizes, indeed systematically surveys, Agesilaus's virtues.

Xenophon's longest and most ambitious creation is also his most peculiar: the *Cyropaedia*, a highly innovative mix of biography, history, fiction, and political philosophy. It is Xenophon's answer to Plato's *Republic*, and Plato seems at one point to be refuting it in his last dialogue, the *Laws*. It is surely a direct stab at Xenophon when Plato has his Athenian speaker assert (*Laws* 694c): "What I now divine regarding Cyrus is that, although he was in other respects a good and patriotic general, he was entirely without a correct education, and had paid no attention to household management." This is essentially a challenge to a central thesis of the *Cyropaedia*, that one of the principal secrets of Cyrus's success was that he was given the ideal education.

It should be obvious from this brief survey that Xenophon was one of the major writers and thinkers of antiquity. There are a number of themes that run through all of his works, but two of them will be of special concern to us as we examine the *Anabasis*. These are the supreme importance, in good fortune and in bad, of maintaining good relations with the gods, and his interest in the qualities that make for good leadership. Throughout his long life, Xenophon had sought the company of "great men": Socrates, Cyrus, and then Agesilaus. This penchant for seeking out the patronage of the great and powerful (or "wise" in the case of Socrates) is reflected in his emphasis on the nature of effective leadership.

Date of the *Anabasis*

The greatest hindrance to interpreting the *Anabasis* in terms of its historical context is our uncertainty as to when Xenophon wrote it. Theoretically, he could have begun to work on it almost immediately. Scholars have been divided between a publication date in the 380s, the 370s, and the 360s. The only evidence that can be brought to bear on this are allusions in the *Anabasis* itself. Many have argued that the use of the imperfect tense in the description of Xenophon's life at Scillus, as well as the poignantly nostalgic tone of that description, suggests that it was written after he had been forced to leave. If it was written in the 360s, Xenophon, once again an exile, and with his Spartan patrons losing their control over the Peloponnese, may have felt vulnerable and in need of explaining his earlier self to his contemporaries (but see below). If we could securely place the composition of the *Anabasis* in the early 360s, then we could fit it into an overall scheme that would render intertextual references to Xenophon's other works more meaningful.

The *Cyropaedia* also seems to be a work of the 360s. The last chapter refers to two important players in the satraps' revolt that took place in 362/1 BC (8.8.4). Some scholars, however, believe that this entire chapter, book 8.8, was either added later by Xenophon or actually written and appended by someone else. Let us assume, however, that this epilogue was both written by Xenophon himself and was an integral part of his original composition. In effect, it is Xenophon's rant against contemporary Persian impiety, injustice, greed, luxury, and effeminacy. He begins by asserting that everything took a turn for the worse as soon as the elder Cyrus died and his sons began to quarrel. But his concrete example is the impiety of the king in killing the Greek generals who had followed the younger Cyrus: "Trusting in their previous reputation (i.e. of the Kings and their subordinates), they handed themselves over, were led to the King, and were beheaded" (8.8.3). The pointed reference to the arrest and execution of the generals suggests that Xenophon's disillusionment with contemporary Persia was a direct result of his experiences with the Ten Thousand.

However that may be, the *Cyropaedia* is not a historical work but a didactic semifictional biography of Cyrus the Great, a sort of philosophical romance. It is a work of considerable interest to political philosophers and students of the origins of the Greek novel but of only very minor importance to historians; and for that reason it is usually not studied together with the *Anabasis*. As we shall see, however, there is an important degree of intertextuality between the two works concerning the portrayal of the two Cyruses, the older one who founded the Persian Empire and the younger one who attempted to become the second king of that name. Moreover, the two works may be seen as pendants in Xenophon's ongoing exploration of the problem of leadership in a well-ordered society. The *Cyropaedia* presents the ideal ruler in an idealized world of Xenophon's own creation, whereas in the messier and nastier world of the *Anabasis*, Xenophon's own leadership, while still being paradigmatic and effective, does not perfectly control the community of sometimes unruly and greedy troops under his command. It is not unlikely that Xenophon intended that these two works be read together.

Why the *Anabasis*?

It is a traditional question to ask why Xenophon wrote the *Anabasis*. To ask such a question, however, is highly problematic. First of all, Xenophon himself as author might not have been entirely sure of his own motives for writing, and some of the subconscious motivations that might have influenced his work may look to us like conscious ones. Second, he may have had several motives and purposes for writing, and there may be several points he is wishing to make and themes he is attempting to stress. At the risk of oversimplification, the major interpretations of the *Anabasis* are as follows.

Ever since the nineteenth century, it has been fashionable to assert that the *Anabasis* is primarily an apology, in the sense of "apology" as a written defense or justification of one's actions. As such, it is meant to excuse Xenophon for participating in and enriching himself through events that, as an Athenian aristocrat, he should have had no part in. It has been argued that his purpose is to construct a narrative that conceals the fact that he was a mercenary serving for pay. And thus he stresses that he was invited by one friend, Proxenus, in order to make a new friend, Cyrus, but that he never received money from Cyrus (3.1.4). When during the winter of 400/399 he was the leading general of the remnants of the Ten Thousand in service to the Thracian prince Seuthes, the narrative is largely devoted to a demonstration that he did not receive bribes from Seuthes in exchange for manipulating the army, nor did he appropriate for himself the pay intended for the common soldiers. More specifically, if he indeed was exiled for participating in Cyrus's expedition, he may have been attempting to explain his behavior to an Athenian audience who had the power to allow him to return home. As it strikes me, however, that particular motive is undercut by his apparent failure to resettle in Athens, even after the decree of exile was probably rescinded.

On a somewhat less personal level, Xenophon may well have been concerned to counter a common perception that the Ten Thousand were poverty-stricken thugs as ready to plunder Greek cities as barbarian villages. Indeed, Isocrates, in his highly acclaimed *Panegyricus* oration of 380 BC, refers to the six thousand (as he calls them) as "not men picked for excellence, but those who were unable on account of poverty to live in their own cities" (4.146). Xenophon seems to be directly countering such assertions when he offers an explanation of why the army was unwilling to establish a colony along the Black Sea but was eager to return to mainland

Greece: "The majority had not sailed from Greece out of want of livelihood, but because they had heard about the virtue of Cyrus" and thought they could enrich themselves and then return home to their families (6.4.8).

Finally, there is a more distinctly literary motive. The evidence is fairly compelling that another *Anabasis* was in circulation before Xenophon wrote his. The sixth-century AD lexicographer Stephanus of Byzantium provides four entries that cite an *Anabasis* by one Sophaenetus. It is a reasonable inference that this was Sophaenetus from the town of Stymphalus in Arcadia, whom Xenophon calls (6.5.13) the eldest of the generals. Sophaenetus plays a minor and not altogether credible role in Xenophon's account. Although he contributed a thousand hoplites to Cyrus's army (1.2.3), his few appearances in the *Anabasis* speak to his unimportance and lack of competence. He is left in charge of the base camp when they attack the camp of the Persian commander Tiribazus (4.4.19), and he later incurs a fine for neglect of duty (5.8.1). In his one recorded utterance, he refuses even to consider crossing a ravine in order to attack the cavalry of the Persian satrap Pharnabazus and the Bithynian infantry (6.5.13). Xenophon "hastily interrupts him" and successfully advocates this very plan of action (6.5.13–21). A less subtle writer would have belittled Sophaenetus more directly; Xenophon's methods are indirect. The reader is given an image of a too feeble and too cautious general, someone whose strategies could not possibly have saved the Greeks. A modern theory has accordingly evolved that Xenophon has largely omitted Sophaenetus because Sophaenetus had given him a minor role in his own *Anabasis*. Xenophon is simultaneously exacting revenge and setting the record straight.

Some modern scholars have denied the authenticity of an *Anabasis* by Sophaenetus, arguing that it is either a late rhetorical exercise or an excerpt from a military handbook or collection of stratagems. But I do not think we need be as skeptical as that. The citations, brief as they are, all concern the names of peoples and places, and this reminds one more of Xenophon's narrative than of any other type of composition. What I find difficult about this kind of explanation is that it assumes that Xenophon, who was a well-known figure and surely writing long after Sophaenetus's death, would have taken such great pains to refute a work that most probably was of minor importance. It really is an extreme version of biographical interpretation to explain the genesis of a literary masterpiece purely in terms of personal rivalries.

What all of these variations on a theme have in common is the presumption that Xenophon felt the need to defend himself against attacks, whether they came from other writers or from public opinion, either that of the common soldiers who served with him, that of his aristocratic peers who looked down on mercenary service, or that of his fellow citizens, who had exiled him as a traitor. The problem, however, with seeing the *Anabasis* as primarily, even exclusively, a work of apology (whomever it is aimed at and whatever attacks it is meant to refute) is the time lag between the expedition of Cyrus and the composition of the work. If the *Anabasis* was written as long after the events described as almost all historians now believe, then his banishment from Athens may already have been revoked (perhaps after the alliance between Sparta and Athens in 369, or even earlier as a consequence of the King's Peace of 386), he had earned fame as the writer of several other books (probably his Socratic dialogues), and he was almost too old to play a role in political or military affairs. So, unless he was excessively worried about his posthumous reputation and waited some thirty years to address that concern, the overriding purpose of the work is unlikely to be apologetic. Historical context is important for the understanding of any work of literature; but that does not mean that biographical facts or inferences can be used to explain the most important aspects of a work's meaning and genesis.

I would not wish to subscribe to any of these positions as stated, since all of them are too one-dimensional. The *Anabasis* is both a portrait of a Greek army on the move and a demonstration of the lessons to be learned from its experience. It is also a self-portrait of Xenophon himself, who here both explains his role in preserving the Ten Thousand and insists that he maintained his own incorruptibility in the process. Divination (the seeking of advice from the gods) both justifies and validates that role and, in the last part of the work, proves his innocence against charges of making money along the way. He emerges as the god-sent savior whom the gods (principally Zeus in his various manifestations) duly rewarded in the end, after much trial and tribulation. At the same time that the *Anabasis* looks backward as an exoneration both of Xenophon himself and of the men under his command, it also looks forward by way of example. In the bleak aftermath of the Peloponnesian War, Xenophon depicts Greeks from various cities that had fought against each other, cooperating both to save each other's lives and to ward off a common enemy. The theory that Xenophon is using the *Anabasis* as a vehicle for promoting some version of "panhellenism" (the idea that the cities of mainland Greece could and should be fighting Persians and not each other) is critiqued in chapter 7. For now it is enough to point out that the Ten Thousand's unity of purpose was fragile, and Xenophon had to work hard, and at great personal risk, to keep it intact, to keep these disparate Greek forces together. So there is also an implied warning in the *Anabasis* about the difficulties involved in making Greeks work together toward a common goal.

The Anabasis as "Memory Place"

Although there are many and various themes that run through the *Anabasis*, I want to end this chapter by suggesting a particularly urgent and overarching motive for committing the story to writing. The Ten Thousand mercenaries formed a body whose esprit de corps and group identity was created and solidified by the trial and ordeal of their shared experience. But for group identities to survive over time, there need to be places of memory that can serve as loci for their identity. As Karl Hölkeskamp has astutely observed, "every group which has an image of itself as a group aims to take permanent possession of . . . specific, meaningful locations, which are symbols of its identity and fixed points of reference for its memory" (2006: 482). What could have served as a "memory place," a *lieu de memoir*, for the Ten Thousand? The trophies they erected over their defeated enemies, even the mound they heaped up atop Mount Theches when they first saw the sea, were places that none of them, either singly or in groups, were likely ever to see again. In his great speech of self-defense before the army, Xenophon refers to himself as someone "who, with the gods being gracious, set up with you many trophies of victory over the barbarians" (7.6.36). There is an allusiveness to this assertion, since the narrative itself has only recorded two such trophies (one on top of a mountain pass, 4.6.27; the other near Calpe Harbor, 6.5.32). Doubtless there were many others, set up in places remote and distant, and subject to decay, vandalism, and ultimately oblivion.

Since the Ten Thousand traversed a vast distance and then dispersed and would never again, either collectively or individually, visit the sites of their victories and monuments, there were no "memory places" that might serve as loci for the preservation and commemoration of their deeds. In this circumstance the text, which both records their actions and describes the monuments they erected, acts as the primary, indeed sole "memory place" both for the participants themselves and for posterity. Xenophon alludes to this potential function of his narrative indirectly in several passages. Most of these are references literary critics would call "metatextual," that is, they are comments that reflect on the nature of the text itself. In simpler terms, Xenophon was surely self-consciously aware that his text had the ability to confer praise and blame and to seal the reputation of its characters for the future, since the story itself reflects this self-awareness.

Soon after the Greeks have learned about the death of Cyrus, a delegation from the king demands that they surrender their weapons. Clearchus addresses the one Greek member of that delegation, Phalinus, in a way that affirms the ability of the text to immortalize his answer (2.1.17–18): "In the name of the gods, give us whatever advice seems to you to be fairest and best, advice which will bring you honor in times to come, when it is recounted that Phalinus, having once been sent from the King to order the Greeks to surrender their weapons, gave them the following advice when they were deciding what to do. And you know that whatever you advise will of necessity be spoken of in Greece." Phalinus attempts to avoid this trap by giving an evasive answer, but the narrator points out his intention to equivocate in case the reader should be taken in.

An even more striking example appears much later on in the story. The Greeks have just crossed a ravine and are on the point of engaging with the enemy army. "When they had crossed, Xenophon went up and down the phalanx, saying, 'Men, remember in how many battles, with the gods on your side, you have been victorious by coming to close quarters and remember what happens to those who flee the enemy, and keep in mind too that we are at the very doors of Greece. Follow Heracles the leader and call upon each other by name. For surely it is pleasant, by saying and doing something courageous and noble now, to provide a memory of oneself among those whom one wishes to be remembered by" (6.5.24).

Yet if the *Anabasis* was a memory place for courageous and noble deeds and words, it was a memory place whose entrance was closely guarded by the author himself. In the passage just quoted, Xenophon the character says it is pleasurable to leave behind a memory of one's words and actions, but the narrator restricts such memory to Xenophon's own words and actions. He does mention Timasion's successful command of the cavalry in this particular battle (6.5.28); but otherwise Xenophon as character takes center stage in both word and deed. The soldiers called on each other by name, but Xenophon, as author, records only his own name—thus condemning them to obscurity while memorializing himself from his own day until ours.

Xenophon, in his capacity as the author of the text, exercises a tight control both over who and what is remembered and over how they are remembered. No text, of course, is completely hegemonic, insofar as no text can completely control how readers will respond to it. But the author's control becomes more secure as the generation of eyewitnesses and participants passes and subsequent generations of readers are more dependent on what he has chosen to record.

Current readers may not be persuaded by how Xenophon treats a particular actor or incident in his narrative—they may suspect apology, distortion, bias, omission, and exaggeration. Nevertheless, they cannot supply the names of actors and incidents that are not named in the text. Out of the thirteen thousand Greek mercenaries who fought for Cyrus, only sixty-six are listed by name and nationality, and fifty-two of these are officers (including seven Athenians other than Xenophon). The unnamed are lost to memory and to history.

When he wishes, Xenophon, like Herodotus, can grant immortality to someone by mentioning his name even with regard to a small detail. Such is the case with Aeneas of Stymphalus, who tries to stop one of the Taochians from jumping off a cliff, but is dragged over too (4.7.13). Sometimes even an individual who often rendered good service to the army is mentioned only once. The most unusual example occurs in the incident in which the generals send Democrates of Temnus to reconnoiter a mountain where enemy campfires had allegedly been spotted. The narrator then explains: "For this Democrates even before seemed to speak the truth about many such things, both the things that were, that they were, and the things that were not, that they were not" (4.4.14–15). If the last part of this sentence sounds odd, it does so with good reason; it is a version of a famous remark by the sophist Protagoras of Abdera (quoted by Plato at *Theaetetus* 152A) that "man is the measure of all things, of the things that are, that they are, and of the things that are not, that they are not." The allusion may be lost on the vast majority of modern readers, but the well educated among Xenophon's ancient Greek audience could hardly have missed it.

Finally, there is a still more profoundly personal reason why someone chooses to record the events of his or her own life. The past is as elusive as the shade of his wife that Aeneas vainly attempts to grasp in Virgil's *Aeneid*. Ultimately, the most effective way to revivify and preserve one's past experiences is to commit them to writing. Xenophon may have told the story of the *Anabasis* many times before he set it down. But it is his written narrative that permanently recaptures what he and the others, including his friend

Proxenus and his patron Cyrus, suffered and accomplished. The *Anabasis* is far more, therefore, than just a static memorial. Every time this work is read, the past, or at least Xenophon's version of the past, comes alive again.

Further Reading

Xenophon has been the subject of renewed and ongoing interest among scholars. Although outdated in many respects, the most accessible general introduction to Xenophon in English is Anderson (1974). Breitenbach (1967) is a foundational text in the modern study of Xenophon; Higgins (1977) offers new readings of many passages in Xenophon's corpus (not always persuasively); and Dillery (1995) interprets the *Hellenica* and *Anabasis* within their historical context. Three important collections of essays have appeared in recent years: Lane Fox (2004b), Tuplin (2004c), and Gray (2010). Lendle (1995) is a commentary on the entire *Anabasis* (in German), and Stronk (1995) on book 7 (in English). Both are stronger on historical than on literary problems. Most books on Xenophon (including the prefaces to translations) contain a brief account of his life. The fullest treatment is Delebecque (1957), although it is highly speculative. In particular, he argues (199–206) that the *Anabasis* was written in two halves at different times and for different reasons (the first half ending at 5.3.6: see also Delebecque 1946–47). Needless to say, almost all critics now, and quite rightly, consider the work to be an artistic whole. Badian (2004) provides an incisive critique of the evidence for Xenophon's life; but the best short account is Krentz (1994: 1–4). A recent study of the date of Xenophon's exile is Green (1994, citing earlier scholarship). Tuplin (2004b) is a detailed treatment of Xenophon's estate at Scillus. For the Persian background to Cyrus's expedition, see Briant (2000). Excellent treatments of the Greek historical background are Cartledge (1987; very detailed), Cawkwell (1976 and 2005; concise and provocative), and Waterfield (2006; aimed at the general reader). For an analysis of mercenary service under Cyrus, see Roy (1967 and 2004) and Dalby (1992).

Lee (2007) gives a brilliant and evocative reconstruction of the actual conditions of service on the expedition. Cawkwell (1972 and 2004) argues that Xenophon was writing in reaction to an earlier *Anabasis* by his fellow general Sophaenetus; this is disputed by West-lake (1987) and Stylianou (2004).

·2·

Xenophon as Author, Narrator, and Agent

An autobiography is the truest of all books; for while it inevitably
consists mainly of extinctions of the truth, shirkings of the truth,
partial revealments of the truth, with hardly an instance of plain
straight truth, the remorseless truth is there, between the lines,
where the author-cat is raking dust upon it which hides from the
disinterested spectator neither it nor its smell . . . the result being
that the reader knows the author in spite of his wily diligences.
—*Mark Twain (letter to William D. Howells, March 14, 1904)*

The *Anabasis* at the Boundaries of Genre

The *Anabasis*, on any reckoning, is a highly unusual work. It has
been called a war memoir, a coming-of-age story (in which the
character Xenophon makes the journey from innocence to experience),
an adventure story, a travelogue, a political (panhellenist) tract, and an
extended personal apology. The *Anabasis*, of course, may contain all of
these elements without necessarily being essentially defined by any
one of them. Moreover, these are mostly modern categories and it is
not at all obvious that such terms would have made any sense to
Xenophon's contemporary audience. If Xenophon wrote the first war
memoir, he was certainly unaware of that fact, since no such genre
existed until modern times. In any case, even by modern standards, it is
not quite a memoir, since Xenophon does not even introduce himself

until almost a third of the way through. It goes without saying that memoirs are usually (but not always) written in the first, not the third person. In memoirs of self-discovery, as Emily Fox Gordon has recently observed (2010: 221–22), "The drive towards narrative closure, which seems to be encrypted in human DNA, is realized in an emotionally satisfying conclusion." As most critics have lamented, neither Xenophon's own story nor that of the Ten Thousand collectively receives "an emotionally satisfying conclusion." Nor is the *Anabasis* merely an adventure story, since it addresses serious themes and concerns. There are didactic elements, but no reader, ancient or modern, would place the *Anabasis* in the same camp with Isocrates's *Panegyricus* (a call for a panhellenic campaign against Persia) or his *Antidosis* (a personal apology in the guise of a fictive law court speech).

In both style and content Xenophon is a deceptively simple author, but that simplicity is itself a finely wrought literary strategy. Although it most closely resembles what his contemporaries would have judged to be a work of historical narrative, it differs in important respects from previous productions in that genre. As in the *Cyropaedia*, there is a considerable amount of generic innovation, whereby Xenophon presses the boundaries of his contemporary audience's expectations of genre. The professional historians of today tend to employ the concept of genre very strictly. If a work conspicuously contaminates information derived from "evidence" with imagined scenes and conversations, then it will inevitably get bad reviews from fellow historians, as did Edmund Morris's *Dutch: A Memoir of Ronald Reagan* (1999) and Marla Miller's *Betsy Ross and the Making of America* (2010).

In the ancient world, there was no collective body of "professional" scholars who could impose standards. At the same time, the expectations of a historical work's various audiences were not the same as those of modern readers, at least since the emergence of "scientific," evidence-based history during the nineteenth century (Tucker 2004: 44–45). As Christopher Pelling has aptly pointed out, generic expectations, especially for prose literature, were never totally fixed in antiquity, and readers had only general expectations of what they would find when they picked up a work. So a reader "will have a provisional idea of what may be expected, but will not be surprised to find one or several of the usual features to be absent, or present in an unusual or off-key way" (Pelling 2007: 80). A text such as the *Anabasis* continually manipulates what the reader is expecting, even as it fits into the broad generic category of "history." To judge from his penchant for literary innovation, Xenophon certainly was not worried about breaking any tacit rules or normative expectations. He was an innovator of a most singular kind—one who lets the innovations speak for themselves without any cues from the author that the reader is about to experience something new.

The most innovative aspect of the *Anabasis* is the tight focus on a single event and, increasingly from book 3 onward, on a single individual. By the time one gets to book 7, the story is virtually a biography. Throughout the fourth century there was a growing tendency to emphasize the deeds and historical agency of a single individual, which culminated in the historians who wrote about the expedition of Alexander the Great. This concentration on the individual first developed in encomiastic literature, particularly in the eulogies of dead rulers such as the *Evagoras* of Isocrates (c. 370–365 BC) and Xenophon's own *Agesilaus* (c. 360 BC). One can see it too in the development of the philosophical literature about Socrates, such as Xenophon's *Memorabilia*. But none of these other works are really equivalent to the *Anabasis*. Xenophon has combined the war monograph with elements of the apologetic defense speech in anticipation of the individual-focused history that would be produced after his death by Theopompus of Chios in the *Philippica* (centered on the deeds of Philip II) and Callisthenes of Olynthus in the *Exploits of Alexander*.

Nonetheless, Theopompus and Callisthenes, it is fair to infer from the fragments of their histories (their works no longer survive), told the readers up front what their works were about. Quite remarkably, the *Anabasis* lacks a preface and begins in story mode (in a way resembling the once-upon-a-time formula): "Darius and Parysatis had two sons, an older one, Artaxerxes, and a younger one, Cyrus." Xenophon nowhere in the *Anabasis* tells us why he wrote it or what its purpose or themes are. Herodotus, despite the storytelling manner of his narrative technique, begins by informing his readers what to expect: "This is the setting forth of the investigation of Herodotus of Halicarnassus, in order that human accomplishments should not be forgotten through time, or that great and marvelous deeds, some displayed by Greeks and others by barbarians, should be without fame, both other deeds and the reason they fought against each other."

Xenophon quite easily could have given us a similar signpost, something like "Here are recorded the deeds of Cyrus's Greek mercenaries, so that their discipline and love of freedom, which sustained them on their perilous march to the sea, may not be forgotten and may serve as an example to others." Given how Herodotean Xenophon is in other respects, such a declaration, right at the start, would not have been out of place. Even that, to be sure, would not encompass his entire intent, but it would be a start. As it is, we can infer that such was one of his many motives in writing, but certainly there were others. One might say that Xenophon has provided what the rhetorician Lucian, writing in the second century AD, later calls a "virtual preface" (*How to Write History* 23, 52). His contemporary readers, to judge from the practice of other historians, would have expected a formal preface.

Xenophon does not tell the reader who wrote the *Anabasis*, what it is about, why it was written, or what methods were employed in its composition. Now the first two items may not be as problematic as they seem. There may have been an indication of authorship on the papyrus rolls that contained the work (the ancient equivalent of a modern title page). And even if, unlike in his other works, the first paragraph does not indicate what the story is going to be about, it is soon obvious that it is about the attempt of Cyrus the Younger to wrest control of the Persian Empire from his older brother and the fate of the Greek mercenaries who accompanied him. As for purpose and methods, since they have to be inferred from the text itself, the task of inference is much harder. If we assume that the implied author (the sensibility behind the narrative that readers construct for themselves) and the narrator of the *Anabasis* are one and the same person, and that person is Xenophon, then we can further assume that he wrote from his own memories of what took place. So the *Anabasis* becomes, in effect if not in strict form, a work of autobiography. (The further question whether he supplemented his memory with notes taken at the time or with other written accounts will be discussed in chapter 3.)

As for purpose, that too has to be inferred from what Xenophon says, and from what he does not say. Here the question of themes and motives is important. If we can detect certain themes that are repeated throughout the work, then we can conclude that the implied author is leading us in a certain direction and prodding us to draw certain conclusions, or at least to ask certain questions. So looking for repetitions of ideas and motifs is informative. But it is also illuminating to look for gaps in the text, the things Xenophon does not tell us or leaves unsaid that may throw light on his interests and purposes. Another way of looking at this problem, and perhaps a more fruitful way, is to ask not why Xenophon the historical author wrote this particular work but what ideas Xenophon the implied author is attempting to convey. In other words, what does the *Anabasis* mean? A related question has to do with Xenophon's audience. This surely included his fellow Athenians as well as Greeks from other cities. And it is essential not to overlook posterity. Like Herodotus and Thucydides, Xenophon can imagine this work being read in the future, so its themes and purpose are not strictly limited to readers of his generation.

The most sensible generic description of the *Anabasis* has been articulated by John Marincola, who calls it "a narrative history of recent events, focalized around an individual group, which tells of dangers, survival, and return against enormous odds and powerful foes. Here adopting the 'story' format eschewed in the *Hellenica*, Xenophon writes a contemporary account with a unity of plot, imposing a beginning and end on a set of events" (1999: 316). The only adjustment I want to make to this characterization of the work concerns the words "return" and "end." Xenophon's ending is not entirely satisfying, and somewhat arbitrary, because the story concludes without either Xenophon or the men under his command actually returning to their homes in mainland Greece. It is even questionable how eager Xenophon was to return to mainland Greece, since he seriously considers using the Ten Thousand to establish a colony along the shore of the Black Sea (5.6.15–17) and he later describes Calpe Harbor as an ideal site for a settlement of ten thousand men (6.4.1–6).

Moreover, the narrative itself does not bear out the assertion, often made in speeches, that the majority of the rank and file were anxious to return to their native communities in mainland Greece and to their parents, wives, and children. At the end of the *Anabasis*, the vast majority of the survivors are eager to sign up for military service with the Spartan commander Thibron in Asia Minor (7.6.8). The western coast of Turkey (where many of the Ten Thousand had served in garrison duty before joining Cyrus's expedition; 1.2.3) may have been considered part of Greece, but the home cities of the Ten Thousand were across the Aegean in mainland Greece. The longing to return "home" has every appearance of being a literary device that gives coherence and a recognizable theme to the story of the Ten Thousand. It also influences the audience to feel sympathy with their plight, causing us to view them not as mercenaries forever seeking plunder and profit through war, but as soldiers (much like those who fought at Troy) who long for their absent families and who will brave any hardship to return to them.

The theme of return is put under a spotlight immediately after the arrest of the Greek generals. The long and ornate pair of sentences that opens book 3 and so graphically expresses the hopeless situation of the Ten Thousand ends by expressing the deepest concern of the soldiers: "they were attempting to rest wherever each of them chanced to be, being unable to sleep because of grief and longing for their home communities, parents, wives, children, whom they believed they would never see again" (3.1.3). Toward the end of book 3, this theme recurs, as Xenophon, in a short speech, encourages his men to reach the summit of a mountain before the enemy does (3.4.46): "Men, consider that you are now racing toward Greece, now toward your children and wives; now, having toiled but a little, we shall make the rest of the journey without having to fight a battle." The narrator, it has been argued (Bradley 2001), by stressing the theme of homecoming, exploits the disparity in knowledge between himself, his characters (including the character Xenophon), and the reader in order to build impossible expectations. Rather, I would say that he is engaging in a cruel irony, since most contemporary readers must have known that "the rest of the journey" would be punctuated by many battles and skirmishes. And even if someone did not know the perilous story of the Ten Thousand's march through central Turkey and along the coast of the Black Sea, their expectations would have been conditioned by the epic poem *Nostoi* (or *Returns*, no longer extant) and by Homer's *Odyssey*, both of which centered on the theme of the Greek heroes' hazardous— and for many, fatal—journeys back from Troy to their homes in mainland Greece. Odysseus, it should not be forgotten, returned alone, all of his men having perished en route.

That said, one should not assume that none of the Ten Thousand makes it home to his family within the narrative world of the text. We are told at 2.3.3–4 that some of the soldiers (perhaps as many as five hundred) sold their arms while the army was tarrying at Byzantium and sailed home as best they could. This statement is confirmed by Diodorus Siculus, who twice says that some of the Ten Thousand returned to their native homes in mainland Greece (14.31.4–5; 14.37.1). The majority of the survivors, however, perhaps some five thousand in number, stayed on in Asia as mercenaries in Spartan service. The real denouement of the story of the Greeks' return to their homeland does not take place in the *Anabasis*, where one might reasonably have expected to find it, but appears indirectly in the *Hellenica*. We there learn that in 395 BC King Agesilaus gave the command of the Cyreans to a newly arrived Spartan named Herippidas (*Hellenica* 3.4.20). At the battle of Coronea in Boeotia in 394, this Herippidas was in charge of the "mercenary contingent" in Agesilaus's army (*Hellenica* 4.3.15). If these later troops were still the Cyreans, then it is strange indeed that the reader has to infer the final homecoming of the remnants of the Ten Thousand to mainland Greece.

Why is it that Xenophon never finishes the story explicitly but lets the final dispersion of the Ten Thousand dissolve into narrative thin air? Is it because he prefers to concentrate on their exploits against barbarians rather than their final action as a self-contained unit in a battle against their fellow Greeks? From a panhellenist point of view, that might be considered an ignominious conclusion to their years of service against "barbarians" and the praise and glory they had won (5.7.8; 6.6.16; 7.6.32). That is perhaps the case; but the plot of the *Anabasis* has an obvious precedent in Homer's *Odyssey*, as many scholars have pointed out, and Xenophon's audience would have seen the structural and thematic parallels. Although the correspondence with the plot of the *Odyssey* is not exact, it is close enough for Xenophon to draw on this particular master-plot in order to achieve an effect of normalization by the end of the work. This normalization entails the themes of the hero's return journey, his defeat of his enemies, and his coming of age from an untried young man to a seasoned commander. The hero, needless to say, is Xenophon himself. Yet even as Xenophon evokes the *Odyssey* as his model, he adapts it to create, in the *Anabasis*, a new "master-plot" (or archetypal narrative) in Western prose literature: the escape story. Though neither Xenophon nor his men—unlike Odysseus—have made it home at the end of the story, they do escape from a host of life-threatening dangers and find safety under Spartan service.

The *Anabasis* as Microhistory

An essential problem that would have faced anyone setting out to recount the expedition of the Ten Thousand was that it was unique—in such a way that it could not seamlessly be inserted into the grand narrative of the type of Greek history written by Thucydides and by Xenophon himself in his *Hellenica*. Book 2 of the *Hellenica* ends with the amnesty at Athens after the overthrow of the Thirty Tyrants. At the beginning of book 3, the narrator reports Cyrus's demand for assistance from the Spartans and their compliance. He then refers the reader to the work of one Themistogenes of Syracuse (a pseudonym for Xenophon himself) for the narrative of Cyrus's expedition and the safe arrival of his Greek mercenaries at the sea (see below). And after this reference to Themistogenes, the narrator does not elaborate further on the expedition but resumes his narrative of events in Asia Minor with the appeal of the Greek cities there to Sparta for assistance, out of their fear of the Persian satrap Tissaphernes and desire for freedom. He then provides a brief narrative of the expedition of the Spartan general Thibron, who absorbed Cyrus's Greek mercenaries into his own army and who was soon replaced by another Spartan commander, Dercylidas (3.1.1–8). In this way, the expedition of the Ten Thousand is neatly inserted into the much broader and more comprehensive story of the *Hellenica*, while the *Anabasis* story's full import as an event unto itself is not explored.

Thus, in our terms, the *Anabasis* is an example of microhistory (which treats of an isolated event in great detail) and the *Hellenica* of macrohistory (which provides a grand narrative). What this means is that in the form that Xenophon wrote them, the two-year story of the Ten Thousand could not be structured as a part of Xenophon's forty-nine-year history of Greece without creating an immensely awkward digression, simply because the *Anabasis* and the *Hellenica* are very nearly the same length. They each comprise seven books (250 and 272 modern pages, respectively, in the Oxford Classical Texts). For Xenophon, as for us, microhistory and macrohistory need to be composed separately if each is to be coherent.

Xenophon's motive for essentially creating the genre of microhistory is not difficult to infer. He saw the succession of Spartan commanders' military interventions on behalf of the Greeks living in Asia Minor as integral to the history of Greece. Cyrus's expedition and the exploits of the Ten Thousand he considered extraneous to that history. How, then, could the *Anabasis* be "historicized," that is, integrated into a larger narrative of Greek history? He chose to give it separate treatment that would highlight its uniqueness. In that treatment, he gives minimal background information so as not to deflect attention away from the experience of the Ten Thousand to the overall scheme in which it is enclosed. Other historians, who wrote on a grander scale and with a different emphasis, made other choices. Ctesias of Cnidus dealt with Cyrus's rebellion in his twenty-three-book history of the Persian Empire, and Ephorus of Cyme covered the same ground as the *Anabasis* in his comprehensive thirty-book universal history (see chapter 3). Nonetheless, neither Ctesias nor Ephorus could have provided anywhere near the same amount of detail as did Xenophon, given the length of the *Anabasis* in relation to their histories.

The *Hellenica* narrates events from where Thucydides leaves off (411 BC), until the anticlimactic battle of Mantinea (362 BC). That battle, according to Xenophon, was generally expected to settle the disputes over the hegemony of Greece but ended up resolving nothing. It has been aptly pointed out that Xenophon's choice of beginning and end attests to a sense of history that is open-ended and inconclusive. The *Hellenica* begins with the simple "And after these things" and ends with the seemingly pessimistic "There was still more uncertainty and confusion in Greece after the battle than there had been before. Up to this point let it be written by me. The events after these shall perhaps be a concern to someone else." The *Anabasis's* final sentence is open-ended and inconclusive in the same way. Following the story of Xenophon's capture of the Persian Asidates and his possessions, a single sentence brings the whole work to a strikingly abrupt end: "Meanwhile, Thibron arrived and took over the army, and mixing it with the rest of his Hellenic force, he made war against Tissaphernes and Pharnabazus [another Persian satrap]." At one and the same time, this ending brings the story full circle (in that the Ten Thousand are once again at war with Tissaphernes and are back in Asia Minor, whence they had set out with Cyrus) and points to an ongoing story (the ultimately futile military exploits of Thibron, Dercylidas, and Agesilaus against this same satrap). Ironically, the Ten Thousand originally set out from Sardis to fight against the Persian king and end up being enlisted by Thibron at Pergamum in Asia Minor, not so very far from Sardis, to fight against the representatives of the same king.

Finally, would ancient readers have recognized the *Anabasis* to be, according to their own generic distinctions, a work of history? The *Hellenica* begins with the words "after these things," signaling to the reader that it is a continuation of Thucydides's history of the

Peloponnesian War. So whatever genre Thucydides's history belonged to would by implication embrace the *Hellenica* as well, regardless of the obvious differences of tone and style between the two. Likewise, the opening of the *Anabasis*, despite its lack of a preface, signals that it is an account of events in chronological order. As for the *Cyropaedia*, an ancient reader of it would have very quickly perceived that it was a different kind of work from the *Hellenica* or *Anabasis* by the time he had read the first few chapters, or even after he had finished the preface (despite the apparent reference to research at *Cyropaedia* 1.1.6). The generic difference would have been obvious, not ambiguous (that is to say, the ancient reader would have understood the *Anabasis* to be history and the *Cyropaedia* to be political philosophy).

Consequently, there is no reason to think that the emphasis on philosophical truth, as opposed to historical truth, completely carried over from the *Cyropaedia* to the *Anabasis*. In other words, there is no need to problematize the distinctions between *Cyropaedia* and *Anabasis*, arguing that they both deal with historical and philosophical truth in an undifferentiated way. Rather, an ancient reader would have inferred from the content of the works themselves that they were doing different things and had different aims and purposes. Although living much later, Cicero got it exactly right when he wrote to his brother Quintus that in the *Cyropaedia* "the famous Cyrus was portrayed by Xenophon not in accordance with fidelity to history, but as a model of just rule" (*Letter to His Brother Quintus* 1.1.23).

The *Cyropaedia*, in contradistinction to the *Hellenica* and *Anabasis*, actually has an introduction in which the author, using the first person plural, explains why he wrote it and what it is about. He is interested in the problem of how to rule others successfully, and he has found in the example of Cyrus the Great the most successful ruler of all time. He therefore intends to examine the nature and education of Cyrus in order to discover why he was so successful: "Believing this man to be worthy of admiration, we have considered who he was by birth, what his nature was, and with what education he was brought up, that he so far excelled in governing human beings. We will try to relate, therefore, both what we have learned and what we think we have perceived about him" (1.1.6). Of course, the reader soon discovers that even if the *Cyropaedia* resembles Plato's *Republic* in its investigation of the best way to organize society, it is unlike it in form (since the *Republic* is purely a dialogue) and indeed unlike any other work of classical Greek literature. For it quickly turns into a romanticized biography of the ideal ruler, replete with extensive dialogue, elaborate battle scenes, and embedded novellas. It is, in other words, a cross between political philosophy and a quasi-historical novel. Those who look for an undercurrent of Persian oral history in the *Cyropaedia* in order to explain its divergences from the *Histories* of Herodotus are looking in vain. If Cyrus conquers Egypt, rather than his son Cambyses, or dies in bed of old age in his palace at Babylon, rather than of wounds on the battlefield, it is because Xenophon has made up these details in order to suit his didactic and philosophical purposes.

Xenophon's didactic purpose is revealed in an interesting, and unnoticed, connection between the *Anabasis* and the *Cyropaedia* that relates to the battle of Cunaxa itself. Cyrus the Younger was taken off guard on the day of the battle. Both he and his forces had to arm themselves very quickly, and his Greek contingent barely had time to draw up in battle formation (*Anabasis* 1.7.19–1.8.14). The battle was lost because Cyrus rashly dashed forward against his brother, striking him but also being struck down himself (*Anabasis* 1.8.26). Xenophon learned from these mistakes, and the appropriate lessons appear, both explicitly and implicitly, in the *Cyropaedia*. When Cyrus the Great was a mere boy and was participating in his very first battle, he too attacked the enemy recklessly and was only saved by his grandfather's intervention (*Cyropaedia* 1.4.21). To judge by his later actions in the *Cyropaedia*, it was a lesson he never forgot. Two of the items of advice Cyrus's father gives him in the long closing section of book 1 of the *Cyropaedia* are always to provide sufficient provisions to one's troops (1.6.10), and to catch the enemy in disorder and unarmed (1.6.35). Both are the precise opposite of what happened at Cunaxa: the Greeks ran out of provisions on the march through the Arabian desert (1.5.6) and Cyrus's army was caught unprepared on the day of the battle. The lessons learned from history are here articulated in a work of political philosophy.

The Voice of the Narrator

Like Homer's *Iliad* and *Odyssey*, the story of the *Anabasis* is told by an "external" third-person narrator; that is, one who does not participate in the events, and who, unlike his characters, knows how the story ends. It has been well observed that the third-person narrator mediates the relationship between Xenophon the author of the text, the character who is called Xenophon in the text, and the historical actor Xenophon who participated in the actual events the text purports to narrate. I would stress that we must always keep in mind that the character "Xenophon" is not identical with the historical actor Xenophon, in just the same way that the events narrated in the text cannot be identical to the events that actually took place but are a representation of them.

Why did Xenophon not simply employ a first person narrative voice, of the type that we are familiar with in modern memoirs? There is no single answer to that question. As far as we can tell, it would have been against the prevailing conventions for Xenophon to refer to his own role in events in the first person, and thus to seem to be vaunting his own accomplishments. Although he was a radical innovator in literary terms, his social attitudes and values seem to be those of his elite upper-class contemporaries. Both Herodotus and Thucydides use the first person singular on occasion, especially when they talk about method, but the third person dominates from the first sentence until the end. When Thucydides relates his own actions as a general in 424 BC, he does so in the third person (4.104–106). If we consider the *Anabasis* to be a work of history, there certainly was no precedent for a historical narrative in which the dominant narrative voice was in the first person.

Quite apart from the cultural and generic acceptability of telling the story from an impersonal perspective, the use of the third person gave the account a much greater appearance of objectivity. The *Anabasis*, like the *Hellenica*, has no preface, and the narrator remains unnamed. This anonymous narrator is also an unobtrusive narrator, letting Xenophon the character take center stage (he is mentioned some 230 times!), while simultaneously creating the impression that the text is unmediated. The illusion is that we are witnessing events as they unfold without the mediation of a narrator who has a vested interest in presenting them in one way or another. At the other extreme, we can compare the highly obtrusive and analytical narrator in the *Histories* of Polybius (written during the second century BC), who is constantly advancing his own opinions. (Modern readers, however, may be more familiar with the intrusive narrators in Henry Fielding's *Tom Jones* or George Eliot's *Daniel Deronda*.)

In addition to employing an unobtrusive and anonymous narrator, did Xenophon take an even more extreme step in order to objectify the account of his own achievements? It is widely accepted that he may have attempted to distance himself even further from his narrative by actually attributing the work to someone else. He refers to the expedition of Cyrus in his *Hellenica* (3.1.2) as follows: "How Cyrus gathered an army and having this army marched inland against his brother, and how the battle took place, and how he was killed, and how after this the Greeks arrived safely [*apesōthēsan*] at the sea, has been written by Themistogenes the Syracusan." Most modern commentators assert that this brief summary applies only to the first four books of the *Anabasis* on the grounds that the Greeks "arrived safely at the sea" when they reached Trapezus at the end of book 4. On the other hand, hardly anyone believes that there actually was such a book written by a Syracusan writer of that name. To my mind, however, it is an overliteral interpretation to understand the last part of the summary as specifically referring to the period that concluded with the arrival at Trapezus. The phrase "arrived safely at the sea" could easily include the narrative of books 5–7 if one does not press them for too much precision. Indeed, a few sentences later (3.1.6) we are told that "the soldiers who had marched inland with Cyrus, having arrived safely [*sōthentes*: the uncompounded form of the verb used above], joined Thibron."

Who was this Themistogenes? The preferred explanation is that Xenophon created Themistogenes as a fiction in order to make the record of his achievements more persuasive. In making this argument, scholars are taking their lead from Plutarch (*Moralia* 345e): "Xenophon was himself the subject of his own inquiry, recording his generalship and his successes; and he attributed the authorship to Themistogenes of Syracuse, in order that he should be more trustworthy in writing about himself as another person and giving as a favor to a third party the reputation for the writing." But before we accede too quickly, we should bear in mind that Plutarch was writing some five hundred years after Xenophon wrote the *Anabasis*, and that he may have had no more information on this topic than we do. In other words, he is merely guessing. There is something odd in the argument that Xenophon employed a pseudonym to give the account of his achievements greater plausibility but then did not actually include that pseudonym in the text of the *Anabasis* itself.

I obviously have trouble believing that Xenophon actually published the *Anabasis* under the pseudonym Themistogenes, if one means by that that he was concealing his authorship. My suspicion is that when he referred to the work of Themistogenes in the *Hellenica*, he expected readers to know that he, Xenophon an Athenian, was the author. I take this to be a polite and rhetorically self-effacing reference to his earlier work, and one in keeping with Xenophon's accustomed reticence. Apart from the *Anabasis*, he appears as a character only in one other of his works, in a brief passage of his *Memorabilia* (see chapter 5). In the *Hellenica* (3.2.7) the unnamed commander of the Cyreans, in a brief but stern speech, effectively counters a Spartan accusation that the Cyreans, while serving with Thibron in Asia Minor, were responsible for pillaging the territory of the Greek cities they were supposed to be helping. This commander was undoubtedly Xenophon himself. Near the end of the *Hellenica* (7.5.15–17) he narrates a cavalry skirmish that preceded the battle of Mantinea in 362 BC and notes that "good men died." One would never guess from this account that one of those "good men" was his own son Gryllus. Yet Gryllus, as discussed in chapter 1, was otherwise honored by "countless" eulogies and was even depicted on a painting in the Stoa of Zeus Eleutherios at Athens, with a copy at Mantinea.

Clearly, Xenophon's reticence to name either himself as a mercenary commander in Spartan employment or his son who died valiantly fighting for Athens on behalf of Sparta explains his self-effacing use of a pseudonym in the passage of the *Hellenica* quoted above. A contemporary reader would not have been fooled by this device. By the 360s, Xenophon was too famous to have passed off his own work as someone else's, and it is possible that by his time papyrus rolls either began with a title (as do modern books) or had labels attached bearing the author's name. If so, I have no doubt that the label or title page would have read "Xenophon the Athenian." If it had read "Themistogenes," or if readers really believed the statement in the *Hellenica* that Themistogenes was the author, then, we may reasonably ask, how did anyone ever discover that Xenophon was the true author? Modern scholars cannot have it both ways—the *Anabasis* cannot both be a late work and an anonymous one.

If I am right in concluding that Xenophon did not publish under a pen name, then this also has an important consequence for our understanding of Julius Caesar's decision to refer to himself in the third person in his two books *Gallic War* and *Civil War*. It makes it extremely likely that Caesar has borrowed this device, which was unusual in a personal narrative in Latin literature, from Xenophon. As in the *Anabasis*, it has the effect of turning Caesar's subjective personal narrative into an apparently objective historical account.

It is important to emphasize the fact that only three of Xenophon's fourteen works lack a preface of some kind: *Anabasis, Hellenica,* and the short philosophical dialogue *Hiero.* In all of his other works he employs, at least at the beginning, a first person narrator, and it is always clear from the opening paragraph what the work is going to be about. Nine of his works begin with "I/me" and two begin with "us/we." The "I" in these sentences is simultaneously that of the narrator, the historical author, and the implied author (the implied author, as stated above, being the sensibility behind the narrative that readers construct for themselves as they read). One should not rule out the equation of author and first person narrator in his Socratic works (*Memorabilia, Oeconomicus,* and *Symposium*) on the grounds that the historical Xenophon cannot have been present at all of the conversations the narrator claims to have heard, since anachronism and fictionalization are characteristic features of the genre of the Socratic dialogue.

The opening of the *Anabasis* is highly unusual, even by the standards of Xenophon's own customary practice, in neither specifying the subject matter of the work nor indicating anything of the mentality of the narrator. It was certainly customary for historians writing before him to begin by stating their name and country and as well as the subject matter of the work at hand. So began the *Genealogies* of Hecataeus of Miletus: "Hecataeus of Miletus says: I write down the following things as they seem to me to be true; for the stories told by the Greeks are, in my opinion, both numerous and ridiculous." Herodotus and Thucydides, too, began their *Histories* in a similar, if less tendentious, fashion: "This is the setting forth of the investigation of Herodotus of Halicarnassus . . . as to why Greeks and barbarians fought against each other" and "Thucydides an Athenian wrote about the war between the Peloponnesians and the Athenians." Xenophon, by contrast, never begins a work, whatever the subject matter, with his name and country. The *Hellenica*, as mentioned above, begins with the stark "after these things." In his two other long works, he only gives the subject matter. The *Cyropaedia* begins: "The thought once occurred to us how many democracies have been overthrown by those preferring to live under any other form of government than a democracy" (and so too with other forms of government, with the exception of the monarchy of Cyrus the Great). The *Memorabilia* starts: "I have often wondered with what arguments those who indicted Socrates persuaded the Athenians that he was worthy to be put to death by the city." The opening of the *Anabasis* is really in a class of its own, and that may be part of Xenophon's overall rhetorical strategy of making the text appear like an unmediated, and therefore unbiased, window into reality.

Nonetheless, the third person is not an omniscient voice but, in some respects, the equal of a first person, and that first person sometimes breaks through. There are a small number of first person interventions in the *Anabasis*. Near the very beginning of the work, after the narrator has described the Greek forces Cyrus has collected, he starts the narrative of the expedition proper with the transitional phrase "Cyrus, having the soldiers whom I have mentioned, set out from Sardis" (1.2.5). More intrusively, in Cyrus's obituary near the end of book 1, four first person interventions are used to validate the claims about Cyrus's popularity (1.9.12, 22, 25, 28). The narrative strategy behind this clustering is to give greater authority and emphasis to the claims that are being made about Cyrus's worthiness to rule. This occasional use of "I," however, is restricted to books 1–2. From book 3 onward, we hear the voice of Xenophon the character ever more frequently. By the end of the *Anabasis*, the distinction between the narrator's voice and Xenophon's voice has virtually collapsed; or, to put it a bit differently, the narrator's voice is often drowned out by the direct speech of Xenophon the character.

If one considers the *Anabasis* as a whole, because there are so many speeches by Xenophon in direct discourse (principally in books 3, 5, and 7), there is a very large first person presence in the text. The combination of third person narrative with first person speech acts tends to give a greater plausibility to each of them because the narrator is not the same as the speaker. The narration seems truthful because it is supported by the speeches, and the speeches seem truthful because they are supported by what appears to be a disinterested narrator.

I would like to end this discussion by giving readers something provocative to think about as they turn from this chapter back to the *Anabasis* itself. The purpose in employing an anonymous third person narrator, as claimed here and as all scholars assume, is to make the narrative appear objectively valid and unmediated. But, given that this narrator is neither Xenophon the author nor Xenophon the character, how can we know that he is a reliable narrator? Why should we as readers trust a narrator whose identity is unspecified and unknowable? Here is an example of where we might be suspicious.

The narrator tells us that Xenophon was interested in establishing a colony on the Black Sea because "it seemed to him that it was a fine thing to gain additional territory and power for Greece by founding a city" (5.6.15.). The seer Silanus, with whose assistance Xenophon has made a divinatory sacrifice concerning his idea, has helped to undermine his plan by leaking it to the army and by claiming that Xenophon's motive was "to acquire a name and power for himself" (5.6.17). When the character Xenophon gives a speech in his own defense (5.6.28) he does not really give an explanation for his plan beyond saying that he always sacrifices to ascertain what is best for the army and for himself (without making any mention of doing something for the benefit of Greece). So whose explanation should we believe, that of the anonymous narrator, of the seer Silanus, or of the character Xenophon? Even if we accept the statement, surely based on inference, that Silanus was motivated by a selfish desire to return to Greece as soon as possible with money Cyrus had given him, why should we believe the narrator when he implies that Xenophon's motives were purely altruistic? When Xenophon the character tells the army that he is concerned to do "what is most excellent and best" both for them and for himself, would not that include "acquiring a name and power for himself"? The anonymous narrator may look impartial enough, but, not surprisingly, he is actually serving the interest of Xenophon the author.

Further Reading

Lee (2005) and LaForse (2005) independently came to the conclusion that the *Anabasis* is the first war memoir. In a highly influential book, Booth (1983) developed the concept of the implied author. Gray examines Xenophon's narrative technique in two detailed articles (2003 and 2004), and Tsagalis (2009) investigates Xenophon's use of names. Bradley (2001) is a particularly penetrating analysis of the manipulation of generic conventions in the *Anabasis* and the role of the anonymous narrator (but his treatment of the theme of Xenophon's delayed homecoming is undercut by his failure to discuss Xenophon's plans to found a colony). For ancient concepts of genre, see Conte (1994), Marincola (1999), and Barchiesi (2001). A famous general treatment is Todorov (1990). Gera (1993) is a detailed treatment of generic innovation in the *Cyropaedia*. Marincola (1997) is the fundamental examination of the self-representation of Greek and Roman historians. For the bias against autobiographical discourse and self-praise in Greek sentiment, see Most 1989 (accepted by Tuplin 2003) and Pernot 1998. Flower (1994) explores the fragments of Theopompus of Chios in the context of the fourth-century tendency to emphasize the deeds of a single individual. For the influence of Homer's *Odyssey* on the *Anabasis*, see Lossau (1990) and Tuplin (2003). Scholars generally accept that Xenophon used the pen name "Themistogenes," but MacLaren (1934) is invariably cited. See Batstone and Damon (2006: 143–146) on Caesar's use of the third person (although they do not accept the debt to Xenophon). Work on the *Cyropaedia* has been particularly varied: Due (1989) takes the work at face value, whereas Carlier (1978) and Nadon (2001) give ironic readings (that is, Xenophon's real message is not necessarily what the text seems to be saying). Hirsch (1985) sees the *Cyropaedia* as historically reliable; Stadter (1991) argues much more persuasively that contemporary readers would not have mistaken it for a work of history. Tatum (1989) investigates the relationship between the reception of the *Cyropaedia* and ascriptions of genre.

· 3 ·

Let It Be Fact *and* Let It Be Fiction?

Let it be fact, one feels, or let it be fiction. The imagination will
not serve under two masters simultaneously.
— *Virginia Woolf,* "The New Biography" (Collected Essays)

"Anyone who reads this book is entitled to ask how anyone can
remember events which happened twenty-eight years ago and,
what is even more extraordinary and unbelievable, what happened
on a particular day. It is, of course, impossible, except for some rare
people who have the gift of total recall, which I do not possess."
Thus Eric Newby begins his memoir of World War II, *Love and War
in the Apennines* (1971).

It is very likely that Xenophon was writing at an equally great
remove, perhaps as many as thirty or forty years later. How much
did he remember? Was the problem of recalling the same for him as
for us? I realize that this question is rather simplistic, because Xenophon's intention may not have been to write the most accurate
account that he could. It may not have mattered to him if he could
recreate speeches and conversations as closely as possible to the very
words that were spoken. His narration of precise distances and troop
numbers gives the impression of a concern for accuracy, but that in
itself may be a literary device. Or it may be that he considered such
matters as chronology and numbers to belong to a different category from speeches and dialogues. There is always a tension between
the artistic arrangement of material and its completely accurate

narration. Literary considerations (that is, considerations about the effect the narrative can have on the reader) may override a concern for total accuracy. Transposing events, recording a speech that was not actually made at the time (but perhaps should have been), and other such devices may be thought to create a greater or higher truth (a kind of philosophical truth) that is more important than mundane historical truth.

The distance in time between the events of the *Anabasis* and their recording has spurred an unresolved controversy in modern scholarship about whether Xenophon kept notes while on the expedition or simply relied on his memory when he wrote up the *Anabasis*. Since most scholars accept a composition date in the 360s, the majority opinion is that he must have kept some kind of diary, given his attention to distances traveled and days spent either resting or marching. Xenophon describes the march of the army in books 1–4 in terms of stages (a single day's march) and parasangs (a Persian measure of distance the length of which is controversial). Yet why did he keep a diary, only to wait more than thirty years to work his entries up into a narrative? And if he did not keep a diary, why must we suppose that his memory was so good that he could remember all sorts of detailed information? My own guess is that he did not keep a diary because he was preoccupied with merely staying alive; and that while his memory, like that of most individuals who live in a largely oral society, was better than that of most readers of this book, he invented some of the details that look so precisely accurate to us. What he did was give guesstimates, and that was not considered "cheating" since ancient authors did not foresee that modern scholars, with printed versions of their rather cumbersome papyrus rolls in hand, would attempt to retrace their routes in the field. So the choice is not simply between a Xenophon who kept field notes and a Xenophon who relied on his prodigious memory while looking up distances in some book that described the Persian Empire (such as Ctesias's *Persica*). We are also faced with a Xenophon who relied on his imagination and literary art not only to give his work shape and structure but also to fill in the gaps of what he could not remember in sufficient detail.

Modern scholars often assert that the Greeks had better memories than we do. If that means that they were better at memorizing poems and speeches than we are, then the statement is probably true. But it does not necessarily mean that a Greek could accurately remember more of his past life experiences than the readers of this book can of their own. What we remember and how we remember it is conditioned by the context in which the act of recollection takes place. We do not know how often Xenophon recounted his exploits to others, but if he had been in the habit of doing this often, then the version he codified in the *Anabasis* is, in some sense, the last version that he had articulated to others, rather than his direct memory of what he had experienced at the time (Bloch 1998: 124).

We must not be beguiled by Xenophon's seemingly artless eloquence into believing that there was a direct line between his experience and his recording of that experience. In any and every memoir, a writer does not record precisely what he or she experienced in the past. When we write a description of something that has happened to us, whether it took place ten years ago or ten weeks, we undergo a complex act of reimagining that experience. That reimagining is itself part of a process of attempted recollection, selection of relevant details and omission of irrelevant ones, elaboration for the sake of clarity or dramatic effect, the conflation of details from other experiences either on purpose or by error, and so on. Moreover, what we remember when we recall a past event is actually not the event itself but our last recollection of it. So the description of an event that is described in words on the page, whether by conscious design for artistic effect or because of the nature of memory itself, may bear only a very rough resemblance to what the writer actually thought, felt, said, and did at the time.

All of this leads to a very complex problem: what is the relationship between what actually took place, the context of remembering what took place, the motive for recording what one remembers, and the literary choices that shape that recording? Xenophon certainly took part in Cyrus's expedition. Many years later, he decided to write a narrative. That narrative was probably in some measure a response to other competing narratives, some written (Sophaenetus, Ctesias, Isocrates), some verbal. Once Xenophon decided to give his version, as a distinct account in reaction to other accounts, he used his literary skills to shape his narrative in order to make it vivid, convincing, and interesting. To some extent he was confined by the generic expectations prompted by Greek prose literature, but he was also an innovator in that tradition. The most basic question modern readers are likely to ask is whether the *Anabasis*, in our terms, is essentially a work of fiction or nonfiction. In other words, did Xenophon set out to write what we would call a historical novel or something more akin to modern academic historical writing?

History or Fiction?

Sometimes it can be very difficult, even for us, to distinguish between narrative fiction and narrative nonfiction, unless some external source tells what kind of text we are reading. Modern books contain material external to the text (such as the blurb on the dust jacket) that indicates what type of text (fiction or nonfiction, history or novel) one is about to read. Ancient books, it would seem, did not contain any such external indications of genre. The only indications were internal, what the narrator told the reader about the work, often in the first paragraph in the case of historical works. Xenophon's works, as discussed in chapter 2, lack such indications.

In a modern book the cue that signals a work's genre is often part of the title, which includes the code words "memoir" or "novel" as part of a subtitle. We might also be suspicious of a work that claims to be nonfiction yet ascribes thoughts and words to the characters that the author could not reasonably have had access to. Unfortunately, the general characteristics of fiction and nonfiction, which can act as cues for the readers of modern texts, are not applicable to the writings of Greek and Roman historians. Herodotus in particular freely attributes motives, intentions, thoughts, and words to his actors in a way that strikes us as novelistic. In sum, there are no textual properties, syntactic or semantic, that will help us to decide whether the *Anabasis* was conceived of as a work of fiction or nonfiction. There are certainly features of the text, places where Xenophon expresses uncertainty as to events or motives, that suggest that he was operating under the same conventions of historical investigation as a modern academic historian. The problem, however, is that fiction can and often does imitate the devices of nonfiction while remaining fiction.

Can we get any closer to the truth-status of the *Anabasis* by looking at the question from the point of view of its ancient readers? Did they expect it to represent the truth of actual events as accurately as possible? Did they think in terms of its being falsifiable by comparison with other accounts, whether oral or written? These questions are difficult to answer, and highly controversial among modern critics. At a minimum, the *Anabasis* had to seem plausible to its contemporary readers, and it had to withstand refutation by other participants who might challenge Xenophon's account (though if he wrote the *Anabasis* in his sixties, most of his fellow mercenaries were probably long dead). His audience wanted to be entertained and instructed. Moreover, I would argue, they also expected the basic outline of the story to be free from outright and intentional fabrications that egregiously misrepresented what really took place. Even today, what most audiences expect in historical narrative is not the truth but the intent to tell the truth, and that was probably the case for ancient audiences as well. We also expect historical novelists not to tamper with well known historical facts, unless they are explicitly writing "alternative history" (Cohn 1999: 158-159). Xenophon was free to insert dialogue and speeches, attribute motives, and highlight his own actions in a way that might seem to us to cross the line between fictional and nonfictional narrative, even though modern memoirists tend to include dialogue, even from the writer's childhood, that the writer could not possibly have remembered in any kind of detail.

Finally, does any of this make a difference? Should we be so concerned with the question of what actually had happened? On one level, the philosophical truth of both fictional and nonfictional narratives can be identical, in that each can accurately reflect the perennial problems of human experience. But on another level, the difference is significant because the pleasure that the reader takes in each type of narrative is different. There is a particular pleasure we take when reading a story we are told is literally true in the sense that it recounts real events that happened to real people. Our psychological investment is different from when reading fiction, and that explains why audiences become incensed when they discover that a work advertising itself as nonfiction has actually been either completely fabricated or significantly enhanced. It is for that reason that even the writers of popular (as opposed to academic) historical works make a point of asserting that they have not invented incidents or dialogue. (Bryan Burrough asserts in his book *Public Enemies*: "Please keep in mind one thing as you read: This book was not 'imagined,' as with some recent popular histories. It was reported" [2004: xiv].) In sum, our seemingly unshakeable desire to know whether a particular story is a true story has both an intellectual basis and a deeply emotional one. We as readers care about what happened to Xenophon, and that human empathy is undermined and disappointed if we suspect that his story (like that of James Frey, the infamous author of *A Million Little Pieces*, published in 2004) is not all it purports to be.

An analogous example from another medium might help to crystallize this issue. Robert Capa's 1936 photograph "The Falling Soldier" is an elegant and moving depiction of a soldier at the very moment of death during the Spanish Civil War. The power of this picture to move the viewer is considerably undermined if the allegation is true that the scene was faked, that the soldier did not die at the very moment that the photograph was taken but got up and walked away. As an article in the *New York Times* expresses it (Marsh 2009), "the beauty and the pristine authority of the image would be horribly, tragically undermined if it turned out that this picture had somehow been staged by Capa."

Would we feel the same about the *Anabasis* if we somehow discovered that Xenophon had not risen from a sleepless night to rouse the Ten Thousand to save themselves, if he had not intervened on countless occasions to rescue his men from some seemingly hopeless situation, if he had not been the influential commander (the one to whom the troops had originally offered the supreme command he declined) he claims to have been? Is the power of these scenes diminished if we learn that they were "faked"—that it was others who roused the troops and who provided the strategic advice that got them out of danger?

Of course, all nonfictional writing has components of fiction as part of its fabric, and that includes traditional narrative history as well as literary journalism (or "creative nonfiction" of the type written by John McPhee). No work of history is a transcript devoid of literary artifice. One cannot even write history without engaging in the most basic aspect of fiction writing, which is the creation of a plot that gives a trajectory and a meaning to otherwise isolated events. And whenever one creates a particular plot out of the immense reservoir of individual events, it is necessary for the historian, as for the novelist, to choose which events to include and which to exclude. One thing, however, that distinguishes fiction from nonfiction is fiction's capacity to create alternative or possible worlds that have no necessary connection to "factual events." I would not wish to accept this interpretation myself, but I will pose the possibility, and leave it for the reader to consider, that Xenophon has retrospectively created the role for himself that he would like to have fulfilled in an alternative reality. The *Anabasis* then would not be a record of what, to the best of his recollection, actually happened, but a fictive exercise in wish fulfillment. Such an interpretation might find confirmation in the fact that subsequent writers, such as Isocrates and Ephorus, either did not mention Xenophon or perhaps assigned to him a very minor role. But I want to stress, so as not to be misunderstood, that I personally feel that this is a much less plausible scenario than one of an artful attempt to recapture the reality of Xenophon's experience to the degree that language is capable of representing lived experience.

Even if we grant that Xenophon has not invented actions that did not take place at all, how can we be sure that he has not omitted major incidents that would cause us to estimate affairs rather differently, if we knew about them? After all, in his *Hellenica* he omits to mention some of the most important and consequential events during the years he claims to cover. We would be ignorant of the foundation of the Second Athenian Confederacy, the liberation of the Messenian helots by Thebes, and the foundation of Megalopolis in Arcadia (due north of Sparta) if we had to rely on Xenophon alone. Other literary sources, as well as official documents inscribed on stone, fill in his gaps. If it were not for Diodorus, the fragments of the *Hellenica Oxyrhynchia* (a detailed history of the period from 411 to 395 or 386 of unknown authorship), and historical inscriptions, we would be at Xenophon's mercy. His omissions of important events and people have became notorious, but it is not so clear how they should be explained; that is, are they due to a toxic mixture of bad memory and personal bias or to the literary aim of writing a kind of "paradigmatic" history that stresses moral and political lessons rather than the comprehensive coverage of events? The traditional explanation is to emphasize the former, but the latter should not be underestimated.

To be sure, Xenophon is not the only Greek historian whose coverage of events can strike us as inadequate. Even Thucydides has some outrageous omissions and distortions in his history of the Peloponnesian War (see H. Flower 1992 and Badian 1993), though that has not diminished his reputation as the greatest historian of antiquity. Xenophon has been picked out for special censure because his narrative in the *Hellenica* can be checked against other sources to an extent that the narratives of Herodotus and Thucydides cannot. The *Anabasis*, however, is in a special category when it comes to appraising Greek concepts of historical accuracy. This is because Xenophon, unlike Herodotus or even Thucydides, is writing exclusively about an event in which he was a direct participant.

In the next chapter I will look at some of the gaps and omissions the narrative of the *Anabasis* itself suggests. Undoubtedly, there are many omissions of fact, some of them perhaps quite serious, that we are not, and never will be, in a position to detect. The rest of this chapter will compare Xenophon's account to other extant versions.

Other Accounts of Cyrus's Expedition

Xenophon's account achieves a high degree of verisimilitude, but that does not mean that it is true. Now, of course, the basic outline of events is true, and we know that it is because it is confirmed by other, and independent, sources. That is, a Persian prince by the name of Cyrus hired Greek mercenaries, mounted an expedition against his brother the reigning king, and was killed in the attempt. The Greeks were then stranded near Babylon, some of their generals and commanders were killed by the Persians, and they eventually made their way back to the coast of Turkey, where they entered Spartan service. Xenophon was one of the Greeks who went on the expedition. That much, and it is not much, I am confident to assert is factual. The really interesting things, however, are far less certain.

There are several ways of judging the factual accuracy of the *Anabasis*: in terms of probability (does the story make sense?) and internal consistency (does the narrative contain contradictions within itself?) and by comparison with other extant accounts of the same events. Most readers of the *Anabasis* (even many classicists) may not be aware that there were other contemporary accounts (Sophaenetus perhaps and Ctesias), and one near-contemporary one (Ephorus), of the Ten Thousand that are now lost. We still possess later versions based on them (Plutarch and Diodorus). The *Anabasis* is Xenophon's foray into this arena of conflicting discourses and competing narratives. His version became, and still is, the dominant version, principally because of its literary merits. Later Greek and Roman critics considered Xenophon a far better writer than either Ephorus or Ctesias (the immediate sources of Diodorus and Plutarch respectively), and that partly explains why their works have not survived.

The two other extant accounts of Cyrus's expedition are brief and written many centuries later than Xenophon. The biographer Plutarch, writing in the first century AD, during the height of the Roman Empire, recounts Cyrus's rebellion in his life of King Artaxerxes. Plutarch's account is focalized from the Persian point of view, and in addition to consulting Xenophon, he makes extensive use of two Greek writers who wrote *Persica* (histories of Persia). These were Deinon and Ctesias, whose works are, unfortunately, no longer extant. Since Plutarch is writing biography, his emphasis is also rather different from that of Xenophon. He goes into more detail about the strife between the two brothers and their family background. Much of this information is of dubious historical value, for example the story that Cyrus planned to assassinate his brother during a religious ceremony.

Near the beginning of the fourth century BC, Ctesias of Cnidus, a Greek doctor at the court of the Persian king Artaxerxes II, wrote a history of Persia in twenty-three books. Unfortunately, his work is only known through citations and paraphrases by much later authors. Ctesias was King Artaxerxes's personal physician and treated the wound that was inflicted by Cyrus during the battle of Cunaxa. Ctesias was in an excellent position, therefore, to know what was happening on the other side in the conflict between the two royal brothers. Even though Ctesias's history has been lost, Photius, a ninth-century patriarch of Constantinople, gives a summary of the contents of his *Persica*. It is often assumed by modern historians that there is a direct relationship between the amount of circumstantial detail in a narrative and its accuracy. Thus Ctesias's account of Cyrus's death might be taken to be a more accurate account than Xenophon's, simply because it is much longer and more detailed (see chapter 4).

Yet a huge amount of detail may be indicative of nothing more than an author with a lively imagination and a gift for literary fiction. This comes out even more clearly in Ctesias's lengthy description of Cyrus's mother being informed of his death. As the ancient literary critic who paraphrases this scene realized, Ctesias drew it out "little by little and step by step" for the purpose of creating suspense and forcing the reader to share in the mother's grief (Demetrius, *On Style* 216). The heaping up of circumstantial detail is here a purely narrative device—it has nothing to do with historical truth or accuracy. So whereas Xenophon leaves out factual material for reasons of personal bias, thematic emphasis, and narrative economy,

Ctesias includes fictive material in order to manipulate the emotions of the reader. Even some ancient writers, such as Plutarch, recognized that Ctesias included outright fictions in his history, such as his assertion that a mound of earth shaded by a new grove of date trees miraculously sprang up and covered Clearchus's exposed corpse (*Artaxerxes* 1.2; 18.5).

The primary challenge to Xenophon's account comes not from Plutarch but Diodorus Siculus (14.19–31, 37). The history of the world down to his own time that Diodorus produced, writing in the first century BC, is a synthesis and compilation of earlier sources. It is generally agreed that his immediate source in this part of his work was Ephorus of Cyme, the fourth-century BC author of a universal history in thirty books that narrated events from earliest times down to 340 BC. Diodorus is generally considered to be an epitomizer of marginal competence, and although some have challenged that characterization, it seems accurate enough. To make matters worse, most modern scholars also regard Ephorus as a thoroughly second-rate historian; but that may be too harsh a judgment, given that his work has not survived to be evaluated on its own merits. Nonetheless, when comparing Diodorus's account with that of Xenophon we must be alert to the strong possibility that differences may be due to the fact that Ephorus would have rhetorically elaborated his sources in order to make his own version look original and that Diodorus often introduces inaccuracies in the process of abridgment. We do not know how long Ephorus's account of Cyrus's expedition was, though it was certainly contained within a single book (perhaps book 17 of his history). The problem is that ancient "books" (or papyrus rolls) differed tremendously in length, with Xenophon's books averaging thirty to forty modern (Oxford Classical Text) pages each, while book 1 of Thucydides is eighty-eight pages. Diodorus's account (in the Loeb Classical Library edition), however, is only twenty-one pages in English translation, whereas the *Anabasis* of Xenophon (again, in the Loeb translation) is 302 pages. This is like comparing a grape to a watermelon.

Ephorus's own sources for the story of Cyrus's expedition and the subsequent exploits of the Ten Thousand are a matter of unresolved (and probably irresolvable) controversy. He certainly used Ctesias. Did Ephorus also rely on Xenophon's *Anabasis*, combining his account with that of Ctesias? Or was his other main source the shadowy *Anabasis* of Xenophon's fellow general Sophaenetus of Stymphalus? No matter what Ephorus's sources may have been, it should be strikingly obvious how far removed we are from historical reality when reading Diodorus's narrative; we must make the leap from Diodorus's abridgement of Ephorus to Ephorus himself, and then to Ephorus's sources, which may have comprised a combination of several different authors. All that we really have before us is Diodorus, and it is sometimes very easy for scholars (including myself) to forget that central fact. One thing, however, is clear: if Ephorus, or Ephorus's own sources (such as Ctesias), survived to this day, no one would be reading Diodorus himself.

One area where all sources are manifestly inaccurate concerns the size of the Persian army at Cunaxa. Xenophon's claim that Artaxerxes's army numbered nine hundred thousand men is simply impossible, even though he cites Persian deserters and captives as the source for this figure (1.7.11–13). What is interesting is not the fact of exaggeration (which began as early as Herodotus's claim that Xerxes's infantry in 480 numbered 1,700,000!) but that Xenophon's figure is more than twice the four hundred thousand given by both Ctesias (Plutarch, *Artaxerxes* 13.3) and Diodorus (14.22.2, citing Ephorus). Few armies in history have numbered more than ninety thousand combatants. Is Xenophon's nine hundred thousand pure rhetorical exaggeration, intended simultaneously to exalt the success of the Greek mercenaries on the field of battle and to exonerate Cyrus's failure to kill his brother? Or was Xenophon, despite his military service, very bad at estimating numbers and too ready to believe faulty intelligence gathered from deserters and captives? It is even more difficult to explain why Xenophon gives one hundred thousand for Cyrus's native troops, a number that could not possibly have made the difficult journey through the Syrian desert (modern estimates put his non-Greek forces at around twenty thousand).

It would require a very long and detailed analysis to compare Xenophon, Plutarch, Diodorus, and the fragments of Ctesias on every point of detail; so I am going to focus on three questions that I hope readers will find interesting and provocative. When did Cyrus first tell all of the Greek generals that he was marching against his brother? Has Xenophon lied about the events that led up to Tissaphernes's arrest of the Greek generals? Was Xenophon actually a very minor player in events until the winter of 399, when the army took service under the Thracian prince Seuthes—so minor, in fact, that other contemporary accounts of the retreat of the Ten Thousand omitted his role altogether?

First of all, when did the Greek generals first learn the true objective of Cyrus's expedition? Readers of Xenophon will be surprised to learn that in Diodorus's narrative this crucial fact is revealed *before* the army sets out from Sardis (14.19.9): "Cyrus had disclosed to the commanders that he was marching against his brother, but he concealed this from the troops out of fear that they might abandon his enterprise because of the scale of the expedition." If we accept Diodorus's testimony, Xenophon would here be guilty of a major cover-up. It would mean that his friend Proxenus, who had invited him to take part in the expedition, knew very early on that this was not going to be some minor campaign against the nearby Pisidians, and surely he would have told Xenophon this. Either Xenophon has consistently lied, or Diodorus (or his source) has made a rather significant factual mistake. Plutarch, however, citing both Xenophon and Ctesias, says that "Cyrus marched against the King . . . alleging one pretext after another for the expedition" (Plutarch, *Artaxerxes* 6.4). It is in Xenophon's favor that he is supported by Ctesias and that Plutarch did not know of an alternative account.

Second, how accurate is Xenophon's account of Tissaphernes's arrest of the generals? According to Xenophon, Clearchus requested an initial meeting with Tissaphernes in order to discuss mutual suspicions that had arisen between the Greek and Persian armies (2.5.1–2). Tissaphernes then suggested that Clearchus return for another meeting, this time bringing with him the other generals and captains. Tissaphernes promised that if they came to him, he would reveal the names of the Greeks who told him that Clearchus was plotting against him and his army (2.5.24–25). On the next day, five of the generals and twenty of the captains came to the Persian camp. After the generals had entered Tissaphernes's tent they were arrested, while the company commanders (who had remained outside) were slain (2.5.31–32).

Some modern scholars have argued that the Greeks were actually in violation of their agreement with the Persians because they had sent out unauthorized foraging parties (see 5.2.37), since not all of them had enough money to buy food from the markets that Tissaphernes provided. Tissaphernes, therefore, could claim that the Greeks had broken the truce, since it specified that the Greeks would not pillage the land as long as the Persians provided a market in which they could purchase provisions (2.3.26–28). Yet all the ancient sources, both extant and fragmentary, are in complete agreement that Tissaphernes used treachery and deceit to entrap the generals (Plutarch, *Artaxerxes* 18; Diodorus 14.26.5–7; Ctesias Fragment 27, quoted below). Indeed, in his first speech at the dawn assembly, the character Xenophon states very explicitly that the Greeks, despite being short of money with which to purchase food, have not seized any provisions in violation of the truce (3.1.20).

The conflict with Xenophon's account concerns the attitude of Clearchus to the fatal meeting with Tissaphernes and the roles of Menon and Proxenus in this incident. Xenophon portrays a Clearchus who is eager for the meeting, even against opposition (2.5.27–30). According to the version he gives, Clearchus believes himself to be on very good terms with Tissaphernes, reports to the army that it is necessary for the generals and captains to meet with Tissaphernes, and attends the fatal meeting fully expecting that Tissaphernes will reveal that his rival Menon has slandered him, and he will then be able to punish Menon as a traitor to the Greek cause. In sum, "Clearchus desired to secure the loyalty of the entire army for himself and to put the troublemakers out of the way" (2.5.28).

Ctesias, however, who was a friend of Clearchus, saw these events in very different terms. In Photius's summary of Ctesias we find the following (Fragment 27): "He relates how Tissaphernes plotted against the Greeks, and, having won over Menon the Thessalian, through him overpowered Clearchus and the other generals through deceit and [false] oaths, although Clearchus both foresaw the plot and endeavored to avert it. But the majority, deceived by Menon, compelled Clearchus against his will to visit Tissaphernes; and Proxenus the Boeotian, who himself had already been taken in through deceit, joined the others in advising him to go."

The statement that Clearchus went to the meeting with Tissaphernes "against his will" contrasts with Xenophon's explicit testimony that it was Clearchus who compelled the others to go. As Xenophon describes the situation, "some of the soldiers were speaking in opposition to Clearchus, saying that all of the generals and captains should not go and that they should not trust Tissaphernes. But Clearchus strongly insisted, until he brought it about that five generals and twenty captains would go" (2.5.29–30). Given that Ctesias was highly partial to Clearchus in his history (a bias Plutarch noticed: *Artaxerxes* 13.4; 18) and was not an eyewitness of what transpired in the Greek camp, it is surely preferable to believe Xenophon in this instance.

Ctesias explicitly claims that Menon was complicit in the betrayal of the generals. Xenophon does not go nearly as far as that but provides enough circumstantial material (focalized through Clearchus) for an impartial reader to infer Menon's involvement: Menon was on bad terms with Clearchus and wanted the command of the entire army for himself, he wished to be Tissaphernes's friend, he had been visiting Tissaphernes and Ariaeus, and Clearchus suspected that Menon had been slandering him to Tissaphernes (2.5.23). What is less transparent is the role of Proxenus. One could translate the last sentence of Photius's summary rather differently from the way I did above, simply by shifting a comma: "Proxenus the Boeotian, who himself had already been taken in, through deceit joined the others in advising him to go." In that case, we might see Proxenus as Menon's collaborator in a move to replace Clearchus as the top general of the Greeks.

This reading of Proxenus's complicity in the machinations of Menon and Tissaphernes is actually, and quite unexpectedly, supported by a passage in the *Anabasis* in which Ariaeus (Cyrus's second-in-command, who joins Tissaphernes after Cunaxa) explains why the generals were seized. He says to the surviving generals Cleanor and Sophaenetus, who are joined by Xenophon, since he wishes to know what has befallen his friend Proxenus: "Clearchus, since he was revealed to be perjuring himself and breaking the truce, has his punishment and is dead. But Proxenus and Menon, because they reported his plot, are being held in great honor" (2.5.36–38). This is a lie, since Proxenus and Menon are also executed in due course. The truly interesting thing is that the Persian Ariaeus thought that this would sound convincing, and it could only sound so if Proxenus and Menon were known to be close associates in the power struggle between the Greek generals. The circumstantial case against Proxenus does look like a fairly plausible one, even if this is the only hint of it in the *Anabasis*.

In the preceding paragraph, I accepted Xenophon's statement that Menon was executed along with the other generals. What Xenophon specifically claims is that the others were beheaded, whereas "it is said that Menon, after being tortured alive for a year, met the death of a scoundrel" (2.6.29). Diodorus's version could not be more different: "Tissaphernes sent the generals in chains to Artaxerxes. He executed the others but spared Menon alone, since he alone, because he was quarreling with his allies, seemed ready to betray the Greeks" (14.27.2). Whom should we believe? Xenophon distances himself from his own version by including the qualification "it is said." Moreover, Diodorus's account might seem to get some verification from Plato's *Meno* (in which the two main speakers, Socrates and Menon, discuss human virtue), since Socrates refers to Menon as "the ancestral guest-friend [*xenos*] of the Great King" (78d2–3). Might Menon's inherited relationship with the king of Persia have earned him a pardon or, on the contrary, an even more severe punishment for having violated it? I do not think that we have enough evidence to settle the question of Menon's fate, even if the "poetic justice" of Xenophon's version is difficult to resist.

If there is one scene among the many striking vignettes that no reader of the *Anabasis* will ever forget, it is the dawn meeting of the army when Xenophon is raised from the position of unpaid volunteer to elected general with a major part to play in saving the lives of the Ten Thousand. How can it be, then, that in Diodorus's version Xenophon is not named until the army begins its campaign in Thrace in the winter of 400/399? Even more startling, Diodorus seems to say that after the arrest of the generals, supreme command was given to Cheirisophus: "The soldiers chose more generals, but they gave the command [*tēn hegemonian*] of the whole army to one of them, Cheirisophus the Lacedaemonian" (14.27.1). Many scholars have inferred from this statement that Diodorus must have been using a source that drastically downplayed the role of Xenophon while simultaneously stressing the importance of Cheirisophus.

Is this a case of narrative abridgement by either Diodorus or Ephorus, or was Cheirisophus really made the supreme commander at this point? If the latter, then did Xenophon greatly exaggerate his own role in commanding the army on the subsequent trek to the sea? Even if the Greeks had a somewhat different notion of historical and literary truth than we do, this is just the sort of thing they did not approve of—blatant personal bias that leads to claiming credit for the actions of others. In a praise/blame society, this kind of historical inaccuracy would have been intolerable to Xenophon's contemporary readers.

Nevertheless, it would be a grave mistake to reach the conclusion that Xenophon has grossly inflated his own importance, without looking more closely at what Diodorus does and does not say. First of all, no other general is mentioned by name for the rest of Diodorus's narrative, and there are only two brief references to Cheirisophus (which merely tell us that he was dispatched to get ships but failed to obtain any). Sophaenetus, it must be stressed, is never mentioned at all. In a delayed postscript to the main narrative of Cyrus's expedition, the reader is told that those of the surviving soldiers who did not wish to return to their own homelands, about five thousand in number, "chose Xenophon as their general," who then set out with them to fight in Thrace (14.37.1–4). All of this indicates that it is Diodorus, and not the source he is abridging, who has condensed his narrative to the point of naming no one but Cheirisophus in his account of the return march and only giving Xenophon a role at the end. If one must deal in probabilities, it does seem highly unlikely that this could have been Xenophon's only important role in the entire enterprise (and, ironically, the one that caused him the most trouble and almost cost him his life and reputation). Surely, Ephorus gave Xenophon a role in the narrative before this point; otherwise it would have been difficult to explain why the surviving members of the Ten Thousand should have chosen an untried commander to be their "sole" general for the campaign in Thrace.

One question, however, remains. Even if we concede that Diodorus's source mentioned Xenophon and other generals throughout the narrative and that Diodorus simply streamlines them out, does the narrative of Xenophon's *Anabasis* conceal the fact that Cheirisophus was the overall commander of the army? It has been well pointed out by P. J. Stylianou (2004: 72) that Diodorus's statement about Cheirisophus being given "the leadership" of the whole army (and again called "their leader," *ton aphēgoumenon*, at 14.30.4) seems based on Xenophon's own proposal at the dawn assembly of the army. The character Xenophon suggests the following arrangement (3.2.37): "Let Cheirisophus lead the way [i.e., command the van of the army: *hegoito*], since he is a Lacedaemonian; let the two eldest generals be in charge of each of the flanks; and let us the two youngest generals, I and Timasion, bring up the rear for the time being." It was only much later, when the army was at Sinope on the Black Sea, that the issue of a single commander came up, and Xenophon declined to stand for election so that Cheirisophus could hold the position (for only six or seven days, as it turned out; 6.1.16–22).

It is an attractive suggestion that Xenophon's own narrative is the source of the widely held modern theory that Sophaenetus of Stymphalus (supposedly the ultimate source behind Diodorus) diminished Xenophon's role in the retreat and gave the supreme command to Cheirisophus. But one final important observation needs to be made. When Diodorus asserts that the army chose Xenophon "to be their general" for the campaign in Thrace, he is once again exaggerating and this time giving Xenophon a prominence he did not actually have. It is clear from the *Anabasis* that even if Xenophon was the most influential of the Greek generals, he was not the only person who held that office during the army's service under Seuthes. I am not entirely convinced by Stylianou's argument that Diodorus's account ultimately, through the intermediacy of Ephorus, depends on Xenophon's *Anabasis*. But I do believe that the above discussion has demonstrated that one must not explain Diodorus's own narrative economy in terms of an assumed bias against Xenophon in Diodorus's source.

Even this partial survey of the evidence suggests that external sources cannot be used to falsify the narrative of the *Anabasis*. Modern critics have been suspicious because the account of Xenophon's own role seems just too good to be true. For many readers, it strains plausibility that he always said and did just the right thing and that his tactical insight saved the day time and again. If Xenophon the author could give a defense of this account, he might stress the artistic need to keep the narrative tightly focalized, as well as the difficulties involved in giving unity and coherence to the experiences of so many actors. He might point out that this is, after all, his own story that he is telling. Then, as now, memoir is a special sort of historical narrative with a strong tendency for selecting and interpreting events from the point of view of a single actor. Events are given a particular type of "spin" or perspective, which does not, however, necessarily mean that what is being narrated is factually untrue. Although ancient historians were very quick to accuse each other of bias in reporting events, it is striking that no ancient writer, whether historian or critic, accused Xenophon the author of exaggerating or falsifying the role of Xenophon the character in the *Anabasis*. So perhaps we, too, should consider it sufficiently plausible that a young Athenian aristocrat, who was feeling somewhat uncomfortable in his home town, joined a friend for what he thought was going to be a short adventure in the entourage of a charismatic foreign prince, little knowing that he would soon be impelled to assume a role of leadership in a desperate two-year struggle for survival in lands distant and remote. Life can indeed be stranger than fiction.

Further Reading

The number of books that treat the nature of history is vast, and new ones appear every day. Evans (1997) is a standard treatment; Curthoys and Docker (2005) give an evenhanded survey of the most important trends and works of scholarship. White, in a series of paradigm-shifting books (1973, 1978, 1987), has argued that historians and imaginative writers (poets, novelists, playwrights) use substantially the same techniques and strategies (primarily rhetorical) in the composition of their discourses. Nevertheless, he still acknowledges that in historical writing, stable events lie beneath the various rhetorical versions of them. Far more extreme is the variety of "postmodernism" that posits (to put it simply) that since we cannot actually know the truth of the past (since the past only exists in books), all history is ultimately fiction. Batstone (2009) gives a provocative application of postmodern theory to Roman historical texts, and this is followed in the same volume by an equally provocative rejoinder by Lendon (2009). These two essays lie at extreme ends of the spectrum, but taken together well illustrate what is at stake for students of classical history and literature. Dolezel (2010) attempts to break the deadlock by pointing out that while historiography and fiction each constructs possible worlds, those two kinds of possible worlds show fundamental differences: the former constructs models of the actual past, whereas the latter constructs imaginary possible alternatives to the actual world. Marincola (2001) provides a concise and balanced survey of recent work in the study of the Greek historians. Historians and literary critics have long been divided over the essential nature of Xenophon's *Hellenica*. Cawkwell (1979, and in long series of articles reprinted in Cawkwell 2011) considers it bad history. Gray (1989) and Pownall (2004) attempt to show how Xenophon shapes his narrative in order to provide moral instruction. (These viewpoints, of course, are not mutually exclusive.) Tuplin (1993) is a close reading of the *Hellenica* that combines historical and literary analysis, as does Dillery (1995). Grayson (1975) goes so far as to claim that Xenophon did not even intend to write history. The standard collection of the fragments of the Greek historians is Jacoby (1923–58), but the fragments of Ctesias have appeared in several recent translations: Llewellyn-Jones and Robson (2010) in English and Lenfant (2004), who also includes a Greek text, in French. Ctesias's career is treated by Tuplin 2004a. For Diodorus's account of the Ten Thousand, see Westlake (1987) and Stylianou (2004). Modern reconstructions of the battle of Cunaxa can be found in Anderson (1970), Bigwood (1983), and Waterfield (2006). Bassett (1999) compares the various ancient accounts of Cyrus's death and (2002) argues that the Greeks had broken their oaths to Tissaphernes. Stylianou (2004) is convinced that Xenophon kept a diary on the expedition; Cawkwell (1972 and 2004) is equally firm that he did not. Xenophon's use of the parasang both as a unit of measurement and as a literary device is analyzed by Rood (2010a).

·4·

Style and the Shaping of Narrative

Le véritable éloquence consiste à dire tout ce qu'il faut, et à ne dire
que ce qu'il faut. (True eloquence consists in saying everything
that is necessary and in not saying what is not necessary.)
                              —*La Rochefoucauld*, Réflexions

Xenophon the author traverses generic boundaries just as successfully as Xenophon the general does geographic ones. This
is because Xenophon is a master of literary style on many levels. He
shows great skill and imaginative power in all of the various components that go into crafting an engaging work of literature: plot
and themes, characterization and focalization, sentence structure
and word choice are all managed with an unpretentious elegance. "Style" is a tricky concept to come to grips with because it
means different things in different contexts. There is "historiographical" style, which refers to the way an author tells the story
(with or without speeches and conversation, with direct speech or
indirect speech, with a first person or a third person narrator, with
or without digressions). Then there is "oratorical" style, which includes the types of arguments and rhetorical devices that are
used. And, finally, we can speak of "linguistic style," which entails
word choice and the arrangement of words within a sentence,
grammatical constructions, and so on (Dover 1997: 1–4). Obviously
there is considerable overlap between these categories, and it is in

combination that they give an author his particular "style," the sum total of his rhetorical, linguistic, and historiographical strategies.

Xenophon is a master of style in that he is adept at choosing precisely the right words, put into the right order, to convey the ideas and images he wishes to communicate. It is easy enough to be misled by his unadorned and simple manner of expression into assuming that his was an artless elegance. T. E. Lawrence (a.k.a. "Lawrence of Arabia") wrote to his biographer that his *Seven Pillars of Wisdom* was "not a human document like Xenophon's *Anabasis* but an artificial straining after art" (Meyers 1977). Lawrence failed to apprehend just how successfully Xenophon concealed the artificiality of his art. It was not without justification that his contemporaries referred to him as the Attic Bee and Attic Muse because of the sweetness of his diction (Diogenes Laertius 2.57).

Scenes

The arrangement of material in the *Anabasis* has been devised with great care (see below). But what is most memorable is not the overall scheme but the individual episodes and vignettes, ranging in length from a few sentences to several pages, which give the text its energy. Plutarch praises Xenophon's vividness in describing the battle of Cunaxa and states (*Artaxerxes* 8):

> Since many writers have reported this battle, and since Xenophon all but shows it to us with our own eyes, and by the vividness of his description makes his reader always a participant in the emotions and dangers of the struggle, as though it belonged not to the past but to the present, it would be folly to describe it in detail, except in so far as he has passed over things worthy of mention.

The scene in which Cyrus attacks his brother is especially vivid and crisp, and contains a powerfully terse description of Cyrus's death (1.8.26–27):

While being with these few cavalry, he caught sight of the king and the mass of troops around him. And at once he did not restrain himself but, having said "I see the man," he rushed against him and struck him on the breast and wounded him through his breastplate, as Ctesias the doctor says, and he also says that he himself treated the wound. As he was striking [his brother], someone hit him with a javelin under the eye with great force.

This three-sentence description of how Cyrus was killed contrasts sharply with Ctesias's overly circumstantial and verbose treatment of this same episode, in which a wounded Cyrus wanders all over the battlefield. Plutarch gives (*Artaxerxes* 11) what he calls "a much abbreviated version" of Ctesias's narrative (which is still two pages long in the Loeb edition) and then wryly concludes: "Such is the account of Ctesias, in which, just as with a blunt sword, he is long in killing Cyrus, but kills him at last." There is, however, an ambiguity in Xenophon's concise narrative that is not easily resolved. Some accounts (but *not* Ctesias's) claimed that the king had also wounded Cyrus, and royal propaganda claimed that the king himself had killed him (*Artaxerxes* 10.3; 16.1). Despite its vividness, Xenophon's single sentence describing Cyrus's death leaves this unresolved, since he does not specify the "someone" who struck Cyrus.

It was not only that Ctesias gave a very long description of the death of Cyrus in contrast to the few sentences in Xenophon. Just before narrating the scene of Cyrus's final charge and death, Xenophon relates how Cyrus personally killed the commander of the six thousand cavalry who were stationed in front of the king. He merely writes: "He is said to have slain with his own hand Artagerses their commander" (1.8.25). Plutarch, again citing Ctesias, turns this into a formal duel in Homeric fashion, with an exchange of spear throws and Artagerses railing against Cyrus in a nine-line speech (*Artaxerxes* 9). Ctesias's fondness for elaboration also comes out in his long-drawn-out depiction of the messenger informing Cyrus's mother about her son's death (as paraphrased by Demetrius, *On Style* 216; also discussed in chapter 3). If Xenophon is minimalist and sometimes does not tell us all that we might like to know, Ctesias is maximalist and often, it would seem, told rather too much.

Xenophon's style is completely different from that of Ctesias, who (to judge from the extant fragments) employed an artificial selection of words and images all too obviously calculated to create scenes of special pathos. Xenophon, too, can use words to express pathos and to communicate to the reader the emotional intensity of a particular situation, but his methods are more restrained and far more subtle. The first two sentences of book 3, in which he describes the feelings of helplessness and depression among the Greeks, as well as their inability to sleep or eat, after they have learned of the arrest of their generals, beautifully convey their predicament in such a way that one can recreate the scene, with its attendant emotions of grief and despair, before one's very eyes:

After the generals had been seized and the captains and soldiers who accompanied them had been killed, the Greeks were in a state of great despondency, as they reflected that they were at the king's gates, that many hostile tribes and cities surrounded them in every direction, that there was no longer anyone who would sell them provisions, that they were at least ten thousand stades [a thousand miles] from Greece, that there was no guide for the road, that impassable rivers blocked their route home, that the barbarians who had marched with Cyrus had also betrayed them, and that they were left on their own without even a single cavalryman as an ally, so that it was very clear that if they were victorious in battle they would not be able to kill anyone, whereas if they were defeated, not one of them would survive. Reflecting on these things and being discouraged, few of them tasted any food that evening, few lit a fire, many did not go to their quarters that night, but were attempting to rest wherever each of them chanced to be, being unable to sleep because of grief and longing for their home communities, parents, wives, children, whom they believed they would never see again.

Both in Greek and in English translation this is a powerful and effective depiction of soldiers who have lost their will to fight and who despair of ever again seeing their homes and families.

Focalization

The story that the *Anabasis* relates is told from a particular point of view. That point of view is always tightly focused, first from the vantage of Cyrus and the Ten Thousand and then increasingly from that of the character Xenophon. It is as if in a movie the camera is focused on the protagonists and never (or hardly ever) cuts away to show us what other characters in the story are doing. The overall structure of the *Anabasis* is dictated by the movements of the Ten Thousand as they travel from Sardis to Mesopotamia, to the Black Sea at Trapezus, along the coast until they cross the Bosporus and enter Byzantium, then proceed to Thrace, and finally end up back again in Asia Minor.

The tight focalization, however, can lead to some surprising narrative gaps that would be hard to justify in a more traditional work of narrative history. Tissaphernes leaves the Greeks for twenty days, in order, he claims, to get the king's permission to lead them back safely to Greece. The narrator does not tell us what Tissaphernes was doing those twenty days. For that we have to turn to Diodorus (14.26.4–5), who fills in the gap with the information that he married the king's daughter and promised to destroy the Greeks with Ariaeus's help.

Xenophon seldom switches to a scene that takes place elsewhere. As a general rule, we are introduced to what others have been doing and planning as and when they come into contact with the Ten Thousand. The trial of the Persian grandee Orontas (1.6.1–11), for instance, is focalized through Clearchus, whom Cyrus invited to attend it. After Clearchus left Cyrus's tent, "He reported to his friends how the trial of Orontas had been conducted; for it was not a secret" (1.6.6). What then follows is a vivid transcript of the proceedings in direct discourse, as if the trial were taking place in real time before our very eyes, rather than being reported second-hand by a less than reliable narrator. For Clearchus's reliability is implicitly questioned by the detail that Cyrus asked for his opinion first and that the seven Persian nobles who were judging the case immediately concurred with his opinion "that Orontas should be put out of the way as soon as possible" (1.6.9). Given what we are told of Clearchus's ambition and craftiness, as well as his readiness to serve Cyrus's interests, one hesitates to take his account, no matter how vividly recounted, at face value. Cyrus, according to Clearchus's version of the trial, executed Orontas because he could no longer trust him after three acts of unprovoked betrayal. Would not the historical Orontas, the one who in real life suffered and was executed, have proclaimed in his own defense that Cyrus himself was untrustworthy and guilty of treason?

In keeping with the tight focalization, Xenophon does not cite sources by name, for that would break the illusion of seeing events through the eyes of the participants. There is, however, one notable exception. Xenophon twice cites Ctesias's testimony for the confrontation between Cyrus and Artaxerxes during the battle of Cunaxa, and he does so in a striking way (1.8.26–27). Often ancient writers will cite another account in disagreement over a minor detail, but Xenophon actually defers to Ctesias. He points the reader to Ctesias "the doctor" for an account of how Cyrus wounded the king ("he says that he himself treated the wound") and for the details of the Persians who died while protecting the king ("for he was with the king"). This reference underscores the tight focalization of Xenophon's account. The implication is that his account depends on what the implied author has either seen for himself or extracted from his fellow participants in Cyrus's army, and that one should consult Ctesias (who was also a participant) for an account focalized from the Persian side. This is how Plutarch interpreted Xenophon's brevity, explaining that he turned to Ctesias for an account of Cyrus's death because Xenophon treated it "simply and briefly, in as much as he was not present" (*Artaxerxes* 9.4). At the same time, however, Xenophon directs us to Ctesias for the very reason that Ctesias is a hostile witness and thus a credible one. As such, Ctesias validates two claims that a skeptical reader might be inclined to doubt, given the small number of cavalry that accompanied Cyrus on this final charge (six hundred against six thousand): that Cyrus dealt the king a very serious blow and that many of the Persians stationed around the king were killed.

As the narrative progresses, there is a shift in focalization from the experience of the Ten Thousand collectively to that of Xenophon as the main character in the story. This occurs rather abruptly near the beginning of book 3, signaled by the words "There was an Athenian in the army named Xenophon." At the conclusion of his dawn speech to the assembled army, Xenophon proposes that they march in a square formation, with Cheirisophus leading the van, the four eldest generals commanding the flanks, and he and Timasion (since they are the two youngest of the generals) sharing the command of the rear guard of the army (3.2.37–38). Notoriously, however, from this point until they reach the sea at Trapezus, it is Xenophon alone who seems to be in command of the rear guard and who deftly leads his men in a series of adventures (4.1.6, 15). Timasion, by contrast, disappears from the entire narrative of the march through the mountains of the Carduchians and the snow-covered plains of western Armenia and only reappears late in book 5, when he attempts to thwart Xenophon's plan to found a colony on the Black Sea. Now, even if this can be explained by the fact that the army was marching in column throughout the action covered in book 4 (as opposed to marching in a square), the narrator has made a deliberate choice to focus on the words and actions of Xenophon and to exclude Timasion completely (who, even if he was marching with his contingent in front of Xenophon's, must have been doing and saying something).

Even the single most famous scene in the *Anabasis* (4.7.21–27), when the army catches sight of the sea from the top of Mount Theches, is largely focalized through Xenophon's personal experience. The focalization shifts deftly from the soldiers at the front of the army, who first view the sea, to Xenophon and the soldiers in the rear. "When the soldiers in the front got to the top of the mountain and looked down upon the sea, a great shouting arose. When Xeno-phon and the rear guard heard this they thought that other enemies were attacking them from the front," but as the shout became ever louder and nearer "it seemed to Xenophon to be something greater, and mounting his horse and taking along Lycius and the cavalry, he went to the rescue; and very quickly they heard the soldiers shouting 'The sea! The sea!' and passing the word along." This is a masterful example of shifting focalization, as we see events through Xenophon's eyes and even hear the famous shout through his ears. The focaliza-tion from the rear of the army also allows the narrator to delay the climax of the scene for as long as possible, while the repetition of certain key words (especially "shouting" and "shout") slows the pace and creates suspense.

At one point, due to an outbreak of ethnic tension, the army temporarily splits into three parts (one of which is commanded by Xenophon), and this necessitates that the focalization switch back and forth between them. The way the narrator relates the subse-quent fate of these parts (before their eventual reunification) reminds one of action movies, such as *Star Wars*, where several different strands of the story are kept in play, punctuated by cliff-hangers (6.3.1–26).

Focalization, however, is not always straightforward. In one pas-sage, it seems to be ambiguous. When the army fords the Euphrates at Thapsacus, the narrator mentions that no one got wet above the breast. This apparently was extraordinary enough at this time of year to call for comment (1.4.18): "The people of Thapsacus said that the river had never before been fordable on foot except at that time, but only by boats, which Abrocomas, who was marching in advance of them, had burnt in order to prevent Cyrus from crossing. It indeed seemed to be something divine and the river plainly seemed to yield to Cyrus on the grounds that he would become king." The observation about the low water level is unambiguously focalized through the local inhabitants, who may be wishing to flat-ter Cyrus. But whose point of view is expressed by the verb "it seemed"? Is it the narrator's inference or that of the people of Thap-sacus? Does Xenophon leave this obscure because the omen proved to be false, in that Cyrus never in fact became king? Or is the narrator attempting to raise the expectations of his readers that Cyrus will defeat his brother and usurp the throne, an expectation that will be thwarted by Cyrus's own rashness in the battle scene that is the climax of book 1? Although the story is told from the vantage of the Ten Thousand with Xenophon at center stage from book 3 onward, various shifts in focalization (as when Seuthes scouts out a mountain pass at 7.3.41–44) give the story greater variety and verisimilitude.

Narrative Economy

Xenophon can seem to a modern reader a frustratingly allusive author, capable of dropping a name or mentioning an incident in passing without giving the details or elaboration we would so dearly like to have, either because we need that information in order to appreciate the historical context or merely out of historical curiosity. For example, what about the Spartan Dracontius, "who had been exiled from home as a boy because he had accidentally killed another boy with the stroke of a dagger" (4.8.25)? This might have occasioned an interesting digression, and it might have told us something about the training of Spartan youths or Spartan homicide law. But we must bear Xenophon's purposes in mind, which are not the same as ours. And his sense of relevance, too, will be different, since he was not writing with a modern audience in mind. Yet, even so, some omissions are very difficult to explain either in narratological or in ideological terms. It is extremely odd, for instance, that Xenophon notes the death of Cheirisophus as an aside ("Cheirisophus had already died from drinking a drug that he took for a fever," 6.4.11) but fails to give him any sort of obituary in which he comments on his personal qualities. Is this because Xenophon was not present at his death, and thus it lay outside the focalization of the narrative?

Although the beginning of book 1 is tight, economical, and sufficiently informative as an introduction to the subsequent action of the story, there is something important that is missing. Most historical works give at least minimal indications of time, whether absolute or relative. The *Anabasis* begins with the illness and death of Darius without giving any indication of when this took place or of how much time elapsed either between his illness and death or between Cyrus's visit and his later expedition against his brother Artaxerxes. The action then moves very promptly to the setting out of Cyrus's expedition. The uninformed reader might be very surprised to learn that Cyrus was summoned in 405 and that his expedition took place four years later in the spring of 401. The chronological relationship between these events is made explicit in the *Hellenica* (2.1.13 and 3.1.1), so did Xenophon expect his readers to have read book 2 of his *Hellenica* before turning to the *Anabasis*, or were these events common knowledge? In this respect, the *Anabasis* more closely resembles the *Cyropaedia* as a work of creative fiction than it resembles the *Hellenica*, a work of narrative history. The beginning of the *Anabasis* is a minimal, if artful, sketch. It resembles the beginning of a novel, not a history.

There is a strong sense of narrative economy throughout book 1. Xenophon keeps the story going and only interrupts the narrative with speeches. Where another author would be tempted to digress, Xenophon sticks to the story at hand. Some of his omissions are probably due to an attempt to suppress embarrassing material, for example not stating by whose authority the Spartan Cheirisophus joined the expedition at Issus with seven hundred hoplites (the narrator merely says that "he had been summoned by Cyrus": 1.4.3). It is left for us to infer that he was officially sent by the Spartan government as part of a concerted effort to support Cyrus's rebellion by land and sea (as Diodorus states explicitly; 14.21.1–2).

When Xenophon does digress, even briefly, it is for a reason. And so he mentions the flaying of Marsyas by Apollo and the retreat of Xerxes from Greece in adjacent sentences, perhaps implying that Marsyas's defeat by the Greek god was a mythic forerunner of Xerxes's defeat at Salamis (1.2.8–9; an idea that may have been suggested by Herodotus 7.26). Near the end of book 1 he passes up an opportunity for a salacious digression that Herodotus (or any one of a number of fourth- and third-century BC historians) would have found irresistible. He states very flatly that Cyrus's Phocaean concubine was captured in Cyrus's camp by the king's forces (1.10.2). He merely says that she was "clever and pretty," which, given what other sources tell us, is a striking understatement. What he could have added is that her name was Aspasia, that she first became Cyrus's (who nicknamed her "the wise") and then Artaxerxes's favorite, that Artaxerxes dressed her up in the clothing of his favorite eunuch, and that he made her a priestess of Anaïtis at Ecbatana when his son requested her for himself (Plutarch, *Artaxerxes* 26–27; *Pericles* 24.7). All of that would have been interesting both to his ancient audience and to us, but it also would have slowed down his taut narration of the battle. Likewise, the story of how Cyrus came to esteem Aspasia (as told by Plutarch), though revealing of the prince's character, would have seemed out of place, given the economy and focus of the narrative.

Because Xenophon is not writing traditional history, he does not tell us what happened later to the vast majority of the characters in the story, except for the rare aside. There are very brief references, for instance, to Episthenes's future relationship with a boy (4.6.3) and to the later execution of Dexippus (5.1.15; see below). The one major exception, of course, is the excursus about Xenophon's own future life at Scillus. Most readers would have known that Tissaphernes was later executed by the king (as Xenophon himself reports at *Hellenica* 3.4.25), but the full story of Cyrus's concubine Aspasia could not have been common knowledge. Xenophon's treatment of Parysatis, Cyrus's mother, is very brief, hinting at her power, influence, and wealth. For her horrific cruelty to those implicated in her son's death, which must have been notorious, one had to turn to Ctesias (Plutarch, *Artaxerxes* 14–17).

Nor does Xenophon relate all that happened during the expedition or even all that he had personally experienced. In the narrative of the dispute over his foiled plan to establish a colony on the Black Sea, he refers to one of his opponents, Thorax the Boeotian, "who was *always* fighting with Xenophon concerning the generalship," but this is the first and last incident in which Thorax plays a role or is even mentioned (5.6.25). The reference to him is a tantalizing indication of the amount of material Xenophon does not tell us, and an indication that there was opposition to Xenophon's generalship that is not mentioned prior to book 5. This raises the possibility that for thematic reasons Xenophon selected his material so as to emphasize Greek cooperation in books 3 and 4. Book 7 has every appearance of containing a full and detailed account of the campaign of the Ten Thousand with Seuthes in Thrace, yet the final expedition against Salmydessus (a Thracian city on the Black Sea) is narrated in a single sentence (7.5.14): "After they had subdued this region they returned." Had nothing happened worth recording?

It is, to be sure, in the power of the narrator to decide who gets mentioned in a text and how often. There are a number of obvious major characters: Cyrus in book 1, Clearchus and Tissaphernes in book 2, Xenophon and Cheirisophus in books 3 and 4, Seuthes in book 7, and Xenophon himself in books 3–7. There are also a number of minor characters who surface now and again throughout the narrative as they play some particular role in the story. One such minor character is much more pervasive than the others, popping up at key moments from near the beginning of book 3 and making a final appearance right at the end of book 7. This is a captain of the rear guard, Xenophon's friend Agasias of Stymphalus. A glance at all of these passages makes it clear that Xenophon has purposefully singled him out, because of friendship and a desire to commemorate his valor certainly, but also for thematic reasons.

The key appearance of Xenophon on the public stage is his midnight speech to Proxenus's captains (3.1.26–32). One person dares to oppose his call to action, a Boeotian speaker named Apollonides. Agasias then makes his debut with a timely intervention, pointing out that this man is not a Greek because his ears have been pierced like a Lydian's. In four subsequent appearances, Agasias displays uncommon valor in battle, volunteering for dangerous operations (4.1.27) and always wanting to be the first man to enter an enemy stronghold (4.7.8–12; 5.2.15). Although, in competition with other captains (who are also named), he is not the first man to enter the fortress of the Taochians, he is singled out for sole mention during the attack on the outer palisade of the mother-city of the Drilae (an especially warlike people living near the Black Sea). This last scene is especially remarkable because Agasias is not only the first over the wall but "he put aside his weapons and climbed up only wearing a tunic."

Later on, when Xenophon tries to resist the army's efforts to give the supreme command to him rather than to the Lacedaemonian Cheirisophus, even more of the soldiers insist that he accept it, but only Agasias is named and given a speech (6.1.30). It is a speech that gets loud applause because of its pointed wit: "Will the Lacedaemonians also be angry if, when guests come together to dine, they do not choose a Lacedaemonian to be master of ceremonies? If that's the case, then it is not even possible for us to be captains, it would seem, since we are Arcadians." In contrast to this calculated prominence, Agasias's role in events can also be diminished when a fuller disclosure might serve to discredit him. Almost immediately after the conferral of the supreme command on Cheirisophus, the Arcadians and Achaeans defect from the army, and Agasias is one of those involved in this affair. Yet Agasias is merely named as one of the ambassadors to Heracleia, and the leading role in the sedition is credited to others, Lycon and Callimachus (6.2.4–10). Fuller vindication of his role in this unfortunate affair can be found in the detail that he is one of the two captains responsible for passing the resolution that anyone who in future proposes to split the army should be punished with death (6.4.11).

Agasias's largest role in the story takes place when the army is tarrying at Calpe Harbor (6.6.5–37). When the Lacedaemonian Dexippus, who has earlier deserted the Ten Thousand, attempts to arrest one of Agasias's men, Agasias both rescues the man and orders his troops to stone Dexippus. This leads to Agasias's arrest by Cleander, a high-ranking Spartan, who has the authority both to execute Agasias and to outlaw the Ten Thousand. Agasias delivers two earnest speeches in which he manages to defend both himself and Xenophon on all charges of wrongdoing. It is in this episode that the narrator makes explicit something we might reasonably have inferred long ago, that this Arcadian captain owes his persistent role in the narrative to a special connection (6.6.11): "Agasias, whom Cleander was demanding, had been a constant friend to Xenophon, and that was the very reason why Dexippus was slandering him." It is also the very reason why the narrator keeps mentioning him.

Finally, and most emphatically of all, Agasias is the second-to-last member of the Ten Thousand to be named in the *Anabasis*. The last, of course, is Xenophon himself. When the Greeks, under heavy fire from archers and slingers, were retreating from their unsuccessful attack on Asidates's tower, "Agasias the Stymphalian captain was wounded, though he kept fighting the whole time against the enemy" (7.8.18–19). Nearly half of the soldiers are wounded on this retreat, but it is Agasias, unsurprisingly by now, who is commemorated.

Xenophon knew how to honor, and how to remember, his friends. But he could also, if his grudge was strong enough, repay an enemy. The future fates of minor characters with whom he came into conflict remain unrecorded (for instance, Silanus the seer, Neon the general, and Heracleides the agent of Seuthes). In the case of Dexippus, however, whose slanders endangered the lives of both Xenophon himself (6.1.32) and Agasias (6.6.11), the narrator gets his revenge in the court of history. The eventual consequence of Dexippus's treacherous behavior is revealed at the point of his first appearance in the text (5.1.15). He is assigned a warship with which he is supposed to capture merchant ships on which the Ten Thousand can sail home; instead of doing that, he takes the ship and runs away. Most often, the narrator would let it end there, but he here adds: "He later suffered a just penalty; for when he was in Thrace with Seuthes and was engaged in some intrigue, he was put to death by Nicander the Lacon" ("Lacon" is another term for Lacedaemonian). Dexippus's punishment for his treachery is succinctly described in a single sentence. We know nothing of this "intrigue" or of the identity of Nicander. Xenophon's contemporary readers may have been able to fill in the details either from common knowledge or from other historical texts, but that is not really important. The essential "fact," so crisply communicated and permanently commemorated, is that the vile scoundrel eventually met the death that he deserved.

Narrative Gaps and Inconsistencies

Scholars are always eager to read inconsistencies in a text in terms of authorial intention. And so it is often assumed that inconsistencies in the story line, contradictions between details, unfulfilled narrative promises, or references to things that are not actually mentioned, if one is clever enough to perceive it, are all purposeful and are all part of the author's intent to make us think about the narrative and its messages. In other words, they are inserted in order to provoke a reaction on the part of the reader or to suggest an interpretation of the text that lurks beneath easy readings that lie on the surface. In that sense, they are subversive, and subversiveness has an appeal to literary critics. In some cases, this may well be the case. Some of the "panhellenist" passages discussed in chapter 7 may fall into this category. But if you talk to authors themselves (whether novelists or historians), you discover that such narrative phenomena are often accidental—due to oversight or haste or simply to shifts in emphasis over a long period of composition. Unfortunately, we can never be certain when such things are done on purpose or, as it were, by accident.

Perhaps we can call some slips "innocent" rather than purposeful. Xenophon is vague and inconsistent when it comes to noting shifts in the command structure of the army. For instance, in one place the narrator implies that Cleanor was the eldest of the generals (2.1.10), and in another he says Sophaenetus was the eldest (6.5.13). This is more than just a simple slip, for Cleanor is explicitly called a general in book 2 (2.5.37), only to be elected general as the replacement for Agias in book 3 (3.1.47). In order to make sense of this, one has to presume that Cleanor was actually Agias's second-in-command (*hupostrategos*) and that Xenophon is speaking loosely in calling him a "general" (*strategos*) before his actual election to that post. So, too, Xenophon never tells us when Agias became a general, and one has to infer that he was the replacement for Xenias, who deserted while Cyrus was still alive. Finally, Phryniscus suddenly appears as one of the generals in book 7 (7.2.1)! Here again, one has to infer that he replaced Sophaenetus, who was last mentioned in book 6

(6.5.13) when Xenophon the character squashed his battle plan at Calpe Harbor. Those who read the *Anabasis* as a gripping story may not even notice these gaps in the narrative. But students of the *Anabasis* as a source for Greek history are compelled to do quite a lot of hard work in order to explain the shifts in command. Most such gaps in the text are fairly trivial, but it is truly amazing that Xenophon does not tell us when or why Sophaenetus was replaced by Phryniscus, given the tense relationship between their two characters in the story. We need to conjecture that Sophaenetus either abandoned the army, perhaps taking some of his contingent with him, or died before the Thracian campaign of the winter of 400–399. If the latter, then the *Anabasis* attributed to a Sophaenetus by Stephanus of Byzantium (see chapter 1) must have been written by someone else of that name.

Another peculiar "slip" occurs in the obituary of Clearchus at the end of book 2. Xenophon first describes him near the very beginning of the work (1.1.9), giving the minimal amount of background information: "Clearchus was a Lacedaemonian exile. After meeting him, Cyrus admired him and gave him 10,000 darics [Persian gold coins]." In Clearchus's obituary the reasons for his exile are given, followed by "When he was already an exile he came to Cyrus, and the arguments by which he persuaded Cyrus have been written elsewhere, and Cyrus gave him 10,000 darics" (2.6.4). These "arguments," as it happens, are *not* recorded elsewhere, and this looks very much like a cross-reference gone awry (and such slips can be found in modern books too). Yet I am tempted to think that this is not an inadvertent editorial oversight. Rather, Xenophon has purposefully created a gap in the narrative in order to make his readers imagine what kind of arguments Clearchus would have employed in order to persuade Cyrus to give him such a huge sum of money. We are being asked to do some of the narrator's work here and to fill in the gap on the basis of what we have already been told of Cyrus's and Clearchus's characters. And the arguments and motives we are invited to provide might not be particularly flattering to either of them. It is also possible that Xenophon expected his contemporary readers to bring in extratextual knowledge about this event, since there was a fuller and far more hostile tradition (recorded at Diodorus 14.12) about how Clearchus came to be an exile: he had attempted to make himself tyrant of Byzantium, was expelled by an army sent from Sparta, and only then joined Cyrus.

There are other gaps in the narrative, however, that seem to me to be anything but innocent. These gaps are intended to promote a particular version of events. That is, gaps and omissions can be used to lead the reader to interpret and understand events in a particular way. During the onset of the winter of 400/399 BC, the army faces a major decision. Since the season of the year prevented anyone from sailing home, they need to decide where and whom to serve for pay. They have two choices. They can either march to the Chersonese, where they will find employment as mercenaries under Spartan service, as advocated by both the general Neon and by Aristarchus, the Spartan governor of Byzantium, or they can work for the Thracian prince Seuthes. The adjoining narrative has made it completely clear that the character Xenophon wants the army to take service with Seuthes, and he has already sacrificed to that end (in order to get the gods' advice) and has even been on a semipri-vate mission to Seuthes (7.2.15–38). The generals decide to call a meeting of the army, but Xenophon is the only person who gives a speech (7.3.1–14). He represents the decision to join Seuthes as the obvious and most attractive one. We never get to hear the argu-ments in favor of the Chersonese option, either from Neon or from Aristarchus's representatives, except as they are paraphrased by Xenophon himself, and he does this by employing a negative con-trast, enumerating all of the bad things Aristarchus will no longer inflict on the army if they make the difficult march to the Cher-sonese (Aristarchus says that he will no longer sell you into slavery, deceive you, or allow you to starve). Xenophon ends his speech with the suggestion that they find provisions before putting the issue to a vote.

As the army marched off in search of food, "Neon and others from Aristarchus tried to persuade them to turn back. But they would not listen" (7.3.7). Once again, we are denied access to their arguments. Furthermore, there is a narrative gap here, for it was stated above that the soldiers of Neon were not present at this meeting, since they were encamped about ten stades away (just over a mile); so the reader is led to assume that Neon has only just arrived. The next thing we are told is that Seuthes encounters the army on its march and takes them to some villages where they can find food (we are not told whether this was a chance meeting, but the way Xenophon interacts with Seuthes strongly implies that Xenophon orchestrated this encounter). Seuthes then makes his offer of employment to the army, and a very one-sided debate follows in which it is reported in indirect speech that the soldiers very much liked what Seuthes had to say. The scene then quickly comes to an end: "Xenophon said, 'If anyone wishes to speak in opposition, let him speak; but if not, I will put this issue to the vote.' When no one spoke in opposition, he put it to the vote, and it was approved. He immediately told Seuthes that the army would campaign with him" (7.3.14). Fait accompli!

Now let us back up for a moment and see how the narrative has prepared us for this scene. Earlier in the story, at a time when Xenophon was absent, the generals quarreled over where to go (7.2.1–4). Two of them, Cleanor and Phryniscus, were bribed by Seuthes; Timasion wanted to cross back to Asia (this turned out to be impossible), "thinking that in this way he could return to his home"; and Neon wished to lead the army into the Chersonese, "believing that if they came under Lacedaemonian control, he would be in command of the entire army." As the narrative proceeds, Xenophon rejects bribes from Seuthes, Neon camps apart from the rest of the army with about eight hundred men, and Xenophon then learns that Aristarchus is intending to have him arrested (7.2.10–16).

So by the time we reach the moment of real decision in the scene I described above, the reader has been led to believe that Neon is acting out of exclusively selfish motives (as he has done in even earlier episodes: 6.2.13; 6.6.23), that Aristarchus is plotting against Xenophon, and that Xenophon himself has resisted several attempts by Seuthes to bribe him (more on this in chapter 6). In this scene, moreover, he tells us that Neon and the representatives from Aristarchus spoke, but we are not permitted to hear their arguments. Why have their speeches been suppressed? Is it because they gave advance warning of Seuthes's unreliability as a paymaster, a warning that later came all too true? Xenophon as author/narrator controls the narrative, Xenophon the character controls the meeting of the army, and we readers are simply told that the decision to follow Seuthes was unanimous! Was there really no opposition to this course of action? Did the general Neon have no supporters at all who were willing to speak up? By presenting the decision as the obvious and unanimous one through the suppression of other voices and other arguments, the narrative gives the strong impression that no one forewarned them about what kind of person Seuthes really was (ruthless, crafty, greedy, and dishonest!). And given that at the very end of the *Anabasis*, literally in its last sentence, the remnants of the Ten Thousand do undertake Spartan service, one might wonder if they would have been better off to have chosen service under Sparta earlier on (even if that really meant that Neon and not Xenophon would have been in charge). Finally, this is the last reference to Neon in the *Anabasis*. Did he lead his eight hundred men to the Chersonese after all? How did they fare there? Of course, I am raising questions no one can answer. The interesting thing is that it is possible to perceive, even as we read a carefully crafted and highly manipulative narrative, that we are not being told the whole story.

Speeches

The speeches in the works of the ancient historians aim at effective truth rather than verbatim truth. A speech was not intended to be a transcript of what was actually said but was meant to be true to the occasion. About 25 percent of the *Anabasis* is composed of speeches. In books 1 and 2 the character Xenophon utters a total of some eight lines, and most of the speeches are delivered by Clearchus, Tissaphernes, Cyrus, and Menon. In books 3, 5, and 7, by contrast, about half of the text consists of speeches, and the vast majority of them are delivered by the character Xenophon.

The inclusion of so much direct speech in the narrative has several purposes. Most obviously, it renders the story more vivid and entertaining. This aspect of Greek historical writing is an inheritance from Homeric epic. But speeches also serve other, subtler functions. They provide characterization. For instance, Cleanor's speeches are always impassioned and emotional, Cheirisophus's are laconic and to the point, Cyrus's are rhetorically clever and calculated to persuade, and Tissaphernes's are masterfully deceptive. Xenophon's speeches, not surprisingly, tend to be didactic (especially in books 3 and 4) and apologetic (in books 5 and 7). Sometimes speeches are used to provide information that the narrative has omitted, and this can be a highly effective narratological device. And, finally, words spoken in direct speech can be aimed at two audiences simultaneously, both the internal audience of the text and the external audience of readers and listeners. This is especially true of Xenophon's lengthy defense speeches in books 5 and 7, which are aimed at persuading both the internal audience (the Greek army and Seuthes) and the external audience (his contemporary and future readers/listeners).

That said, not all of the speeches in the *Anabasis* seem to be directed at the internal audience as opposed to an external one, and in that sense they are not really true to the occasion at all. The character Xenophon's last major speech in the work, directed at Seuthes, probably falls in that category (see the discussion in chapter 6). Clearchus's speech to Tissaphernes at the end of book 2 is not so much directed at Tissaphernes as at Xenophon's contemporary and future readers. Xenophon wrote this speech in order to counter charges that Clearchus was plotting against Tissaphernes, and he has Clearchus say things and make the sorts of arguments, such as appeals to Greek notions of piety, that the historical Clearchus is unlikely to have made in those circumstances (2.5.1–23).

At the same time, however, the exchange between Tissaphernes and Clearchus is a brilliantly vivid recreation of a private meeting that reveals Clearchus, the professional soldier, to be easily ensnared by the subtle courtier. In earlier episodes Clearchus has displayed a shrewd cunning, manipulating the Ten Thousand when they have mutinied at Tarsus (1.3) and outmaneuvering Phalinus when he attempts to get the Ten Thousand to surrender their arms to the king after Cunaxa (2.1.7–23); but Clearchus's hatred of Menon and his desire for the sole command have here dulled his wits. Tissaphernes, for his part, shows himself to be a consummate liar in front of two different audiences. He convinces Clearchus that he really does seek the friendship of the Greek mercenaries and wishes to employ them for himself, and he even hints that he might use them to make himself king ("Only the king is allowed to wear the tiara upright on his head, but perhaps, with you Greeks at his side, another might easily wear it upright on his heart": 2.5.23.) On the other hand, his insistence that the Persians need not resort to impiety because they can easily destroy the Greeks is aimed at the reader, inasmuch as that assertion will only be disproved by the narrative after Clearchus's death.

Xenophon can also adjust patterns of speech to suit the background of the speaker. When the Persian Ariaeus offers advice (2.2.11–12) to the Greeks about the road back to the sea after the death of Cyrus, he speaks in short, choppy, awkward sentences, which are very unlike the longer syntactical constructions of a native speaker from an equivalent social class. So, too, the Arcadian captain Agasias, presumably a hearty soldier without much formal education, speaks in inelegant, awkward sentences (6.6.17–24). When Agasias defends himself for ordering his men to strike the traitor Dexippus, he concludes his defense before the Spartan governor Cleander with a sentence that is not quite grammatical: "Consider, if you now kill me, on account of a man who is terrible and base will be killing a good man" (6.6.24: here the verb "killing," *apoktenōn*, should be a future infinitive in indirect statement, not a future participle).

Xenophon shows his virtuosity as a composer of speeches in a rhetorical showdown between his character and a professional orator (5.5.7–25). The city of Sinope on the Black Sea sent a delegation to the Ten Thousand, who were encamped near their colony of Cotyora. One of the ambassadors, Hecatonymus, "who was considered to be a clever orator," begins by praising the Ten Thousand in lofty panhellenist tones ("being Greeks you are victorious over barbarians") and then ends with a threat. "We do not deem these things to be proper [i.e. harming the city of Cotyora]. But if you continue to do them, we will be compelled to make Corylas [the king of the Paphlagonians] a friend, as well as the Paphlagonians and anyone else we can" (5.5.12).

Xenophon then defends the actions of the army and effectively puts Hecatonymus into checkmate, both rhetorically and in terms of Realpolitik, by issuing a threat that echoes his own. "If it also seems best to us to make the Paphlagonian a friend (and we hear that he desires your city and your strongholds on the coast), we will attempt, by helping him to obtain the things that he desires, to prove ourselves his friends" (5.5.22–23). The last sentence of each speech ends with the word "friend(s)" as the next to the last word, and I have tried to capture something of the force of that in my translations. Hecatonymus is introduced as a good speaker, but Xenophon is shown to be a better one. That Xenophon has won this debate is certified by the internal audience, since the other ambassadors disapproved of Hecatonymus's speech, and one of them, answering for Hecatonymus, says to Xenophon, "We see that everything that you said is true."

The speeches in Xenophon are tailored to fit not only the circumstances in which they were delivered but also the character of the speaker. Aristotle's nephew, the historian Callisthenes of Olynthus (who died in 327 BC), said of speeches in historical works (Jacoby *FGrH* 124, Fragment 44): "It is necessary for anyone who sets out to write something not to disregard the character of the speaker, but to compose speeches that are appropriate both to the person speaking and to the situation." Xenophon, for the most part, has accomplished this consistently and artfully. We should, however, beware of reading his speeches as transcriptions of what was actually said. In a few cases, such as the private interchange between Clearchus and Tissaphernes, he was not present. But even when he reports a speech he gave himself, he is surely not giving us his very words, which he could not possibly have remembered precisely. Rather, he is giving us a speech that serves to fashion a particular image of himself, one that represents what he would like us to think that he said, or even what retrospectively he wishes he had said.

Characterization

Xenophon is an expert at depicting a person's character through narration. Long before we read their obituaries, the narrative itself has revealed Cyrus as being ambitious and manipulative, Clearchus as quick-tempered and severe, Proxenus as mild and reasonable, and Menon as cunning and self-interested. Xenophon does not need to say explicitly that someone is a scoundrel as an authorial intervention—the story itself can do this for him, and in this he is much more believable than most other Greek historical writers, including Thucydides. Nor are there intrusive bestowals of praise in the *Anabasis*.

The two major exceptions to this overall pattern are his obituaries of Cyrus and of the slain generals (1.9; 2.6), but these serve to bring closure to portions of the narrative and to offer a sort of benchmark by which to measure Xenophon himself after he becomes one of the new generals (see chapter 5). Nonetheless, the harshness of his appraisal of Menon (2.6.21–29) is unparalleled elsewhere in the *Anabasis* and is indeed almost unmatched in Greek historical writing (the censure of the court of Philip II by Theopompus of Chios is even harsher and is quoted with disapproval at Polybius 8.9.5–13). Menon is a thoroughly base commander whose only concern is the acquisition of money and power by any means, a person who "took pride in the ability to deceive, in the fabrication of lies, and in the mocking of friends." The sharpest sting comes at the end: "One might be mistaken about him," the narrator concedes, "regarding things done in secret; but the things that everyone knows are as follows." He then gives an exposé of Menon's socially unacceptable sexual practices (2.6.28).

The narrator occasionally sums up a person's character by a single attribution of motive or emotion, often as an explanation for why he opposes Xenophon. Silanus slanders Xenophon out of a self-interested desire to return to Greece with a large sum of gold (5.6.17) and Heracleides out of anger and fear of losing Seuthes's friendship (7.5.6). Neon ignores unfavorable sacrifices because he wishes to gratify the soldiers (6.4.23). But the text can also cumulatively build up a portrait of someone in more subtle ways. Seuthes is an interesting case. Our first impression is that he is going to be a generous employer, but little by little a picture emerges of a ruthless and unscrupulous person. He never hesitates to burn the villages of his would-be subjects (7.4.1; 7.4.5). He uses terror to achieve his aims, even if this entails killing an entire population of men, women, and children: "Seuthes told them that if they would not come down from the mountains to live and obey him, he would burn both their villages and their food, and they would perish from hunger" (7.4.5). His cruelty comes out when he slays all of his prisoners "unsparingly" (7.4.6). Finally, Seuthes obviously has no intention of ever giving the Greeks their payment, he repeatedly attempts to bribe the Greek commanders, and he keeps none of his promises to Xenophon. His character is revealed indirectly through his actions.

The analysis of motivation is most penetrating and complex, and comes closest to the conventions of the modern novel, when the narrator turns to the motives of Xenophon himself. Especially remarkable (and unique in Greek historical writing) is the internal dialogue that is reported in direct speech at the beginning of book 3 (3.1.13–14), in which Xenophon rouses himself to action after awaking from his prophetic dream (see chapter 5). In book 6, the narrator once again reveals Xenophon's inner thoughts at a crucial moment, when he weighs the possible positive and negative consequences of accepting the supreme command of the army, and "being quite at a loss what to decide" turns to divination for guidance (6.1.20–22: see chapter 8). This, too, is a form of internal dialogue, but it is presented less directly and much less vividly than in the postdream scene in book 3.

The narrator can also reveal character and simultaneously manipulate audience reactions with the use of humor, and some funny sketches are sprinkled throughout the text. In the scene that immediately follows the army's decision to campaign with Seuthes, Xenophon and the other officers are invited to a banquet at which they are expected to give presents to their new employer (7.3.15–33). This is an especially embarrassing situation for Xenophon, because he is seated in the position of most honor next to Seuthes yet has no possession of any value to give him. When it is his turn to drink to the prince's health, what happens is rather amusing (7.3.26–33): "Xenophon, who by now had drunk a little too much, stood up boldly, took the drinking horn, and said, 'I, Seuthes, give you myself and these my comrades to be your trusty friends, and not one of them against his will, but all of them, even more than me, wishing to be your friends.'" There then follows a rather over-the-top enumeration, in somewhat clumsy Greek, of what the army will accomplish for Seuthes. This scene has been crafted with considerable artistry, as Xenophon (as author) manages to slip in that he was the Greek held in most esteem by Seuthes (7.3.19) while at the same time raising a laugh at his own expense. Another Athenian, in his sole appearance, has just asked for a gift for himself, and Xenophon looks cleverer, and much less self-interested, by comparison. And the narrator partially mitigates the exuberance of Xenophon's pledge to Seuthes with the telling (and probably understated) detail that he had drunk "a little too much."

Elsewhere, the narrator uses humor to lighten the charges the army levels against Xenophon. During the scrutiny of the generals at the end of book 5, Xenophon admits in his defense speech that he struck one of his accusers for attempting to bury a comrade who was still alive (5.8.8–11). When his accuser replies that the man soon died anyway, Xenophon responds, "All of us indeed will die. Should we for that reason be buried while alive?" He goes on to declare to the assembled army that he is more confident than he used to be, "and I drink more wine, but, nonetheless, I no longer hit anyone. For I see that you are sailing in fair weather" (5.8.19–20).

Xenophon's humorous self-deprecation serves to represent him as a person who does not command out of a sense of self-importance but out of duty to those who depend on him for his leadership. Humor, however, can also serve other purposes. It can be used sarcastically against Xenophon's enemies (as when Xenophon tells Seuthes's flunky Heracleides that if he really cared for Seuthes he would have sold his own clothing in order to raise enough money to pay the soldiers their wages: 7.5.5). Finally, it is deftly employed to lighten the narrative and to entertain as an end in itself. In such cases, a humorous incident is a vehicle for a brief character sketch. Two such sketches appear in book 7, and in each case the internal audience, who is Seuthes, is roused to laughter. During the banquet scene, an Arcadian named Arustas, whom the narrator calls "a terrible eater," is too busy stuffing himself with bread and meat to accept a horn of wine, which he tells the cupbearer to pass on to Xenophon (7.3.23–24). A few pages later, Episthenes, who is called "a lover of boys," is willing to be killed in place of a beautiful lad who is among the prisoners Seuthes is about to execute (7.4.22–24). Xenophon, as a writer, can dramatically shift the tone of the narrative, moving back and forth between pathos, humor, suspense, and indignation, by alterations in style and pace.

The Shape of the Story

Since a detailed narratological exposition of the structure of the *Anabasis* is beyond the scope of this study, what follows is highly selective. It has often been pointed out that the *Anabasis* quite clearly falls into two halves, the first of which has been much more widely read and more influential than the second. Books 1–4 emphasize the Ten Thousand working together against common enemies, whereas books 5–7 highlight disunity, bad discipline, and problems both with other Greeks and with the Thracian prince Seuthes. Less obvious is the peculiar way the action of book 7 mirrors that of books 1–2. Just as Tissaphernes successfully plots to kill Clearchus and the other generals in book 2, so in book 7 the Spartan governor Aristarchus unsuccessfully plots to kill Xenophon (7.2.12–16). In book 1 the Ten Thousand fail to make Cyrus a king, but in book 7 they succeed in gaining a kingdom for Seuthes. Cyrus had made the Greek officers and common soldiers extravagant promises, which the narrative suggests he would have kept had he won the battle of Cunaxa. Seuthes, despite his success, breaks his promises to both. It is no wonder that most readers have found book 7 less satisfying than the early books, since there is something unsettling about the Greeks being ill-used by the Spartan authorities and doing their best to serve a prince who is so morally inferior to their original employer.

Although books 1–4 form a thematic unit, there is a significant break between books 3 and 4 as the army leaves the civilized region of Mesopotamia for areas that are less directly under Persian control or completely autonomous. The description (3.5.16) of the Carduchians as warlike, and especially the claim that they once annihilated a Persian army of 120,000 men ("not one of whom returned home on account of the roughness of the country"), sets up the expectation that the narrative of book 4 will be a harrowing one. It also emphasizes in advance and underscores the heroic achievement of the Ten Thousand in getting through the Carduchian land alive.

There are several major temporal dislocations in the *Anabasis*, mostly in the form of flashbacks in time (3.1.4–11; 5.7.13–31; 5.8.2–17); but there is also one highly detailed flash-forward. The latter begins with Xenophon's future dedication to Apollo at Delphi of an unspecified object that he has inscribed with his own name and that of Proxenus; "for he was his guest-friend [*xenos*]." Then follows the idyllic description of the temple, estate, and festival that Xenophon will establish for Artemis at Scillus in the Peloponnese. This digression certainly helps paint the picture of Xenophon as a pious man who discharges his duties both to the gods and to his friend Proxenus. But why does the narrator end by quoting the inscription on a stone stele that stood next to the temple (5.3.13)? "This place is sacred to Artemis. Let the one who possesses it and who enjoys its produce offer the tithe each year as a sacrifice. Let him keep the temple in repair from the surplus. If anyone fails to do these things, it will be a concern to the goddess." Does the injunction "let the one who possesses it" imply that Xenophon is no longer the owner? Is this, then, a comment on his own piety and a statement about those who confiscated the estate from him in the aftermath of the battle of Leuctra in 371 BC: that they will need to try hard to live up to his standard of piety and generosity to the community? Or is Xenophon merely looking to later generations without any implication for the current possessor? It is frustrating that the text provides no answers.

Finally, the *Anabasis* begins and ends with references to two women who are manipulating events behind the scenes, but perceptibly enough to catch Xenophon's attention and to let his audience glimpse their interventions. Just beneath the surface of the text, Cyrus's mother, Parysatis (1.1.3–8), and Hellas, the wife of Gongylus of Eretria (7.8.8–11), are controlling events. Likewise Epyaxa, the wife of Syennesis, the king of Cilicia, intervenes at a critical moment in Cyrus's fortunes, providing him with the money to pay his troops (1.2.12–20). It is significant that Parysatis is a Persian and Hellas a Greek, so one cannot argue that women only make an appearance in the *Anabasis* because Persian women are culturally "other" and consequently more influential than Greek women. There are no equivalent women in Thucydides, for the simple reason that women counted as historical agents for Xenophon, as they did for Herodotus, in a way they did not for Thucydides (for there must have been politically influential women, especially at Sparta, whom Thucydides could have mentioned had he so wished). Ctesias, notoriously, includes much more about Cyrus's mother and other Persian royal women; but that is because the focus of his account is court history. Ctesias witnessed firsthand, even if he embellished them, things that Xenophon simply was not in a position to know. Yet one should always be aware that emphasis (of the sort given to Parysatis, Hellas, and Epyaxa) is as significant in Xenophon as the mere allocation of narrative space.

Closure

When a narrative resolves a conflict, it achieves closure. Closure is something that an author constructs as part of the "emplotment" of the story (that is, the putting together of a series of discrete events into a narrative with a plot). It is not something inherent in the events themselves. The choice of a stopping place is never a neutral one, and it is far more arbitrary than it might appear, especially in a work that purports to be a historical narrative that chronicles events with a factual beginning, middle, and end. One might argue that the choice where to stop is even more important than where to begin, because the ending of a work is decisive for how we retrospectively interpret the work as a whole (Mink 1987:42–60). The end point of the *Anabasis* is neither a particularly obvious nor a thematically and emotionally appropriate one. But closure does not have to come at the end of a story; in fact, it does not have to come at all.

Readers, however, expect a story to have closure, and the end of book 4 provides a type of false closure. The Ten Thousand reach the summit of Mount Theches, and they utter their now famous shout "The sea! The sea!" They embrace each other, weep, and spontaneously build a stone mound (4.7.25). Then, after their arrival at the Greek city of Trapezus on the Black Sea, they hold games (4.8.24–25) and offer the sacrifice to the gods that Xenophon himself, in response to an ominous sneeze, earlier has proposed they make "whenever they first arrived at a friendly land" (3.2.9). But the reader is very likely to know something that the characters in the story do not, that their journey and its hardships are far from over. Nonetheless, although both the narrator and the historically informed reader know more than the participants in the story, the illusion of an ending at the end of book 4 has had a tremendous hold on the reception of the *Anabasis* from antiquity until the present. As Tim Rood (2004a: 2) has eloquently expressed it, "the Greeks' shout has gripped the imagination of readers of the *Anabasis* because it is the climax to a long narrative of toil and suffering. Its appeal is a reflection of our desire for the satisfaction of closure." It would be erroneous to assert, as some critics have, that the story is any less gripping or exciting in books 5–7; it is just that we, like the participants themselves, want the story to have a happy and uncomplicated ending with the arrival at Trapezus.

It is not at all surprising, therefore, that generations of students should have ended their reading of the *Anabasis* with book 4. Sighting and reaching the sea is a "natural ending" to the narrative of the march through inhospitable lands toward safety. Once the sea has been reached, it becomes unclear what the next goal will be or how it will be reached—that is, where home actually is and how the Greeks will get there, if they ever do. Moreover, the narrative itself suggests an ending at this point, with the games and celebrations of the Greeks. And the description of the games, which brings book 4 to a close, ends with a sentence that could well have ended the work as a whole, had the Ten Thousand really come to the end of their toils: "There was much shouting, and laughter, and cheering."

There are numerous and firm hints in this narrative, however, that final closure to the toils of the Ten Thousand is not at hand. Their arrival at Trapezus should be a moment for rejoicing as they reach their first Greek city. The people of Trapezus do indeed give them tokens of hospitality, cattle and barley, but they also ne-gotiate on behalf of the local Colchians, whose villages the Greeks have begun to plunder (4.8.22–24). This is a rather ominous begin-ning for what the reader was expecting to be a happy homecom-ing. There are other indications, too, that all is not as it should be. The figure of the Spartan Dracontius, who is chosen to admin-ister the games, is an ambiguous one (4.8.25–28). He was exiled, so Xenophon relates, for accidentally killing another Spartan boy with a knife, and here he deliberately chooses rough terrain for the wres-tling, so that a greater number of contestants will be injured.

Even more ominously, book 5 begins with an assembly scene in which the army debates how to make the rest of the journey. The very first speaker (in his sole appearance) asserts that he is fed up with marching, carrying his weapons, and fighting. He desires "to sail for the future and, stretched out just like Odysseus, to arrive in Greece" (5.1.1–3). The reader might well take this to be a bad omen for the rest of the journey, given that Odysseus took ten years to reach Ithaca and that he did so without any of his shipmates, only to find troubles at home. The speaker was obviously thinking of the last part of Odysseus's journey, when he is soundly asleep in a Phae-acian ship—but his words may signify more to the attentive reader than the speaker intended. They have a meaning that exists outside the text, so to speak, and that indicates that the trip home will not be as easy or as painless as the Greeks at this point seem to think. Our misgivings are increased when the soldiers refuse even to consider Xenophon's proposal that they request the Greek cities situated along the coast to repair the roads, and Xenophon, recognizing their foolishness, persuades the cities to do this on his own (5.1.13–15).

This inauspicious beginning to book 5 is soon confirmed, first by the desertion of the Lacedaemonian Dexippus (5.2.1–2), and then, more significantly, by the nearly catastrophic campaign against the metropolis of the Drilae. The people of Trapezus, more concerned to maintain their friendship with the local Colchians than to provide sufficient provisions for the Ten Thousand, lead them against these people, who are "the most warlike of the peoples who live along the Black Sea" (5.2.1–2). Finally, when Cheirisophus fails to return with the ships he has been sent to procure and the army no longer is able to find provisions, they depart by land on a road that, thanks to Xenophon's initiative, had been repaired (5.3.1).

Closure finally comes at the end of book 7, but here it is the readers who may feel disappointment, if they were expecting Xenophon (despite the proleptic reference to his exile at 7.7.57) to return home safe to Athens, as did Odysseus to Ithaca. If the purpose of closure is to normalize the story, to make it coherent by confirming the master-plot, then the end of the *Anabasis* fails to do that. The story has not ended, and readers are not sure what will become of Xenophon in the future. They know that he will live at Scillus in the Peloponnese, near the site of the Olympic games, but they do not know if he will ever see his native city again. Similarly, the failure of the narrator to inform us of the fate of almost all the minor characters in the story (such as Xenophon's fellow generals, apart from Cheirisophus, and the various named captains) leaves us with an uneasy feeling that the story does not have a proper end, or at least not an emotionally satisfying one. Who could not help but long to know what ultimately befell the four captains Agasias, Aristonymus, Callimachus, and Eurylochus, who are described as "rivals in valor and always contending with each other" (4.7.12)? Did they make it home alive; did they ever see their families again?

In one limited sense, however, the *Anabasis* does have what we might recognize as a happy ending. Xenophon pulls off a successful mission by capturing a wealthy Persian, and on his return to Pergamum "he greeted the god" (Zeus Melichius) since everyone (the

Spartans, his fellows officers, and the rank and file) agreed that he should have the pick of the spoils (see chapter 8). "Consequently, he was now capable even of assisting someone else." That statement, which is the second to last sentence in the *Anabasis*, is highly significant: Xenophon, selfless as usual, sees the possession of wealth as a means of helping others. By honoring Zeus Melichius, he is also guaranteed success in the future, and the very last sentence of the work looks forward to Greeks fighting Persian satraps. This panhellenist tone is further accentuated by the references to Gongylus and Procles, the descendants of two infamous traitors of the Persian Wars, who now wish to help the Greeks. It would be easy enough to see this as an upbeat happy ending that is a good omen for the future. On the other hand, the work does not end as one might have expected it would, if it is indeed based on the master-plot of the return of the hero, with Xenophon getting home to Athens or even to the Greek mainland. And readers will surely know that Spartan interventions in Asia, including that of King Agesilaus, will come to nothing, and panhellenist dreams will be unfulfilled. The ending, therefore, is a triumph for Xenophon and his style of leadership, even as it signals the ultimate failure of his desire to return to his own home. He is now rich enough to help his friends (and what is left unsaid—to hurt his enemies); nonetheless, he will not return in triumph, as did Odysseus, but will live his life as an exile from his native land. Cyrus's defeat was ultimately also Xenophon's.

A Case Study in Narrative Technique

M any of Xenophon's narrative techniques can be illustrated in a single artfully crafted passage near the end of the work (7.7.48–54). These techniques include narrative economy, gaps in the narrative, humor, characterization, and personal apology. The context is that Xenophon has just concluded a lengthy speech in which he chides Seuthes for not paying the Ten Thousand their wages and for bringing Xenophon into dishonor among the soldiers. "When Seuthes heard these things, he cursed the person who was responsible for the soldiers not being given their pay long ago. And everyone suspected that this person was Heracleides. 'For I,' he said, 'never intended to defraud them of it, and I shall pay it.'" The reader knows that Seuthes is lying as usual. The narrator does not need to tell us as much because Seuthes's character has been revealed through a series of such scenes in which he repeatedly makes false promises. The narrative has prepared readers well not to believe him now.

Xenophon then requests that the payment be made through him, so that his former position of honor in the army can be restored. Seuthes, crafty as ever, responds with an offer that Xenophon and a thousand hoplites remain with him permanently, and offers to give Xenophon everything, including the fortresses, that he had previously promised him. Xenophon curtly rejects this offer, twice repeating that "it was not possible" for him to remain, even though Seuthes claims that it would be "safer" for him to do so. Seuthes then has to admit that he only has a small amount of money ("I only have a little bit of silver, a talent [6,000 drachmas], and this I give to you"), as well as six hundred cattle, four thousand sheep, and 120 slaves. He ends by saying, "Taking these things, and taking in addition the hostages of the people who wronged you, depart." The obvious inference is that these "hostages" were from the Thynians who had attacked Xenophon at night in violation of a truce (7.4.12–24), but we are never told whether Xenophon accepts them—the economy of the narrative is too restricted to linger on minor details. Instead, we are subjected to some humor. The exchange ends with Xenophon laughing (at the smallness of the sum?) and saying, "If all this does not cover the amount of the pay, whose talent shall I say that I have? Surely, in my dangerous situation, it would be better for me to be on my guard against stones while on my way back. You heard the threats." The reference to "stones" refers to 7.6.10, where the army threatened to stone Xenophon as a punishment for keeping their pay for himself. Instead of saying outright that Seuthes is once again attempting to bribe him ("this I give to you" is ambiguous), the narrator prefers to employ Xenophon's sense of humor to convey the possible consequences of his returning to the army without the means to pay them in full.

When Xenophon returned to the army (7.7.55–57), the soldiers were delighted and ran to greet him, because they thought that he was going to stay with Seuthes and accept his gifts. The narrator does not explicitly say why Xenophon asserted it was impossible for him to stay with Seuthes (and finally take possession of those oft-promised fortresses), but the reader is led to assume that it was out of his loyalty and concern for the army, and this impression is strengthened by the delight of the soldiers at his return and by his further decision to forgo returning to Athens in order to lead them to Thibron. There is a gap in the narrative at this point, and one that I find very strange indeed. After we hear that the soldiers were delighted to see him, the narrative continues:

> When Xenophon saw Charminus and Polynicus [the two Spartan envoys who had come for the army], he said to them, "This property has been preserved for the army on account of you and I hand it over to you. You dispose of it and make the distribution to the army." They received it, appointed booty-vendors, and proceeded to sell it, *and they incurred a great deal of blame* [my emphasis]. Xenophon, however, did not approach them, but was openly making his preparations to return home.

This episode then ends with his decision, at the request of his friends, to put off his trip home in order to lead the army to Thibron.

The reader is compelled to fill in some significant gaps. Most obviously, it is left unexplained why Charminus and Polynicus are blamed. Presumably it is because the amount realized from the sale of the animals and slaves has fallen far short of the back pay that is due the army, and the soldiers accordingly are angry with them. Earlier on, Heracleides disposed of a much larger quantity of goods for a mere 15 talents (7.3.48: sixteen hundred captives, two thousand cattle, and ten thousand sheep), and now the army was owed 30 talents in back pay (7.7.25). Readers can calculate on their own that even without a swindler like Heracleides taking a cut for himself, not nearly enough money is going to be raised to satisfy a very frustrated and angry band of professional mercenaries. A second gap is more elusive. Are we to take at face value the reason the character Xenophon gives for allowing these two Spartans to take charge of paying the soldiers? He has twice requested of Seuthes that the payment be made through him so that he could regain the respect of the army, so why now let these Spartans take the credit? Are we meant to infer that Xenophon, the clever Athenian, has duped these two unsophisticated and naive Spartans by allowing them to arrange for the sale of the booty (which he knew was insufficient) as if he were doing them a favor, knowing full well that they would draw the wrath of the soldiers? In other words, has Xenophon cleverly diverted that wrath from himself to them? The narrator lets his readers draw their own conclusions.

Further Reading

Genette (1980 and 1988) and Bal (1997) are fundamental treatments of narratology. Herman (2007) is a useful collection of essays. To my mind, however, far the most stimulating and entertaining introduction to this field is Abbott (2008). Dover (1997) discusses the various forms of style in historical writing (historiographical, oratorical, and linguistic). The fullest treatment of Xenophon's linguistic style is still Gautier (1911). Walker (1993) is a stimulating study of vividness in Greek historical writing. Baragwanath (2008) gives a highly sophisticated treatment of personal motivation in Herodotus that is relevant to all the Greek historians. The problem of achieving closure in narrative is discussed in the works on narratology mentioned above; for closure in the Greek and Roman historians, see the essays in Roberts, Dunn, and Fowler (1997) and the useful collection of material by Marincola (2005). Purves (2010) explores Xenophon's manipulation of time and space for literary effect (but more attention to books 5–7 would have been fruitful). Much has been written about the status of speeches in classical historiography (see especially Marincola 2007), but Walbank (1965) remains fundamental. Lee (2004) is interesting on women in the

Anabasis. Lane Fox (2004a: 35–46) attempts to prove that there is a gap of three months in the narrative of book 4 between chapters 4 and 7 (which would be a striking example of Xenophon's evasiveness); but he is refuted by Lee (2007: 29–30). Xenophon's command of the rear guard is briefly evaluated by Roy (1968a). Roy (1968b), reacting against the modern view that Xenophon exaggerated his own importance, argues that Xenophon's narrative was limited by the scope of his personal notes.

· 5 ·

Xenophon Takes Command

> On occasion Xenophon appears to be one of those heroes from
> children's comics, who in every episode manages to survive against
> incredible odds.
>
> —*Italo Calvino,* Why Read the Classics?

A lthough it is dangerous to read a work in purely autobiographical terms, the *Anabasis* can be understood in terms of Xenophon's self-representation. It has, of course, long been recognized
that there is a degree of personal apology in the way Xenophon
presents his own role in the expedition (see chapter 1). But that is
only one facet of his self-presentation, and focusing on apology
alone makes for a fairly simplistic reading of the text. Xenophon has
carefully constructed the *Anabasis* so as to make himself the central
player, the one most responsible for the salvation of the Ten Thousand, but he has done this discreetly and incrementally. That motivation explains the most unusual feature of the work, the fact that
Xenophon does not appear as a major player, indeed is not even
formally introduced, until the beginning of the third book. Xenophon's decision to introduce himself formally only at the moment
of extreme crisis following the arrest of the generals is an extremely
effective literary strategy. The reader has come to believe in the
factual nature of the story, as well as in the objectivity of its anonymous narrator, long before Xenophon introduces himself as the
person who will emerge as the Ten Thousand's unlikely savior. If

Xenophon had introduced himself sooner, the illusion of impartiality might have been broken.

One of the most important themes in the *Anabasis* is leadership, or, more particularly, what constitutes good and bad ways of governing and commanding. It has often been observed that the Ten Thousand constitute a *polis* on the move, and thus it is not surprising that questions of governance are of central importance. But the real lessons come by example, Xenophon's own, as he assumes command (with others) and brings the army to safety. Although there are serious challenges to his authority and integrity, he manages to negotiate his way through these difficulties. In other words, the *Anabasis* has encoded within it paradigms for good leadership. It is certainly the case that sometimes Xenophon seems too good to be true (as noted by Italo Calvino in the epigraph); but isn't such self-presentation the central concern of all autobiographical writing? As H. Porter Abbott has expressed it (2008: 138), "Certainly the history of autobiography, like that of biography, is full of accounts of lives that are a little too good to be true. . . . But in general, if you want to write your autobiography without the sense that you are fictionalizing by displacing yourself with a type that is either more heroic, more honest, more pathetic, more whatever—if you want to do this, it can be hard work."

The whole point of a memoir, after all, traditionally has been to give an author the opportunity to project the image of himself that he wishes to become the dominant one both for his present readership and for posterity. That image usually, if not invariably, is going to be a positive one—one that explains in as sympathetic a way as possible the character's past actions. Autobiography is frequently the defense of an individual who has made some controversial life choices, and Xenophon uses the normalizing function of narrative, including its structures of cause and effect, to make his choices seem justifiable and appropriate. Moreover, Xenophon has constructed his role in the narrative in conformity with an exemplary type, playing the leading role in a master-plot that he has artfully adapted from epic poetry (the trial, escape, and return of the hero). He is the exemplary type of the wise, resourceful, pious, honest, and selfless leader who cares more for the safety and well-being of his men than for himself. He seeks fame and renown, although not at any price. Whereas Odysseus managed only to save himself, Xenophon preserves his men as well. Xenophon the author depicts Xenophon the character in such a fashion not only by way of self-justification but surely as an ideal type for others to imitate. If that indeed was his intent, he would be pleased, since many who have exercised military command have been inspired by Xenophon's example, from ancient times right through to the present.

In many ways the character Xenophon exceeds the expectations of readers whose notions of democratically elected leadership were formed during the Peloponnesian War or gleaned by reading the histories of Herodotus or Thucydides. Xenophon exhibits cunning like Themistocles, the mastermind behind the victory at Salamis, when he uses a combination of deception and persuasion to restrain the soldiers from pillaging Byzantium. But unlike Themistocles, he is never self-serving and dishonest (Herodotus calls Themistocles "greedy for money": 8.112). Like Pericles, Xenophon "led rather than was led by the multitude" (Thucydides 2.65), but he lacks Pericles's haughty aloofness (Plutarch, *Pericles* 7), and unlike Pericles he survives the war that made him famous. He shares a facility for tactical innovation with the fifth-century general Demosthenes and a deep reverence for the gods with Nicias; yet he avoids miscalculations such as Demosthenes's failed plan to capture the heights above Syracuse or Nicias's fatal error in obeying the recommendations of his seers to remain at Syracuse because of a lunar eclipse (as narrated in Thucydides, book 7). Xenophon shares the strengths of these famous statesmen and generals, but he avoids their failures and faults, while maintaining a proper attitude of integrity toward men and piety toward gods. This self-portrait moves beyond apology into the realm of scripting a paradigm of the ideal democratic leader (one who must be both answerable to and in control of the common citizens and soldiers), the counterpart perhaps to Xenophon's ideal monarchic leaders, Cyrus the Great of Persia and King Agesilaus of Sparta.

The Death of the Generals

The obituaries the narrator gives (2.6) of the five generals who were arrested and subsequently executed prepare the way for Xenophon's own emergence as a leader. Even the best of these generals have certain flaws: Clearchus was too severe and was unwilling to be commanded by others; Proxenus was too lenient. Xenophon will emerge in the subsequent books as someone who strikes the mean between them. Proxenus was a student of Gorgias, and his instruction had not properly prepared him for command. Nor had the famed Spartan education given Clearchus the flexibility to deal with politically and diplomatically complex and morally ambiguous situations. Xenophon the Athenian, the student of Socrates, will emerge as the ideal ruler: eloquent, pious, strict but not harsh, with a sure moral compass, putting the interests of his men before his own. Shortly after the obituary of these failed leaders, he places his own formal introduction, emphasizing his connection to Socrates and his piety. Although the other generals were motivated by greed and ambition, Xenophon's reasons for joining the expedition are represented in rather different terms.

Xenophon to the Rescue

The episode in which the narrator explains how and why Xenophon became one of the Greek generals at a crucial moment is one of the most remarkable and carefully wrought passages in all of ancient Greek literature. For that reason alone, it is worthwhile to look at it in some detail. It is too lengthy to quote completely, but I here provide key sections (where Xenophon has chosen the wording with special care) in a translation that is literal enough to catch some of the nuances of the original (3.1.4).

> There was an Athenian in the army named Xenophon, who was accompanying the expedition neither as a general nor as a captain nor as a common soldier; but Proxenus, who was

an old guest-friend of his, had summoned him from home. Proxenus promised him that if he came, he would make him a friend to Cyrus, whom, he said, he considered to be of greater importance to himself than his own homeland.

The narrator here gives Xenophon a magisterial entrance. We have just been told in a pair of long and artfully constructed sentences that the entire army was in a state of total despair after the arrest of the generals, and it is quickly made clear that, from here on, Xenophon will be a major player in the story. But this is not his first appearance in the *Anabasis*. He has already appeared four times in books 1–2. Attentive readers know that they have encountered this Xenophon before, but it will come as a surprise that he is not one of the paid mercenary fighters. Xenophon's original audience probably assumed that he had served as a mercenary under Cyrus, because he had been so employed by the Spartans immediately after the Ten Thousand undertook Spartan service, first under Thibron and then under subsequent Spartan commanders. This formal introduction both subverts previous assumptions and simultaneously signals Xenophon's significance for the rest of the narrative. Yet his significance has already been prefigured, and those previous scenes seem to be preparing the reader for this grander entrance.

Some of what the narrator tells the reader in the introductory sentence quoted above is not new information. In book 2 we see Xenophon and Proxenus taking an evening stroll together (2.4.15), and near the end of that book, after the arrest of the generals, Xenophon goes with Cleanor and Sophaenetus, two of the remaining officers, to find out from a Persian delegation what has happened to Proxenus (2.5.37). He even makes a short speech to those Persians, demanding the release of Proxenus and Menon (2.5.41). Cleanor has spoken first, losing his temper and hurling insults, but Xenophon makes so clever an argument for Proxenus's and Menon's release that the Persians are unable to answer it. From these passages, it is crystal clear that Xenophon and Proxenus were close friends. But the additional information that Xenophon is some sort of volunteer and not actually serving for pay as a mercenary will come as a complete surprise after the way he first enters the story in book 1. Just before the battle of Cunaxa begins, Cyrus rides into the space between the two armies and is looking back and forth at each of them (1.8.15): "Xenophon an Athenian, seeing him from the Greek army, went forward to meet him and asked if he had any orders. Cyrus halted his horse and requested him to tell everyone that both the *hiera* [the campground sacrifice] and the *sphagia* [the battle-line sacrifice] were favorable." Cyrus then asks Xenophon about the noise that is passing along the Greek ranks, and he explains that it was the password "Zeus the savior and victory."

This initial presentation of Xenophon is more important than is usually realized, partly because modern critics tend to undervalue the importance of prebattle sacrifice for the Greeks and partly because there is a striking narrative gap in the text. Xenophon is given a key role in the events leading up to the battle, despite his noncombatant status, inasmuch as he functions as the conduit for telling both the reader and his fellow Greeks that the omens from sacrifice have been favorable. Under normal circumstances, commanders took great care to inform the rank and file about the results of prebattle sacrifices, since it was a way to boost morale in battle. The reader is surely meant to infer that Cyrus does not have time to do this, since the Greek army is still forming up just before the fighting begins. Nonetheless, there is still an odd narrative gap in this episode, and it is not completely obvious how the reader is expected to fill it. What was Xenophon doing both before and after he rode up to address Cyrus? Doesn't it look as if he was going to participate in the battle, and thus was one of the mercenaries, perhaps even an officer, if he had the confidence to ride up to Cyrus? This scene seems to be in implicit, but inherent, tension with the statement at the beginning of book 3 (quoted above) that he was not a soldier. Perhaps an ancient reader would have taken it for granted that one had to be armed if in the vicinity of a battle and so might not have perceived any contradiction or incongruence between these two passages. Even the Greeks who remained with the baggage train in Cyrus's camp had to repel an attack (1.10.3). If I have belabored this point, I have done so in order to illustrate that the way readers fill the gap in a narrative depends on their own horizon of expectations and cultural knowledge, and it is not always very easy to bridge the gap between an ancient reader's expectations and ours.

To return now to the famous scene in book 3, the narrator explains that after Xenophon read Proxenus's letter of invitation, "*he consulted with Socrates* the Athenian concerning the journey" and Socrates in turn advised Xenophon, after traveling to the oracle of Apollo at Delphi, "*to consult with the god* concerning the journey" (3.1.5–7; my emphasis). This was because "Socrates suspected that becoming Cyrus's friend would in some way be a cause for blame from the city's point of view, because Cyrus seemed to have fought with zeal on the side of the Lacedaemonians against Athens." The fact that the same phrase is used of consulting both Socrates and the god of prophecy suggests that Socrates's advice transcends mere human wisdom, and that in turn implies that Socrates correctly prophesied the reason for Xenophon's eventual exile (something modern scholars have endlessly debated). Xenophon took his teacher's advice, but then (as every student of Delphic prophecy knows) famously asked the wrong question of the god: "Socrates reproached Xenophon because he had not first of all asked this, whether it was better for him to go or to stay." Rather, Xenophon asked to which of the gods he should sacrifice and pray in order to have a successful trip and return safely. Although this was not an unusual form of question for oracular consultations, Xenophon had nevertheless formulated his query in such a way as to almost guarantee the response that he wanted by restricting the range of possible answers that the god could give. It was possible, but extremely unlikely, that Apollo (speaking through his prophetess) would respond that there were no gods who could be moved, by prayer and sacrifice, to secure his safe return.

Why does Xenophon not explain his failure to ask the type of question that Socrates had in mind? The answer is left to his audience to infer, since it was too obvious, and in a sense too embarrassing, for Xenophon to spell out. It was because he eagerly wanted to go and would not be put off either by the wisest of men (Socrates) or by the wisest of the gods (Apollo). Xenophon the character makes an appearance only in one other of the author Xenophon's works. The context is a single short episode in the *Memorabilia* (or "Conversations of Socrates": 1.3.9–13), in which the young Xenophon gives the wrong answers to Socrates's questions. It has been well observed that both passages capture the same contrast between the wisdom of Socrates and the ignorance of Xenophon. Moreover, the wisdom of Socrates is confirmed by the outcome of Xenophon's adventure, which was the "blame" and sentence of exile that Socrates predicted (Gray 1998: 98–99). Xenophon, I would emphasize, did learn his lesson from this exchange. Throughout the rest of the *Anabasis*, he never takes any important action (such as whether he should accept the supreme command of the army, found a colony, go home to Athens, or stay with Seuthes in Thrace) without first consulting the gods through a divinatory sacrifice.

But still more seems to be going on in this passage. The narrator not only underscores Xenophon's folly and Socrates's wisdom but exonerates both of them from the charge of being either pro-Spartan or anti-Artaxerxes. Socrates is aware that being considered a supporter of Sparta (even indirectly through friendship with Cyrus) is a bad thing, and he is solicitous of the opinions of the Athenian people; whereas Xenophon, for his part, asserts a few sentences later that he was expecting to be sent home as soon as the expedition against the Pisidians was over. The implication, therefore, is that Xenophon was not privy to a Spartan-backed effort to dethrone Artaxerxes by making Cyrus king in his stead, since he did not know that Cyrus was intending to attack the king or that the Spartans were going to assist him. Accordingly, the consultation of Delphi is not as transparent as it might seem to be. In fact, this scene is an elaborate apology on behalf of Socrates, Proxenus, and Xenophon himself. The scapegoat is Clearchus, who alone knew of Cyrus's true aims (see below). Indeed, this is the second time Proxenus is explicitly stated not to have known the true purpose of the expedition (1.1.11). Xenophon accepts some blame by presenting himself as asking the wrong question of Apollo, but this is a mere smokescreen, the equivalent of confessing to a lesser charge in order to deflect a greater one. Finally, is there also a hint here that just as Socrates did not take pupils for pay (unlike the sophists who traveled from city to city), so, too, Xenophon did not fight for a wage (as did all of the other Greeks on the expedition)? In other words, neither Socrates nor Xenophon were mercenaries.

The narrator does not raise the possibility that Xenophon could have returned to Delphi for a second consultation (perhaps we are to infer that there was no time for that), so Socrates told Xenophon that it was necessary to make the sacrifices the god had specified. Xenophon made the sacrifices and then set sail. The next few sentences are very carefully worded (3.1.8–11):

> Xenophon overtook Proxenus and Cyrus in Sardis when they were on the point of setting out on the journey inland, and Xenophon was introduced to Cyrus. Proxenus was eager for Xenophon to stay, and Cyrus was eager too and told him that as soon as the expedition was over, he would immediately send him back. The expedition was said to be against the Pisidians [note the impersonal subject of the verb]. And so Xenophon made the expedition thoroughly deceived—but not by Proxenus. For Proxenus did not know that the attack was against the king, nor did any of the other Greeks except Clearchus. By the time that they reached Cilicia, however, it seemed clear to everyone that the expedition was against the king. Although the Greeks were afraid of the journey and were unwilling to go on, the majority of them nevertheless continued the march out of a sense of shame both before each other and before Cyrus. One of these was Xenophon.

Two things are worth pointing out. First of all, the narrator leaves it ambiguous whether Xenophon knew about this expedition in advance of his arrival at Sardis, since Proxenus's original invitation (quoted above) had only mentioned the prospect of becoming Cyrus's friend. Secondly, the narrator's insistence that the soldiers followed Cyrus out of shame is actually undercut by the previous narrative. The army has twice refused to go forward, but their fear of the road home and the enticement of higher wages convinced them to follow Cyrus even against the king (1.3.20; 1.4.12). Shame before Cyrus, however, was not given as a motive. Yet it would be incongruous for the narrator to mention greed in the present passage, since he has just asserted that Xenophon was not earning wages for his participation.

Next comes the dream sequence that incited Xenophon to take some action to save himself (3.1.11–13), one of the most famous passages in Greek prose literature:

> When they were in a state of *aporia* ["hopelessness" or "despondency"—a word frequently used to describe the state of mind of the Ten Thousand], Xenophon was distressed along with the others and unable to sleep. But after he had fallen asleep for a short time, he had a dream. A bolt of lightning, preceded by a clap of thunder, seemed to him to fall upon his father's house, and as a result of this the entire house seemed to blaze up. Being thoroughly terrified he immediately awoke, and, in one respect, he judged the dream to be good, because, even though he was in the midst of toils and dangers, he seemed to see a great light from Zeus. But, in another respect, he was also afraid that he would not be able to depart from the land of the king but would be hemmed in on every side by difficulties, because the dream seemed to him to be from Zeus the King and the fire seemed to blaze up in a circle. What kind of thing it is to have such a dream it is possible to consider from the events that took place after the dream. These events were as follows.

Xenophon advances two very different interpretations of his dream, but he seems to favor the first one—that he would be saved from his present danger because he "saw a great light from Zeus," implying that merely seeing that light was in itself a good thing. That, however, is not the most obvious interpretation, and Xenophon does not really elaborate on his reasons for optimism. His strained and unexplained interpretation actually invites his readers to interpret the dream for themselves. What does it mean when one's father's house is blasted by Zeus's thunderbolt? Does it not most obviously signify that one will never see that house again when awake? And is that not precisely what happened to Xenophon?

During the story time of the *Anabasis*, Xenophon the character does not know that Xenophon the historical actor will remain in exile from Athens for a very long time to come, probably even after the decree of exile is officially rescinded. Ironically, the reader does know this (or is in a position to know it). Yet if Xenophon the author was writing the *Anabasis* in the 360s, he would have been aware of the dream's double signification (both escape in the short term and exile in the long term). One signification is indeed revealed immediately by "the events that took place after the dream," when Xenophon rouses the troops to action, and more fully by the end of the *Anabasis*, when he has escaped from "the land of the king" as well as from other hostile territories and enemies. The other signification, the decree of exile against Xenophon, lies outside the chronological horizons of the main story line of the *Anabasis*. It finds its fulfillment in the digression about Xenophon's estate at Scillus, "where he was made a colonist by the Spartans," and by references in the text to his future exile (5.3.4–13; 7.7.57).

After Xenophon awakes from this dream, he engages in a soliloquy that is unique in Greek prose literature, and is a remarkably effective example of internal dialogue (3.1.13–15):

"Why am I lying here? The night advances. It is likely that the enemy will arrive with the dawn. If we fall into the king's hands, what is to prevent us, after we have witnessed all the things that are most cruel and have suffered all the things that are most terrible, from being insulted and killed? As to defending ourselves, no one is making any preparations or taking any thought, but we are lying here just as if it were possible to be at leisure. From what city am I expecting the general to come who will arrange these things? What age am I waiting for myself to attain? For I shall not get any older, if today I give myself up to my enemies." After this he got up and first of all summoned the captains of Proxenus.

I suspect that even the most careful of readers will need to be reminded at this point that, contrary to the implications of this interior dialogue, not all of the generals have been seized by Tissaphernes. In fact, two of them are still alive at this very moment: Sophaenetus and Cheirisophus. But in the scenes that follow, it is Xenophon the Athenian who takes center stage, delivering five speeches: one to the captains of Proxenus, another in answer to a gainsayer, a third to a meeting of the approximately one hundred surviving captains and generals, and then two more before an assembly of the entire army.

By what authority Xenophon can address the hundred surviving officers is not explained. The eldest of Proxenus's captains introduces him rather perfunctorily: "Say, Xenophon, the things that you also said to us." After his oration, the Spartan general Cheirisophus, in his first speech act in the *Anabasis*, validates Xenophon's arrival on the scene in the strongest possible terms (3.1.45): "Previously, Xenophon, the only thing that I knew about you was that I heard that you were an Athenian, but now I praise you both for your words and for your actions, and I wish that the majority were just like you. For it would be a common good." This is an extremely nice touch. It is not the seemingly impartial narrator who praises Xenophon's abrupt intervention onto the stage of history, but rather a very partial Spartan (seeing that the Spartans had very recently defeated the Athenians in a very long and drawn-out war). This Spartan, moreover, praises Xenophon for the two qualities that mattered most to the Greeks from the Homeric poems onward— excellence in giving advice and taking action.

New generals are then chosen, one of whom is Xenophon, taking the place of Proxenus. The soldiers are then assembled, and more speeches are delivered. Cheirisophus's speech before the assembled army is brief and stark, and very Spartan, making just one basic point, "Conquer or die well." This is essentially the Spartan martial ideology of "victory or death," a commonplace familiar from Herodotus's account of the battle of Thermopylae. Cleanor's speech is merely an improved version of Cheirisophus's. He makes the same general points in almost the same order. Neither speech, however, makes any recommendations as to how to effect their salvation. That is left up to Xenophon in his third speech, which he delivers before the army in his very best dress uniform. This speech is very long (five pages) and detailed, and it is followed, after a very brief interjection by Cheirisophus, by another speech of Xenophon of a page in length. After the troops assemble, it is Xenophon who makes the long speeches and who gives the strategic advice. It is even he who suggests that Cheirisophus, since he is a Spartan, should lead the van of the square that Xenophon has proposed the army adopt for the march. All of this is quite remarkable, given that Cheirisophus was a seasoned Spartan commander and already a general in Cyrus's army, while Xenophon has hitherto not even been a common soldier, much less an officer. Xenophon has thoroughly dominated these proceedings, to the extent that some 276 lines of text are spoken by him, in contrast to a total of 44 lines spoken by other characters. Few authors of "historical" narratives have given themselves such an elaborate and dramatic entrance onto the stage of great events.

It is always tempting to rationalize, especially when a scene or sequence of scenes, no matter how brilliantly realized in artistic terms, seems to strain historical credibility. Could Xenophon, in the course of one sleepless night, really have gone from being a noncombatant to one of the newly elected generals? Was he the only one with enough gumption to rouse himself and then call a meeting of the surviving officers? Did Xenophon set up this meeting for the specific purpose of getting his hands on Proxenus's command? What was Cheirisophus, an experienced Spartan commander, doing this whole time? Xenophon himself seems to anticipate these objections on the part of readers when he says to Proxenus's captains, "But perhaps others are contemplating these same things; so, by the gods, let us not wait for others to approach us for the purpose of summoning us to the fairest deeds, but let us be the first ones to rouse also the others to excellence" (3.1.24).

One could easily rewrite this account in accord with what might appear to us a more plausible scenario. For example, we might argue that Xenophon was already in some position of command.

John Lee (2007: 54) has made the ingenious suggestion that Xenophon was actually Proxenus's second-in-command, and that would certainly explain why Proxenus's captains chose him to be their new general in preference to one of their own number. Less radically, it is certainly probable that Xenophon was one of several men who roused themselves over the course of the night, who rallied various units of the army, and who gave inspirational speeches, while his account focuses on his own personal experiences and on the speeches he himself gave. Such suggestions are tempting indeed but, like all "reconstructions," ultimately unverifiable. What the narrator wants us to believe is that Xenophon alone took courage when no one else did, and literally stepped up to take command because he felt that Zeus had promised him deliverance.

Xenophon Saves the Day

In his dawn speech before the army in dress uniform, Xenophon addresses and counters many of the arguments that earlier speakers have raised about returning to the sea without Persian assistance, to wit, their lack of guides, cavalry, a market for provisions, and a means for crossing impassible rivers (1.3.14; 2.1.11; 3.1.2). In the scenes that follow, either Xenophon himself takes credit for an innovation, or it is attributed to the generals collectively. If Xenophon disobeys orders (see below) it turns out all right; if someone else does so, it is a disaster.

Moreover, the narrator alternates between episodes in which the character Xenophon exercises leadership and ones in which it is exercised anonymously by "the generals." For example, at one point (3.3.16–20) Xenophon suggests creating a corps of cavalry and archers, but later on (3.4.19–23) the creation of six mobile companies of one hundred men each is an anonymous innovation, and so is the decision to have peltasts (light-armed spearmen) seize the high ground above the enemy while the army traverses a series of hills (3.4.28). But Xenophon then saves the day again when he proposes the strategy that dislodges Tissaphernes's troops from a spur of the mountain overlooking their route (3.4.37–49). This pattern serves a double purpose. It makes Xenophon's role more plausible and believable by not attributing everything to him alone; at the same time, the anonymity of the other leaders tends to highlight Xenophon's own contribution while denying them a comparable spotlight.

Yet, unlike Thucydides, who in his history lamely excuses his failure to secure the city of Amphipolis against the Spartans (4.106.3–4), Xenophon does not gloss over his own mistakes (even if one sometimes gets the impression that criticisms are included for the sole purpose of being refuted). After the Greeks have crossed the Zapatas River, the rear guard is suffering greatly at the hands of the archers, slingers, and cavalry of the Persian commander Mithradates (3.3.6–20). When the Greeks prove unable to retaliate (since their arrows and javelins are not reaching the Persians), "it seemed to Xenophon that a pursuit was necessary." This proves totally ineffectual, since Xenophon's foot soldiers are unable to overtake any of their Persian opponents. The upshot is that the army travels only a short distance during that day and is once again in a state of despondency (*aporia*). Cheirisophus and the eldest of the generals then censure Xenophon for putting himself in danger without having done any harm to the enemy. Xenophon accepts the criticism, although not without the qualification that he was "compelled to pursue" the enemy rather than watch his men suffer; but he then comes up with a plan for the future that will prevent a repeat of this situation: they should organize a corps of slingers and cavalry. This is a model of good leadership. Xenophon recognizes his mistake, learns from it, and then comes up with a plan for the next encounter. At the same time, it should be noted that he does not take credit for every successful innovation, such as the reorganization of the square that follows (six units of one hundred men each: 3.4.19–24). Later on, he leaves two of his fellow Athenians, the captains Cephisodorus and Amphicrates, on one of the hills he captures in Carduchian territory, and they are killed along with many of their men (4.2.13–18). He could easily have omitted this detail, which does not make him look good.

Xenophon, as we have seen, depicts himself as capable of making a bad, if necessary, decision and then admitting his error. He was also capable of disobeying orders when necessary. Another flashpoint between Xenophon and Cheirisophus occurs at the end of book 3 (3.4.37–49). When Cheirisophus sees that the enemy has occupied the spur of a mountain above the Greeks' line of march, he orders Xenophon to bring the peltasts from the rear to the front of the army. Xenophon, disobeying this order, leaves his men behind and comes in person to find out why they have been summoned. He then explains to Cheirisophus that he has not brought the peltasts because the entire army of Tissaphernes has appeared in their rear, and he comes up with a better plan of attack. Once again, Xenophon sees something that everyone else has completely missed: that if they send a detachment to seize the crown of the mountain, they can dislodge the enemy from the ridge. Even if the exchange between him and Cheirisophus seems a bit strained, Cheirisophus immediately recognizes that Xenophon has come up with a better plan than his own.

When the Greeks and the Persians both make a dash for the summit, Xenophon, who is in charge of the operation, is challenged by a foot soldier, Soteridas, who complains that Xenophon is riding on a horse, whereas he is totally exhausted from carrying his shield (3.4.47–49). Xenophon then gives a splendid and unforgettable display of leading by example when he dismounts from his horse, takes the man's shield, and runs up the hill, even though he is weighed down by the heavy breastplate worn by cavalrymen. It is a grand gesture, equivalent to Alexander the Great refusing to drink water when his men had none (Arrian 6.26.1–3; Plutarch, *Alexander* 42.3), despite the fact that Xenophon found it hard to keep up the pace. In vindication of Xenophon, "the other soldiers struck and pelted and verbally abused Soteridas until they compelled him to take back his shield and proceed on foot." In this way, Xenophon's excellence in giving counsel at the beginning of book 3 is matched by his excellence in deeds at the end of that book. This scene, moreover, is repeated in book 7, when Xenophon dismounts in order to lead the infantry charge against some Thracian villages. When questioned by a surprised Seuthes, he responds, "The hoplites will run faster and more cheerfully, if I also lead them on foot" (7.3.45).

There is, however, a caveat. The recalcitrant infantryman made his complaint immediately after hearing Xenophon's speech of exhortation. These words of encouragement that Xenophon uses to incite his men to reach the summit before the Persians are rather problematic, in that they are proven to be false by the next four books of the *Anabasis*. "Men, consider that you are now racing toward Greece, now toward your children and wives; now, having toiled but a little, we shall make the rest of the journey without having to fight a battle." The narrator, and at least some readers, know what these men do not—that many more battles await them and that a large number of them will never see their children or wives again.

In book 4, another famous incident (4.3.1–34) has a very close affinity with the opening of book 3. The Ten Thousand, having survived their travails in the mountainous country of the Carduchians, are finally poised to cross into the plains of Armenia. But a large force of cavalry and infantry is blocking what is apparently the only crossing point of the Centrites River, and an army of Carduchians is ready to attack their rear as soon as they attempt to ford the river.

The gravity of the situation is underscored by the repetition of the phrase "in a state of great *aporia*" from the opening sentence of book 3: "During this day and night the Greeks remained in a state of great *aporia*. Then Xenophon had a dream. He seemed to be bound in fetters, but these fell from him on their own, with the result that he was set free and able to walk wherever he wished" (4.3.8). Xenophon immediately reports this dream to Cheirisophus, and at daybreak all of the generals sacrifice and obtain good omens on the first attempt. Then, as Xenophon is eating breakfast, two young men approach him with the news that they have discovered another, shallower, place to ford the river that, moreover, is inaccessible to the enemy cavalry. Xenophon and the two youths then poured libations and "prayed to the gods who had revealed the dream and the ford that they also bring to fulfillment the remaining good things." When Cheirisophus hears this news he, too, pours libations.

This passage, with its combination of *aporia* followed by a dream, closely mirrors the dream episode in book 3. There too we read, "there was *aporia* . . . he had a dream" (3.1.11), and there too Xenophon provides the means of salvation for the army. Once again, the gods select Xenophon to be the agent of salvation for the Greeks by sending him a dream that rouses him to action. The divine origin of the dream is confirmed both by the sacrificial omens turning out well on the first attempt and by the immediate appearance of the two young men with news of their discovery. The further emphasis on piety in this section is striking, with the repeated pouring of libations and the prayer for deliverance. It might seem, however, that in comparison with Xenophon's actions in book 3 in rousing his fellow Greeks through his several speeches, his role here is more passive. That is not quite so. The two youths were able to transmit their vital information to Xenophon so quickly "because all knew that it was possible to approach him both when he was having breakfast and when he was having dinner and that it was even possible to wake him when he was asleep in order to speak to him, if someone had something to tell him that was relevant to the war." It is Xenophon's round-the-clock accessibility to everyone and anyone with something important to say that makes divine intervention efficacious. Our impression that Xenophon is being especially praised for this accessibility is confirmed, if confirmation were really needed, by the fact that two famous generals are singled out in his *Hellenica* for a more limited application of the same habit (the Syracusan Hermocrates at 1.1.30 and the Spartan Teleutias at 5.1.14).

In subsequent scenes, when the generals get together to decide what to do, it is always Xenophon who comes up with the best plan. In quick succession he prevails over Cleanor's plan of making a costly frontal assault on forces who are blocking a mountain pass with his suggestion that they seize an unguarded part of the mountain by night (4.6.7–19); he comes up with the plan for storming the Taochian stronghold (4.7.3–7); and he also suggests the strategy of attacking the Colchians on yet another mountaintop by advancing in columns rather than in a phalanx formation (4.8.8–14). In this last incident, it is also Xenophon who gives the prebattle exhortation to the army as he proceeds along the battle line in order to take up his position in command of the left wing.

Let us take the attack on the Taochian village as an illustration of the narratological device that is being deployed in these scenes (4.7.1–14). The Greeks have run out of provisions, and Cheirisophus, who is leading the army, initiates an attack as soon as he reaches a fortress where the Taochians have deposited a large number of cattle. This is to no avail, since the defenders are rolling down stones that are crushing anyone who attempts to approach. Xenophon then arrives with the rear guard, and Cheirisophus says to him, "You have come at a good time. The place must be taken; for the army will have no provisions unless we capture this place." The generals take counsel together, and Xenophon asks what the problem is. He then immediately comes up with the winning plan: to wit, that the soldiers dash between trees and take cover behind them until the enemy have used up all of their stones! Xenophon saves the day by offering what seems, at least in retrospect, to be a fairly obvious piece of advice.

It is only after one reaches book 4 that the author Xenophon's strategy in not introducing the character Xenophon until the beginning of book 3 makes sense. He figures so centrally in book 3 that the reader would feel overpowered by his dominant presence in the narrative were his entry not delayed. A less artful writer would have insinuated himself into the narrative of books 1–2 by having himself give salient advice either to the generals or to Cyrus directly. But when Xenophon the character makes his cameo appearances in books 1 and 2, it is in a passive role. He is right up in front with Cyrus at Cunaxa, but he merely explains Greek practices to the prince. There is no hint, or obvious foreshadowing, of the leadership role he will play later on.

One thing that distinguishes Xenophon from all of his fellow commanders is his concern for the common soldiers and his readiness to share their burdens. The narrator creates this image by showing rather than by telling; it is only much later in the *Anabasis* (in his speeches at the end of book 5 and in book 7), when Xenophon is compelled to defend himself and his previous actions, that the character Xenophon tells his audiences, both the assembled army and his readers, about his earlier solicitude for the army. During the time of action the narrator leaves it implicit, for instance, that by rising to split wood Xenophon sets the example that saves his men. The army is spending the night in the open, and a heavy snowfall covers the soldiers in their sleep (4.4.12–13). "There was a great reluctance to get up because the snow that had fallen upon them while they were lying down, so long as it did not slip off, was keeping them warm. But when Xenophon had the hardihood to stand up without this cloak on and to begin splitting wood, quickly someone else also got up, took his axe from him, and started to split wood. As a result of this the others also got up and began to kindle fires and to anoint themselves." It is left unsaid that if Xenophon had not roused himself (just as he did after his dream at the beginning of book 3), all of these men would have perished.

When caught in a deadly snowstorm in the plains of Armenia a few days later, he addresses the problems of hunger-sickness, frost-bite, and snow-blindness (4.5.1–22). He does what he can to save the soldiers who are too ill to proceed. When they refuse to budge, he grows angry, but also devises a scheme to save them. His behavior contrasts especially sharply with that of Cheirisophus, who is only concerned for the men under his immediate command and does not even inquire until the next day what has befallen the rest of the army. Cheirisophus is implicitly blamed for the deaths of the soldiers who could not keep up. Xenophon comes off as a caring but also resourceful commander who does whatever he can to save each and every soldier regardless of rank or city of origin. To the modern reader, he is reminiscent of Alexander the Great, yet without the vainglory and self-centeredness.

Xenophon subsequently has a falling out with Cheirisophus over his treatment of the Armenian village chief who is acting as their guide and whom Xenophon has treated with considerable solicitude (4.6.3). When the chief fails to lead the army to any villages, Cheirisophus becomes angry with him and hits him, but fails to tie him up, and so he runs away during the night. There is an implied contrast here between Xenophon and Cheirisophus in terms of temperament: one lesson is that unnecessary brutality, as also displayed by the Spartan Clearchus, is a fault in a commander (see chapter 7 for another possible lesson). Xenophon too sometimes loses his temper, but always as a last resort and when it is justified.

At the very beginning of book 5, Cheirisophus leaves the army on a fruitless quest to obtain ships for the journey back to Greece; he returns empty-handed near the beginning of book 6 (6.1.16). Although there are other generals, Xenophon seems to be de facto in sole command for the rest of book 5. It is Xenophon who advises the army, who leads them in battle and gives the prebattle exhortation, and who responds to envoys (especially to those from Sinope, in a series of set speeches). Indeed, even before Cheirisophus's actual departure, we see Xenophon setting out policy at the beginning of the book. When the army refuses to consider his proposal that they request the coastal Greek cities to repair the roads, he recognizes their "folly" and persuades the cities on his own authority. It is a good thing that he does, since when Cheirisophus fails to return before they have run out of provisions, the main body of the army is compelled to proceed by land (5.3.1–3). The narrator merely observes that "the road had been repaired," without reminding us that Xenophon arranged for this against the troops' wishes. In book 4, a pattern was to have the generals jointly consider plans and then for Xenophon to propose the winning idea. In book 5, he is more securely in command. Then in book 6, it is Xenophon who rescues the Arcadians and Achaeans when their secession from the army backfires (6.3.10–23), and it is Xenophon who both proposes the winning strategy and delivers the prebattle harangue in the decisive victory over the forces of the Persian satrap Pharnabazus and the Bithynian Thracians (6.5.7–25).

And what kind of commander is he? His first major solo undertaking is the attack on the fortress of the Drilae (5.2.1–32). The narrator sets the stage for the near disaster of this expedition by telling us that the Greeks of Trapezus, because of their friendship with the native inhabitants, will not lead the army where they can easily get provisions, and by emphasizing the difficulty of the terrain and the extremely warlike character of the Drilae. The scene that follows is rather complex. An advance group of peltasts and some spearmen have got themselves into trouble by crossing a ravine in order to attack a palisade. When they are unable to retreat, they send to Xenophon, who is leading the hoplites, with an explanation of their situation. Xenophon's first action is to cross the ravine with his captains so that he can "consider whether it was better to withdraw the men who had already crossed, or to lead over the hoplites as well, on the assumption that the fortress could be captured." He then consults with his captains and with his seers, who are religious specialists, about the best course of action. "It seemed that it was not possible to retreat without many casualties, and the captains believed that they might be able to capture the place; and Xenophon yielded to them, trusting in the sacrifices. For the seers had declared their opinion that although there would be a battle, the end result of the expedition would be good" (5.2.8–9). The Greeks then proceed to capture the palisade, only to discover that a village of wooden houses and an impregnable citadel lie beyond it. Retreat without heavy losses again seems impossible, since the Drilae are both attacking them from the gates of the citadel and pelting them from the rooftops of the houses. The line of retreat to the initial palisade is along a narrow road that leads from the citadel and goes between these houses.

At this crucial juncture, a pattern that we have seen twice before again emerges (5.2.24–25):

While they were fighting and were at a loss for what to do [i.e., were in a state of *aporia*], one of the gods offered them a means of salvation. For suddenly one of the houses on the right blazed up, since someone had set it on fire. When this house began to collapse, the enemy started to flee from the other houses on the right side of the road. When Xenophon learned about this opportunity which chance had given, he gave orders to set fire to the houses on the left also; and since they were made of wood they started to burn very quickly. And so the enemy fled from these houses too.

In this way the Greeks under Xenophon's command escaped, although, it should be pointed out, without having captured the citadel. The resemblance of this scene to Xenophon's dream at the beginning of book 3 is more apparent in the Greek than in translation. In both places, *aporia* is followed by an omen—a house that "blazes up." Although the narrator does not know which god has set the house on fire and refers to this as an opportunity given by "chance" (*tuchē*), the obvious implication is that Xenophon has once again, and now for the third time, been aided by a divine intervention that he has swiftly both understood and acted on.

In what was almost a total disaster Xenophon reversed the situation by exemplifying the dictum of Admiral Mike Mullen, the current chairman of the Joint Chiefs of Staff: "Listen, Learn, and Lead." Xenophon appears as the contemplative and prudent commander who sizes up the situation for himself but also consults with his captains and with the gods, thus building consensus before taking action. Xenophon trusts in the omens that the expedition will be successful, albeit with fighting. The situation turns critical, but then a god intervenes by setting fire to one of the houses. This gives Xenophon the idea of setting more fires, and his strategy saves the day. We can see here the relationship between divine assistance and human agency working itself out. Xenophon, by trusting in the omens and acceding to the opinion of his captains, has put his men in a very dangerous situation. The gods come to his aid, but only partially; they show the way forward, so to speak. Xenophon then takes the initiative and sees the potential benefit of a "chance" happening. Once again, we see in Xenophon a commander who can learn from his mistakes and think on his feet. When faced with a new situation, he can quickly plan the appropriate strategy.

Yet one can also read against the grain of this narrative; that is, read it subversively. Xenophon consults his captains for actions that have a dubious result but takes sole credit for actions that end in success. After the initial consultation, Xenophon takes a series of strategic decisions on his own, and he only consults the captains once more, when they jointly decide that the inner citadel itself cannot be captured. So one might conclude that the narrator is perfectly willing to share the responsibility for failure but gives to Xenophon alone the credit for success.

Further Reading

Hutchinson (2000) is a popular treatment of the theory and practice of military command in the works of Xenophon. Xenophon's self-representation is well analyzed by Bradley (2001). See, too, Gray (1998, 2003, 2004) and Tsagalis (2009). Tuplin (2003), a wide-ranging essay, concludes that Xenophon's purpose for writing was didactic (providing paradigms of leadership and critiques of panhellensim), not apologetic. Rood (2006) argues that part of the didacticism of the *Anabasis* is Xenophon's portrayal of himself as an ideal leader. For the apologetic aspect of the text, also consult the further reading for chapter 6.

· 6 ·

Xenophon on Trial

> I will leave judgments on this matter to history—but I will be one
> of the historians.
>
> —*Winston Churchill*

A striking feature of the *Anabasis* is that books 5, 6, and 7 each ends with a set of serious accusations against Xenophon, all of which he refutes at length. Even if the book divisions that we have were not created by Xenophon, the placing of these defense speeches at roughly equal intervals is hardly coincidental. Taken together, they comprise a defense of Xenophon's actions and motives that is both comprehensive and cumulative. It is easy to understand why so many readers of the *Anabasis* have been left with the impression that Xenophon was a truly great man who continually put himself in personal danger on behalf of the army he was determined to save.

To be sure, skeptical readers have not let this image go unchallenged, and ultimately, every reader is entitled, and indeed invited by the narrative itself, to judge Xenophon (as author, as historical actor, and as protagonist in a literary text) for himself or herself. But one consideration should be kept in mind. Xenophon has been simultaneously criticized for exaggerating his own importance and influence and for defending his own actions. Yet, if in reality he was a minor figure, then why the need for a self-defense? What memoirists would so greatly exaggerate their own role in controversial events that they then had to justify things that they had never actually done? So either Xenophon was a minor actor who had nothing to apologize for (and the purpose of his speeches is purely didactic rather than apologetic), or he was a major player who was a lightning rod, both during the expedition and even decades later, for personal attacks. But one cannot logically have it both ways.

The personal problems of Xenophon, as a character in the *Anabasis*, begin when he considers founding a colony along the southern coast of the Black Sea (5.6.15–5.8.26). Both speech and narrative are at great pains to demonstrate that Xenophon's first, and only, step is to ascertain from the gods through sacrifice whether he should bring up this issue with the army. The seer Silanus, however, who has assisted Xenophon with the sacrifice, spreads the rumor that Xenophon desires to acquire "a name and power for himself" by establishing a colony. Various officers in the army then join in the attempt to discredit him, each scheming for his own advantage. The general Timasion of Dardanus is the most prominent of Xenophon's opponents, as he schemes to get the people of Heracleia and Sinope (Greek cities on the Black Sea) to provide wages to the army so that he can take them to the Troad, from which he has been exiled. The narrative indirectly imputes two motives to Timasion: that he wants to use the Ten Thousand to effect his restoration to his homeland and that he exploits the situation to get a bribe out of the Sinopeans and Heracleots (5.6.21–23).

Matters come to a head during an assembly of the army during which Timasion and several others attack Xenophon, who at first remains silent but finally is compelled to speak. Just as Xenophon will later extricate himself from being forced to accept the supreme command of the army by deferring to the will of the gods, so here he attempts to use religion as a means of defending himself against the charge that he is taking steps to found a colony without first having consulted the army (5.6.28–29):

> I sacrifice, as you see, as often as I can, both on your behalf and on mine, in order that I may say, think, and do whatever is most honorable and best both for you and for me. And I

was now sacrificing about this very thing, whether it was better to begin discussing this project with you and taking some action or absolutely not to touch the matter. Silanus the seer responded with respect to the most important point, that the omens from sacrifice were favorable; for he knew that I was not inexperienced on account of my always being present at sacrifices. But he said that a kind of treachery and a plot against me appeared in the omens, since he indeed knew that he himself was plotting to slander me to you.

With these few words, the character Xenophon is able to demonstrate a number of important principles: he always seeks the advice of the gods in order to obtain the best, first for the army and then secondly for himself; he sacrificed specifically to find out whether he should introduce the topic of founding a colony to the assembled soldiers (he did not inquire whether the colony was in itself a good idea); and the gods themselves have revealed Silanus's treachery. That would have put an end to the matter, had Timasion not changed his mind (out of fear of the army, since the Heracleots had reneged on their offer to provide pay) and convinced the generals to persuade their captains in private that they should establish a colony at the Phasis River at the eastern end of the Black Sea (5.6.34–37).

At that point, Neon of Asine, with whom Xenophon has a number of clashes throughout the *Anabasis*, falsely accuses him of planning to trick the soldiers into sailing east back to the Phasis River rather than west toward Greece (5.7.1–4). It is not explicitly said why Neon tries to bushwhack Xenophon (out of spite for being left out of Timasion's plan?). In any case, Xenophon needs to deliver a second speech in order to clear himself of this new charge (5.7.5–33). Even then, the army is still so suspicious of him that when they reach Calpe Harbor they refuse to encamp in the most suitable location because they think they have been led there as part of a scheme "by certain people" who wish to found a city (6.4.7). Some even accuse him of bribing the seer Arexion to say that the omens are unfavorable for a departure (6.4.14). It is remarkable that so much narrative space is given to justify a character's actions and motivations in regard to a hypothetical situation. Xenophon never formally proposes to the army that they remain on the southern coast of the Black Sea; indeed, he never moves beyond his initial exploratory sacrifice. We are also told that "the majority" of the soldiers do not want to found a city. So why has this become so large an issue in the text?

One way to answer that question is by rationalizing this narrative as if it were a partial transcript of what had actually happened (and I am *not* advocating that the text must be treated in this way). If we do that and then fill in between the lines, the narrator's explanation for why Xenophon wants to found a city is not entirely convincing. Xenophon's plan, we are told, is to establish an economically viable new city, one that "would add to the territory and power of Greece." The historical Xenophon, we might be tempted to infer, obviously was ambitious to be the leader of the colony, and so it is not all that surprising that Timasion makes a counterbid for leadership (offering to take the soldiers to the Troad, his homeland, where he could enrich them). Did the historical actor Xenophon inadvertently unleash this nasty competition and has the narrative been constructed in such a way as to excuse him while making Silanus, Timasion, and Xenophon's other opponents appear to be the greedy ones out for themselves? Should we blame Timasion for wanting to effect his own restoration (a desire that is repeated at 7.2.2)? It would certainly not be fanciful to conclude that the attention given to this issue reflects a desire to convince the external audience, just as much as the internal one, about the nature of Xenophon's leadership and his degree of responsibility for certain unsavory actions by the Ten Thousand (see below).

Moreover, Xenophon's second defense speech (five times longer than the first one: 5.6.28–34 and 5.7.5–33, respectively) is only partly a rebuttal of the accusation that he is intending by deceitful means to take the army back to the Phasis River. The narrator sets up this speech by telling us that Neon's disclosure of Xenophon's alleged plan has made the soldiers very angry, that they are gathering in small groups, and, most important, "it was very much feared that they would do the sort of thing that they had done to the heralds of the Colchians and the market regulators, who had all been stoned to death, except for those who had escaped to the sea." Xenophon then calls an assembly of the soldiers in order to preempt their gathering on their own. All of a sudden, the entire emphasis of the narrative has switched gears from an attack on Xenophon's personal ambitions to the danger of a mutiny.

Xenophon starts off his speech by demonstrating just how ridiculous the accusation is (how could the army be fooled into sailing east instead of west?), and he attributes it to unnamed men who are jealous of him. In the main body of the speech, however, he dexterously diverts attention away from the colonization controversy by addressing the growing, and serious, problem of indiscipline in the army. He begins with a specific example of indiscipline in the form of a flashback to an earlier incident that was not recorded in the previous narrative. It involves two independent but related incidents: the assassination of three ambassadors from the Colchians and a subsequent spontaneous attack on the market regulators in Cotyora. Xenophon then moves from a lengthy description of these specific examples of lawlessness to a delineation of the general consequences that will befall the army if such indiscipline continues. So this speech is simultaneously apologetic and didactic. It is apologetic in the sense that it demonstrates two things about Xenophon: that he neither attempted to manipulate the army into establishing a new city with himself as founder nor encouraged acts of insubordination and indiscipline. It is didactic in that the speaker explains why discipline is essential to an army's survival, success, and reputation. Xenophon has very effectively manipulated his internal audience, but has he also effectively manipulated his external one? Are we convinced that the Xenophon in this story was not just as self-seeking as Silanus, Timasion, and Neon?

The soldiers, at least, are utterly convinced by this speech, so much so that they propose to execute anyone who in the future incites lawlessness and they decide to subject the generals to an investigation of their past conduct. Philesius and Xanthicles are each fined 20 minas (2,000 drachmas), and Sophaenetus 10 minas "for neglecting the duty for which he had been chosen." If indeed there was a historical and literary quarrel between them, that brief and grammatically awkward notice (and it is possible that a few words have dropped out of the text here) is a deft touch on Xenophon's part. The reader's imagination, which is made less suspicious of bias than it would have been by a longer denunciation on the part of the narrator, is left free to fill in the narrative gap of what Sophaenetus had actually done wrong.

But Xenophon is not yet out of trouble. Some of the soldiers claim that they were struck by him and formally charge him with *hubris* (insolence involving violent behavior). In this way, book 5 ends with yet a third speech by Xenophon in his own defense, although it takes a rather different form from the previous ones, as he cross-examines, rather humorously, one of the soldiers (a muledriver) who claims to have been hit. At the end of the exchange, when the internal audience learns why Xenophon struck the soldier (for attempting to bury alive a soldier whom he had been ordered to carry), they shout that Xenophon gave him too few blows! He goes on to admit that he struck other soldiers, too, either because their indiscipline threatened the safety of the whole army or in order to rescue them from certain death when they refused to march on.

This verbal exchange with his accuser serves as a flashback to the heady days of Xenophon's uncontested leadership. It is a vivid retelling of how he was concerned to save every single one of the Greeks from freezing, starving to death, or being killed by the enemy while the army was struggling through a snow-covered plain in Armenia (4.5.1–36). This incident has a double focus. On the one hand, it points the contrast with the self-serving disunity that has come to characterize the Greek army in book 5; on the other, it is a restatement of Xenophon's own role as the leader who kept the army safe and a defense of his conduct. In literary terms, the story of Xenophon's confrontation with the disobedient muledriver is more effective in the present context than if he had narrated it in its proper chronological place in book 4.

Xenophon's speech is on the surface a defense against charges of *hubris* and overly strict discipline. But in fact it serves a subtler purpose as well, for it effectively counters the charge that comes up later in the *Anabasis* (book 7) that he was too lenient and indulgent a commander (see below). At the level of characterization, it reveals a commander who could learn from his own experiences, who led by example, was fully cognizant of the evils attendant on indiscipline and idleness, and was not afraid to impose corporal punishment if it meant saving lives. And, most important perhaps, Xenophon very effectively brings his defense (as well as book 5 itself) to a close in a way that involves both the internal and external audience in the mental act of remembering his previous good deeds (5.8.25–26):

> "In any case, I am surprised that if I offended any one of you, you remember it and do not keep quiet about it; but if I helped someone in a storm, or defended someone against an enemy, or helped to provide for someone who was ill or in want, no one remembers this. Nor if I praised someone for doing something well or if I honored someone, to the extent that I was able, for being a good man, do you remember this either. But surely it is good and just and pious and more pleasant to remember good things than bad ones." After this they stood up and began to recall these things, and it turned out well.

The narrator drives Xenophon's point home by conjuring up the image of the troops remembering and recalling Xenophon's benefactions toward individual soldiers. It is rhetorically and imaginatively more effective for the army to recall Xenophon's good deeds than for either the character Xenophon or the narrator to do so. This type of narrative economy serves several purposes simultaneously. It allows the narrative to move on, and it encourages the reader to fill in the narrative gap in the way the text itself promotes and authorizes. At the same time, however, the last sentence of book 5, insofar as it suggests a successful closure to events ("it turned out well"), gives a false sense of security. The Ten Thousand recall everything Xenophon has done for them so far, and this assembly, as well as the book itself, ends on a positive note, just as book 4 has.

Is that ominous for what comes in the last two books of the story, as new causes for grievance, and the apologies they elicit on the part of our protagonist, present themselves? Only a few pages into book 6 the army will splinter under ethnic divisions, and Xenophon's leadership will once again be called into question.

The question of motive loomed large in the preceding discussion. Indeed, the attribution of motive is a powerful tool in any narrator's attempt to influence the reader's reaction to the narrative. The narrator's assertion that Silanus leaked Xenophon's interest in establishing a colony because he wanted to return to Greece with money (3,000 gold darics) Cyrus gave him is confirmed by later events (1.7.18; 5.6.18). Silanus desperately attempts to oppose a vote by the army to punish anyone who attempts to run away (5.6.34), and in book 6 the narrator slips in, as an aside, that a different seer is conducting the sacrifice for the generals, because "Silanus the seer had already run away, having hired a boat out of Heracleia" (6.4.13). Nothing condemns so much as treachery, and Silanus's own actions have effectively validated the narrator's account of his motives in opposing Xenophon. Our expectations as to Neon of Asine are also realized by the subsequent narrative, as he continues to oppose Xenophon and attempts to gratify the army, all for his own advantage (6.4.23; 7.3.7). Yet when it comes to Timasion, the narrator does not fulfill our expectations. When Seuthes's agent Heracleides attempts to persuade the other generals to campaign without Xenophon, promising them two months' pay for the army, Timasion responds, "I would not make an expedition without Xenophon, not even if there should be pay for five months" (7.5.10). Timasion's change of attitude toward Xenophon has been so gradual over a long stretch of narrative that this declaration of loyalty seems startling, and for that reason it is all the more persuasive.

More surprising, perhaps, is a slight incongruence between Xenophon's personal motives and his declarations to the army. When the captains press him to accept a supreme command over the army, the narrator reveals Xenophon's internal conflict, as he weighs the pros and cons (6.1.19–25). This is an opportunity to stress Xenophon's total selflessness and unswerving dedication to the welfare of the Ten Thousand as a collective entity. Contrary to expectation, that is not what the narrator delivers: "Xenophon, on the one hand, desired this [the supreme command], thinking that he would be held in greater honor by his friends and that his name would be greater when it reached his native city, and that perhaps he might be the cause of some good for the army."

The incongruity has to do with priority of interest. Silanus has claimed that Xenophon wants "to acquire a name for himself," and here the narrator is asserting the very same thing! In the speech quoted at the beginning of this chapter in which he defends his private initiative in sacrificing in connection with the founding of a colony, Xenophon has put the interest of the army first and his own second ("I sacrifice on your behalf and on my own behalf, I seek what is best for you and for me"). Now, when the sacrifices have unambiguously revealed that he should not accept the command, he says to the army (6.1.26), "I delight in being honored by you, since I am indeed a human being, and I am grateful, and I pray that the gods grant it to me to be the cause of some good for you." And he then goes on to explain why it would be dangerous both for the army and for himself if he should be chosen for the post in preference to a Spartan. The point that I am trying to make is that in his public declarations, the character Xenophon always stresses the army's advantage first and his own second. In his private ruminations, the order is reversed. That should give us pause. Xenophon is beginning to look not so different from the other leaders, whose *primary* concern is their personal reputation and standing. As it turns out, Xenophon is right not to accept the supreme command of the army, but not precisely for the reasons he foresees. Cheirisophus himself can only maintain command for five or six days, and he *was* a Spartan. It looks as if the Achaeans and Arcadians can no longer countenance either an Athenian or a Spartan commanding them, now that they are close to home (or so they believe) and are thinking more about bringing home plunder than about mere survival.

Nonetheless, book 6 concludes with Xenophon willing to sacrifice his life for the army and for his friend Agasias when the Spartan Cleander seeks to arrest Agasias (6.6.5–37). This incident revolves around Agasias's clash with Dexippus, who deserted the Ten Thousand at Trapezus and ever since has done his best to slander Xenophon to various Spartan commanders in the region. Agasias got the entire army into trouble when he rescued a man whom Dexippus was unjustly attempting to arrest and then ordered others to strike Dexippus. Xenophon delivers a speech to the Ten Thousand in which he offers to hand himself over to Cleander for execution if he was responsible for Agasias's actions ("For I hear that Dexippus is saying to Cleander that Agasias would not have done these things if I had not ordered him to"; 6.6.15). Agasias, however, states in the strongest possible terms that none of this was authorized by Xenophon: "I swear," he says to the assembled army, "by all of the gods and goddesses, that Xenophon did not order me to rescue the man" (6.6.17). This entire incident, which may seem a minor affair in itself, functions as a device for clearing both Xenophon personally and the army collectively against charges of lawlessness. Agasias is acquitted on all charges, and Xenophon and Cleander get on so well that they even enter into a formal relationship of guest-friendship. Moreover, Cleander is so impressed by the discipline of the Ten Thousand that he desires to accept an invitation to become their commander and personally lead them back to Greece, but is prevented when his sacrifices over a period of three days fail to get favorable omens. Thus book 6 ends, as did book 5, on a note of false optimism. The rapprochement with the Spartan authorities, Xenophon's popularity and standing with the army, and his chances of returning home to Athens all dangerously unravel in book 7. He will need to make a whole new apology, and his very life will depend on his success.

Xenophon's Thracian (Mis)Adventure

Book 7 is perhaps the least read but, in many ways, the most important book in the *Anabasis*. Xenophon now, if not before, is fully foregrounded as the protagonist. There are two central themes. One is Xenophon's thwarted desire to leave the army and sail home. The other is his rejection of Seuthes's numerous attempts to secure his services through bribery. About a third of book 7 consists of speeches delivered by Xenophon himself. Book 7 is in essence the last act in a great drama that has seen an obscure character (Xenophon) rise to prominence, survive challenges to his authority from various quarters, and then triumph, in however limited a sphere, over adversaries and adversities alike.

The book opens with one of the most dramatic scenes in all of Greek historical writing (7.1.12–31), a miniature gem that can stand comparison to anything written by Herodotus or Thucydides. When the Spartan admiral Anaxibius attempts to shut the Ten Thousand out of Byzantium, in a rage they break into the city. "When Xenophon saw what was happening, fearing that the army might turn to plundering and that incurable evils might befall the city, himself, and the soldiers, he began to run and he entered the city gates with the mob." Meanwhile, the inhabitants flee in terror, and Anaxibius summons reinforcements. This leads to an exceptionally dangerous situation:

> When the soldiers saw Xenophon, many of them rushed to him and said, "Now it is possible for you, Xenophon, to prove yourself a man. You possess a city, you possess triremes, you possess money, you possess men in such numbers. Now, if you should wish to do so, you would both profit us and make yourself great." Xenophon responded, "You speak well and I shall do these things."

The reader, who is by now familiar both with Xenophon's abilities as a leader and with his moral values, knows that he will not do "these things" that the soldiers have urged. Rather, he will use his rhetorical skills to calm them and to bring them to their senses by pointing out the terrible consequences that would follow if they gratified their anger by punishing the Spartans who are present and plundering a blameless Greek city. It would be better to suffer injustice, he tells them, than to be deprived of their homecoming to Greece, a theme repeated from his exhortation that they should not disregard Cleander's demands (6.6.11).

When the soldiers say to Xenophon, "Now it is possible for you to prove yourself a man and to make yourself great," are they tacitly suggesting that he has not been a "man" so far, that his previous accomplishments have not been sufficient to make him truly great? In other words, is the army collectively accepting the claim of Silanus, that Xenophon is chiefly motivated by a desire to acquire a name and power for himself? If so, the vivid narrative of this incident has refuted a narrowly negative view of Xenophon's character and motivations. Like most Greeks of his social class, he wanted to achieve and leave behind a good reputation, but not at any price.

The apologetic tone of book 7 is more pronounced and pervasive than anything that came before. Xenophon keeps trying to leave the army, but either the gods (6.2.15) or men more powerful than himself (7.1.4; 7.1.8–11; 7.1.38–39; 7.2.8) or his sense of duty to his friends in the army (7.7.57) will not let him. The continual thwarting of Xenophon's desire to sail home both assimilates him to Odysseus, whose homecoming was continually delayed by one circumstance or another, and sets up an excuse and justification for his service with Seuthes, who was alleged to have paid him a lot of money while the troops got little. From start to finish, book 7 constitutes a defense of Xenophon against charges of being self-serving.

Now, if not earlier, the reader might have some real doubts about the narrator's reliability. In particular, there is something vague about the reasons that are given for Xenophon's decisions to put off sailing home. When he is actually en route, traveling in company with the former Spartan admiral Anaxibius, all of a sudden Anaxibius reverses his previous policy and bids Xenophon to return to the army and lead it back into Asia (7.2.7–8). Anaxibius's less than creditable motive, that he wants to spite the Persian satrap Pharnabazus for ignoring him now that his term of office has expired, has to be inferred from the narrative. Pharnabazus has earlier made an agreement with Anaxibius that if he gets the Ten Thousand out of Asia "he would do for him whatever he asked" (7.1.2), but he is now negotiating with Aristarchus (the new governor of Byzantium) without having made good on his promises to Anaxibius. More alarming is the fact that the narrator leaves

Xenophon's motives for returning to the army completely vague, merely saying that "Anaxibius urged Xenophon with every contrivance and machination to sail to the army as quickly as possible." There is a large narrative gap here, and filling it in is not a simple matter.

What kind of arguments is Anaxibius likely to have used and why did Xenophon obey him? Was the character Xenophon motivated by fear of disobeying a prominent Spartan, or by loyalty to his former comrades, or by ambition to make a bigger name for himself? Likewise, when he delays his return for the last time, we are told (7.7.57): "Xenophon . . . was openly making his preparations to return home. For the decree of exile had not yet been passed against him at Athens. But his friends in the army approached him and begged him not to depart until he should lead the army away and hand it over to Thibron." Here we are prompted to infer that it is loyalty to these friends, rather than a more self-interested consideration, that is motivating Xenophon.

There is something else suspicious about the way Xenophon's delayed homecoming has been treated by the narrator. In the passage mentioned above, the narrator shares with the reader a piece of information the character Xenophon does not yet know, that a sentence of exile will be passed against him at Athens at some unspecified time in the future. This may be true, historically speaking, but surely Xenophon had some inkling that his association with Cyrus (as Socrates indeed had warned him) and other actions on the campaign might not look too good to his countrymen back home. Was he then hesitant to return, fearing that he might face prosecution for some offense? This consideration comes out during his final speech to the army, when he complains (7.6.34), "I am hated by Seuthes on your account, the man who I hoped, by rendering him good service with your help, would set aside a fair place of refuge for me and my children, if I should ever have any." This "fair place of refuge" is a reference to the three fortresses on the coast of the Propontis that Seuthes repeatedly promises to give Xenophon. Contemporary readers would have noted with interest that two of those fortresses are the same ones that were held by Athens's most notorious "traitor," the fifth-century general and statesman

Alcibiades (also a pupil of Socrates), who retreated to them after he was deposed from his generalship in 406 BC (*Anabasis* 7.7.8; *Hellenica* 1.5.17; Nepos, *Alcibiades* 7.4).

It has been remarkable all along, in book 5 at Cotyora, in book 6 at Calpe Harbor, and in book 7 with Seuthes's offer of estates, how ready and willing Xenophon is to stay in Asia. There is an unresolved tension between this willingness and his attempts to sail back home. Perhaps Xenophon, both character and historical actor, was easily enough persuaded to stay with the remnants of the Ten Thousand in Asia, since even after he handed the army over to Thibron he continued with them under Spartan service, only returning to Greece in 394 with King Agesilaus. By then, since the Spartans were departing from Asia, his options had finally run out.

Now that we have grounds to doubt the narrator's reliability on the important question of Xenophon's intentions, we might also be skeptical of another persistent theme in book 7. Both narrator and character assert that Xenophon never took bribes or gifts from Seuthes (the same Greek word, *dōron*, has both meanings). Right from the start of book 7, we see Xenophon rejecting bribes from Seuthes and negotiating for the common soldiers. But at the same time, he seems to arrange for Seuthes to meet the men on their way out of Perinthus, so that they will accept his offer and reject Spartan service (7.3.7). The suspicion arises that Xenophon has maligned the Spartans Anaxibius and Aristarchus (the latter allegedly was scheming to have him arrested) in order to justify his own actions and decisions in accepting service with Seuthes.

References to bribery are strategically placed throughout book 7. The first of these has the function of refuting in advance the later charge that Xenophon profited from his service with Seuthes. And so, right at the beginning of the book, when Seuthes's agent Medosades attempts to bribe Xenophon to use his influence to get the army to cross from Asia to Byzantium, Xenophon responds that there is no need for Seuthes to pay either him or anyone else to do what the army is going to do anyway (7.1.5–6). Xenophon has to rebuff Medosades a second time, when Seuthes is "promising Xenophon whatever he thought would persuade him" to bring the army to him from Perinthus

(7.2.10). These two incidents are placed in advance of Xenophon's eventual dealings with Seuthes in order to establish Xenophon's innocence in the reader's mind right from the start. It is only when the Ten Thousand are forbidden by Aristarchus from crossing back to Asia from Perinthus that Xenophon negotiates with Seuthes.

Those face-to-face negotiations between Xenophon and Seuthes begin with a scene in which Xenophon rehearses with Medosades his previous attempts at bribery (7.2.23–30). It is difficult to understand the point of this interrogation, unless it is aimed at the external audience and is meant to drive the point home that Xenophon's ultimate decision to bring the army to Seuthes had nothing to do with bribery but everything to do with necessity. At this point, there is simply no other option that is as attractive and potentially as lucrative, since the narrator depicts Xenophon as being reluctant to lead the army to the Spartan-controlled Chersonese and as being completely taken in by Seuthes's generous promises of payment and benefaction for the soldiers. Yet even here there is a hint, for the careful reader, that Seuthes may not be as generous as he pretends to be. He says to Xenophon, "To you, Xenophon, I shall give my daughter, and if you have a daughter, I will buy her according to Thracian custom, and I shall give to you Bisanthe as a residence, which is the most beautiful of my strongholds on the sea" (7.2.38). Some scholars have mistakenly taken this passage as evidence that Xenophon must have been old enough to have a daughter of marriageable age, but that completely misses the point. The *real* point, however, will not have been lost on contemporary readers, who would have known from Herodotus (5.6.1) that marriage in the Thracian fashion entailed the groom paying a large sum of money to the bride's parents. So what Seuthes is essentially proposing is that Xenophon pay him a large sum of money in exchange for marrying his daughter. Since Xenophon is not old enough to have a daughter that Seuthes could marry (and he later says that he had no children as yet; 7.7.38), any suggestion of a reciprocal exchange is bogus. The reader, if not Xenophon the character, is alerted to the slipperiness of any offer made by this cunning prince.

But if Xenophon did not accept gifts from Seuthes, others apparently did. Here the narrative strategy is to shift the culpability onto others, thus making Xenophon look even better by comparison. Even before his initial meeting with Xenophon, Seuthes persuades the generals Cleanor and Phyrniscus to bring him the army, giving Cleanor a horse and Phyrniscus a woman (7.2.2). During their service in Thrace, Xenophon refuses a gift of three pairs of mules and some oxen, saying "it is enough for me to receive something later" and bidding Seuthes to give the animals to the other generals and to the captains. The generals Timasion, Cleanor, and Phryniscus each take a pair of mules. Xenophon's declaration that he will wait before accepting anything is explained by the fact that there is only enough money realized from the sale of plunder to give the soldiers two-thirds of their pay for the previous month. Xenophon is outraged (and shoots a barbed quip at Heracleides for failing to raise sufficient funds); the reaction of his fellow generals is not recorded (7.5.1–5).

It is at this point that Xenophon's problems really begin. All parties are now thoroughly angry with him (7.5.6–8; 16). Heracleides begins to slander him out of fear of losing his influence with Seuthes; the soldiers hold him personally responsible for their loss of wages; and "Seuthes was annoyed with him because he was insistent in demanding the wages for the soldiers." The narrative from this point on is focused on demonstrating three propositions: that Xenophon made no personal profit; that he did his utmost to exact from Seuthes the pay agreed on for the army; and that as a result of his honesty and solicitude, all parties concerned were extremely angry with him. And this situation arose despite the fact that the Ten Thousand, under Xenophon's leadership, had won back for Seuthes his ancestral kingdom. The only essential point the narrative leaves unclear is whether Seuthes himself is guilty of withholding payment from the army or whether he has been cheated by Heracleides, since Heracleides was in charge of selling plunder for coined money and is accused of embezzling some of the proceeds (explicitly so at 7.6.41 by the captain Polycrates).

Two lengthy speeches bring the story of the Thracian campaign to a close. The first is delivered before the entire army, the second to Seuthes in private a little later. In these speeches Xenophon, as both author and character, must address once and for all the charge that he has been enriched by Seuthes and has conspired with him to cheat the common soldiers of their wages. If some of the other generals were also accused, the narrative tells us nothing of it. The rhetorical overkill and the sophistic argumentation in these speeches have put some readers off. And in one spot Xenophon might seem to slip. He says to Seuthes that he has been falsely accused by the Ten Thousand of having received gifts (*dōra*) from him, and then goes on to say, "You, however, before I had rendered you any service, welcomed me with a pleasure that showed in your eyes, and voice, and hospitality (*xénia*), and you could not get your fill of promising all the things that were still to come" (7.7.46). It has been argued that the term *xénia* (here translated as "hospitality") is a code word for socially acceptable and tangible gifts that Xenophon had been given. One critic has asserted: "In a spectacular volte-face, Xenophon finally admits that he has received many hospitality presents from Seuthes—not once but many times. . . . In a few lines, Xenophon manages a virtuoso exercise in ideological gap-bridging, grounded in the ambiguity of *xenia*. His apparent duplicity reflects the implicit distinction, widely held in aristocratic circles, between hospitality presents, which are a legitimate form of *xenia*, and the *dōra* which embody the attempt and the temptation of corruption, and which must be eschewed at all costs" (Azoulay 2004: 294).

The Greek word *xenia*, depending on the accent, can mean two different things: as a feminine noun (*xenía*) it denotes the institution of ritualized guest-friendship; as a neuter plural substantive (*xénia*) it means the gifts that are exchanged as part of that relationship. Now it is true that *xenía*, in theory at least, could entail the bestowal of material goods on a guest-friend, and it is also true that the designation "guest-friend" can be a polite cover for a more mercurial and unequal relationship. Four of the seven original Greek generals are called Cyrus's guest-friends (*xenoi*), although they were simultaneously mercenaries receiving a wage (1.1.11;

1.3.3). Xenophon refers to himself as Seuthes's "friend" (*philos*; 7.8.43), but it is perfectly clear that they have concluded a formal relationship of guest-friendship (just as Xenophon did with the Spartan Cleander while at Calpe Harbor). In other words, Xenophon and Seuthes were *xenoi*.

In actual use, however, the word *xénia* invariably refers to the food and drink that is given to a guest by his host (as it does elsewhere in the *Anabasis*). So what Xenophon is referring to in this passage is conviviality. In Xenophon's case, the narrative makes it very clear that he, as well as the other generals, accepted invitations to Seuthes's banquets (where, ironically, they were expected to give *him* gifts, and Timasion gave Seuthes a silver cup and a valuable carpet; 7.3.15–33). And so Xenophon is not being inconsistent or engaging in sleight of hand (or, rather, of phrasing) when he goes to great lengths to convince us that he accepted no gifts at all (no horses, no women, no mules, not even an ox) and that when he got back to Lampsacus he was so broke that he even had to sell his horse to raise travel money (7.8.1–6). If he was willing to admit that he had accepted disposable gifts under the socially acceptable label *xénia*, then why did he end the campaign in penury? Finally (and this may seem to be a fine point), Xenophon never says that he did not draw the wages due to him as a general in charge of mercenaries: what he repeatedly stresses is that he did not receive presents, gifts, the wages due to the army, or the coastal fortresses that Seuthes kept figuratively dangling before his eyes. Moreover, he states in his speech to Seuthes that if the soldiers had received their full pay, then he would have been willing to accept "the things that you had promised to me" (7.7.39–41).

Is it likely that Xenophon was so sloppy a writer that after all of the artistry that went into building up his case for personal integrity, he would undermine it by including this one word, *xénia*? This is not a transcript of a private conversation (which Xenophon could hardly have provided years or decades later) but a composition carefully crafted to convince the external audience that he left Seuthes's employ empty-handed. This claim, moreover, is backed up in the most authoritative way that was available to him. For in his speech before the assembled troops, Xenophon exclaims, "I think that I am a long way from possessing your wages. For I swear by all of the gods and goddesses that I do not even possess the things that Seuthes promised me for myself. He is present himself and listening, and he knows if I am swearing falsely. And so that you may be even more surprised, I swear in addition that I have not even received the things that the other generals received, nor even as much as some of the captains" (7.6.18–19). The explanation that follows is not very compelling—that Xenophon had decided to share Seuthes's poverty in order that he could make him an even bigger friend after Seuthes gained power. Yet it would not have been very easy, any more than for some politicians today, to prove his case. In the last analysis, the judgment call depends on how willing we are as readers to be persuaded by Xenophon's self-representation as a man of exemplary piety, a person who would never, indeed could never, swear falsely. He again invokes the gods when making a similar declaration to Seuthes in private (7.7.39). In the later scene involving the sale of his horse, he confides to his incredulous seer that he has no money, and his claim is verified by a divinatory sacrifice to Apollo (7.8.3). Religious belief and practice play a key role throughout the *Anabasis*, both in the representation of Xenophon and in giving shape and structure to the narrative (see chapter 8). Some modern readers may take the intrusion of religion to be a cynical device for manipulating naive or superstitious readers, which would itself be a naive and unsophisticated way of viewing Greek religious practices and beliefs.

I now want to return to Xenophon's speech before the army and the way this scene is introduced (7.6.1–44). This final crisis in Xenophon's leadership is prompted by the arrival of two Spartans, Charminus and Polynicus, who have come to fetch the remnants of the Ten Thousand for service under Thibron in a war that Sparta has just declared against Tissaphernes. Heracleides and Seuthes immediately see this as a golden opportunity to dismiss the Greeks without their back pay and so invite the two Spartans to a private banquet. Heracleides confidently predicts that as soon as the soldiers hear their generous terms of payment, they will abandon Xenophon without a second thought. When Heracleides and Seuthes bring the two Spartans to the army, where they make their pitch for employment, an Arcadian soldier (whose name is not given) stands up and with extraordinary bitterness charges Xenophon with having profited at the troops' expense (7.6.9–10):

> "We would have joined you long ago, Lacedaemonians, if Xenophon had not used persuasion to bring us here, where we have never ceased campaigning by both night and day through an awful winter. He profits from our toils. Seuthes has enriched him in private, while depriving us of our wages. And so, if I should see Xenophon stoned to death and punished for the way in which he has dragged us about, I would consider that I had my pay and would feel no anger at all over the toils that I have endured." After him another speaker stood up and talked in the same way, and then another.

Why does the narrator not provide the name of this disgruntled soldier? The obvious answer is that Xenophon, as author, chose not to immortalize his accuser. It is also possible that the speech is a complete fabrication, inserted into the narrative for the sole purpose of providing an occasion for the character Xenophon to deliver a speech in which he answers all of the charges that were still lingering against the historical Xenophon. Yet if that were the case, it would be strange indeed that the first charge made by the speaker remains unanswered. Would the soldiers have been better off if Xenophon had yielded to Neon's recommendation and led the army to Spartan service in the Chersonese? As I have noted, since the narrator never tells us what happened to Neon and the eight hundred hoplites who followed him, we cannot answer that question. We are told about the hardships Xenophon's soldiers suffered during the winter campaign in Thrace; most disturbingly, and all too reminiscent of the frostbite suffered in Armenia (4.5.12–14), "the noses and ears of many of the Greeks froze off" (7.4.3). Neon's troops in the Chersonese certainly would have experienced a more hospitable climate. In any case, Xenophon gives a long defense speech, as if on trial for a capital offense, in which he does his rhetorical best to answer the other charges. Moreover, the narrator constructs this scene as the stage on which the dishonest Heracleides, who has done so much both to slander Xenophon and to defraud the army, finally gets his comeuppance.

This anonymous common soldier, so like Thersites, who attacks Agamemnon in book 2 of the *Iliad*, is not personally rebuked or struck by Xenophon, as Thersites is by Odysseus. Here, as elsewhere, Xenophon consistently proves himself superior to his Homeric prototypes. Unlike Odysseus, he always puts the interests of his men before his own, and that is why he is more successful at saving their lives. He could return home alone, as Odysseus did, but repeatedly chooses not to abandon the soldiers who need his leadership. One of the secrets to his success is that he is a less boastful and self-centered leader than Odysseus. He is just as clever, as in the banquet scene, when he does not have a gift for Seuthes other than himself and his men (7.3.26–31), but far more modest. Although brave and fearless in battle, he is also unlike Achilles, in that he repeatedly sacrifices opportunities for increasing his "fame" for the common good (a point reiterated in many episodes).

The whole Thracian episode so far has been a sort of prelude to this long speech, and the narrator has laid the groundwork very carefully. We have seen Xenophon work on behalf of the troops tirelessly and unselfishly, but the unscrupulousness of Seuthes and of his henchman Heracleides has thwarted his every effort. And the soldiers not only blame Xenophon for their hard winter service and lack of pay but even think that he has become rich at their expense. If these accusations had not been made in real life, it is very difficult to understand why Xenophon as author would paint them so vividly and give his namesake-character the immensely challenging task of refuting them.

Although this speech contains some striking exaggerations of "fact," it would be going too far to assert that the character Xenophon is "lying": none of his statements are inconsistent with the previous narrative, not even those that add information that is new. The differences are trivial, but effective in terms of his need to persuade. Xenophon twice received one messenger from Seuthes, not many (as now claimed); he returned to the army because the Spartan Anaxibius persuaded him to do so (although that does not preclude his assertion here that it was due to concern for the soldiers); he has not previously mentioned that the gates of Perinthus were shut against the Ten Thousand or that separate units of cavalry and peltasts were disbanded during his absence with Anaxibius. Narrative displacement is a normal tool of good storytelling, just as rhetorical exaggeration/oversimplification is of forensic rhetoric. Contemporary readers would not have found such "inconsistencies" troubling.

The main thrust of the argument is to assert, once again, that Xenophon sacrificed his personal interests and his reputation, and incurred the displeasure of Seuthes, the Spartans, and the army, in his efforts to secure the well-being of the common soldiers, who are now totally ungrateful. Xenophon argues that they should be grateful that they have received any pay at all, given that before they joined Seuthes they were not even able to find provisions, and grateful too because of the renown they have won in conquering barbarians in both Asia and Europe. One may wonder how well Xenophon's accusation of ingratitude would have been received, had anything like these words been spoken in reality, and especially if the troops now really regretted that they had not followed Neon instead of Xenophon. Yet, regardless of the actual sentiments of the army on this point, Xenophon concludes the speech by once again painting a picture of himself as the ideal commander, one who tirelessly toiled on behalf of the army while vigorously opposing any action that would make them enemies to other Greeks (7.6.36). The speech closes as follows (7.6.37–38):

Now that you have an easy passage and are able to sail where you have long desired to go, and the mightiest are in need of you, and pay is at hand, and the Lacedaemonians, who are judged the most powerful men on earth, have come as your leaders, do you indeed think that now is the critical moment to kill me as quickly as possible? But you were certainly not so minded when you were in difficulties. Rather, you used to call me "father" and you promised that you always would remember me as a benefactor.

The irony in this statement is that the text itself becomes the memory place in which Xenophon's role in the exploits of the Ten Thousand Greeks, despite the soldiers' own shortness of memory, will be preserved for all time. That shortness of memory was also stressed at the end of the closing speech of book 5. The text itself, however, guarantees that Xenophon will always be remembered as the army's "benefactor and father." Such is the power of narrative.

Quite a lot of artistry, if not sophistry, has gone into the composition of this speech. But part, indeed a large part, of its effectiveness is due to the way it is framed by the surrounding narrative. It is important to examine how this has been done, since the narrative framing is just as important a component of the defense as the actual speech.

In the prelude to the assembly scene, as noted above, the two Spartan ambassadors have a private meeting with Seuthes (7.6.1–6). Xenophon brilliantly projects a positive image of himself by shifting the focalization to one of his enemies, who presents his virtue as a vice. When the Spartans Charminus and Polynicus ask Seuthes, "What kind of man is Xenophon?," he replies, "In other respects he is not bad, but he is a friend to the soldiers [*philostratiōtēs*], and for this reason things are more difficult for him." Seuthes thinks that this is a valid criticism of Xenophon, and Heracleides, less graciously, accuses him of pandering to the troops (of being a demagogue). What the reader should think is made clear a few pages later.

As soon as Xenophon has finished delivering his defense speech, one of the same Spartans, Charminus, proclaims that he can vouch for Xenophon's honesty (7.6.39). He stands up and says, "Well, by the twin gods, I do not think that you are justly angry with this man; for I can bear witness for him myself. When Polynicus and I asked Seuthes what kind of man Xenophon was, he was not able to find any other fault in him, but he said that he was *too much* a friend to the soldiers [*agan philostratiōtēs*], and for this reason things are more difficult for Xenophon *both when dealing with us Lacedaemonians and with him.*" The very remark that Seuthes intended as a criticism, that Xenophon was too fond of the common soldier, has now been turned into proof of his innocence. Actually, what Charminus remembers Seuthes saying is not exactly what he did say but a slightly exaggerated and fuller version of it (the differences are in italics). In this way the narrator turns the criticism into a compliment by shifting the focalization from a Thracian prince, who is only concerned with his own advantage, to a Spartan commander, who understands Xenophon's conception of how a general ought to treat his troops. All of this would have been much less effective, and less convincing, had the Xenophon of this narrative said something like "The only criticism that one can make of me is that I am a friend to the soldiers." Coming from the mouth of an enemy, and then being reaffirmed in public assembly by a high-ranking Spartan citizen, makes this description of Xenophon appear objective and verifiable. At the same time, the fact that Seuthes makes this remark and that the Spartans believe it is proof for the audience that Xenophon was not in fact receiving money from Seuthes and did not deceive his fellow Greeks. With this device, the narrator externally verifies both Xenophon's innocence and his virtue. The narrator has depicted him as being a man of principle, even though the less scrupulous mistake scruple and fairness for weakness and pandering.

Xenophon's speech, validated as it was by Charminus's remark, completely turns the tables on Seuthes and Heracleides. Another Arcadian soldier, Eurylochus, demands that the Spartans retrieve their pay for them, and Polycrates, an Athenian, "prompted by Xenophon," asserts that Heracleides has defrauded them of their wages by keeping the proceeds from the sale of booty for himself, and urges the soldiers to grab hold of him, "For this man at least is not a Thracian, but being a Greek, he is wronging Greeks." Heracleides and Seuthes then flee (7.6.42–44), and Seuthes sends his personal interpreter to Xenophon (so as not to be misunderstood?) in an attempt to win over Xenophon by a mixture of bribery (promising to give him all the things he previously promised if he remained with a thousand hoplites) and warning (revealing secret information that Thibron was intending to kill him). But Zeus the

King reveals through sacrifice that Xenophon should turn down Seuthes's offer (which Seuthes makes again at 7.7.50) and remain with the army. Xenophon then goes on an embassy to Seuthes, with Spartan permission, in order to ask him for the pay still owed to the Greeks.

The long speech of Xenophon to Seuthes (7.7.20–47) is perhaps a case of rhetorical overkill, but it does reiterate in detail Xenophon's position, that he was doing what he thought was best both for Seuthes and for the army. That speech is part friendly advice (securing a kingdom depends on maintaining a reputation for trust-worthiness), part threat (either the Ten Thousand or the Spartans may use force to exact the payment), and part personal plea (Xenophon wants Seuthes to restore him to his former position of honor in the army). Xenophon repeats this plea in the conversation with Seuthes that follows, but Seuthes is unable to pay the back wages in full. On one level, it is this speech in combination with the previous one to the army that restores Xenophon's reputation, both with the soldiers (who "rejoiced and ran to meet him" upon his return) and with readers past and present. Seuthes decides to pay up, and this looks good for Xenophon, but there is still a cloud hanging over his head because the amount given does not add up to the 30 talents owed. Xenophon indirectly passes the blame on to the two Spartan commanders, letting them handle the sale of the livestock and captives that Seuthes offers by way of payment, as well as the distribution of the proceeds (7.7.55–57; discussed more fully in chapter 2).

The speech of Xenophon to Seuthes is the last long address in the *Anabasis*, and for that reason alone it bears a great deal of weight in shaping the reader's response to him. Some readers, however, have found it too "preachy." As G. H. Nall described it in his school commentary (1903: 82) on book 7: "A severe lecture, quite unsuited in style to the person addressed and the circumstances under which it was delivered." But we should not be too quick to convict Xenophon of having broken the historiographical principle that speeches should suit the occasion. The mixture of friendly advice, implied threat, and personal appeal could be considered appropriate, given Xenophon's situation. Yet, if the general arguments are suitable to the occasion, the rhetorical and linguistic style in which they are expressed is arguably too ornate and too abstract to have been spoken to a foreigner whose rudimentary knowledge of Greek required the assistance of a professional translator. This impression is heightened by the employment of sentiments and themes that reappear in other of Xenophon's works, especially in the *Cyropaedia*. For instance, Xenophon says to Seuthes about the importance of friendship (7.7.41–42), "I believe that no possession is more honorable or more splendid for a man, and especially for a ruler, than valor, justice, and generosity. For the one who possesses these things is rich because he has many friends, and rich also because still others want to become his friends. And if he is successful, he has those who will rejoice with him; but if he should fail in something, he does not lack those who will assist him." Readers are required to suspend their disbelief that Xenophon would have addressed Seuthes with words so rhetorically polished and abstract, and so similar to views expressed by Cyrus the elder in the *Cyropaedia* (7.2.13–22).

Nonetheless, the last five books of the *Anabasis*, despite challenges to Xenophon's authority and integrity both from other officers and the common soldiers, demonstrate what the obituaries of Proxenus and Clearchus suggest, that he is the golden mean between a style of command that is too accommodating (not wishing to chastise but only to praise) and one that is too severe. And, unlike Menon, who was only out for his own advancement, he put the interests of his men before his own. The *Anabasis* is the testament of what Xenophon suffered and achieved on their behalf.

Further Reading

The brilliant classical scholar Eduard Schwartz (1889: 161–193) made the earliest case that the *Anabasis* has an apologetic purpose. He has been widely followed. Dürrbach (1893) argues that Xenophon greatly exaggerated his own role and importance in events. Erbse (1966) thinks that Xenophon's aim was to show that he had not been an accomplice of Cyrus, since that was the grounds for his exile. Azoulay (2004) interprets the *Anabasis* as a basically dishonest defense against two types of accusation: the rank and file accused Xenophon of corruption at the time of the expedition; much later his fellow aristocrats accused him of being a paid mercenary. Braun (2004), by contrast, argues that Xenophon's blindness to the misdeeds of Cyrus and Clearchus was due to his personal desire for making a fortune while following them. (I agree with his characterization of Cyrus as a fratricide, but Braun relies too heavily on the tradition about Clearchus that derives from Ephorus and is now found in Diodorus and other late sources.) The standard treatment of guest-friendship is Herman (1987).

·7·

Reading the *Anabasis*

The past is never dead. It's not even past.
—*William Faulkner,* Requiem for a Nun *(act 1, scene 3)*

Literary texts can mean different things to different readers, quite apart from whatever ideas and themes the author may or may not have intended a work to convey. They can also have different levels of meaning for the same reader. This capacity to sustain different readings/meanings is what literary critics refer to as a text's polyvalence. Nevertheless, as I argued in the introduction, it is not the case that all readings and interpretations are equally valid or indeed that a text can mean anything at all. Although a literary text is open to a number of different readings, it is not open to any and all readings. In other words, there is a plurality of possible readings that can legitimately arise from the inherent structures of a text, but not an infinity of possible readings. As Wolfgang Iser has argued in his influential book *The Act of Reading* (1978), the subjective element in interpretation is not arbitrary, since it is guided by the structures the text contains.

If a reader tried to argue that the *Anabasis* suggests that Artaxerxes was more worthy of being king than Cyrus and that the Ten Thousand would have been better off had they surrendered their weapons to him after the battle of Cunaxa, I find it difficult to imagine that any rational reader would be persuaded by this interpretation, since it goes against the grain of what the text, both explicitly and implicitly, says. Not all texts, however, exhibit a completely consistent internal coherence, so it is possible to argue for an interpretation that seems to go against the grain of one part of a text, if it is supported by some other part or parts. And any given narrative sequence may contain cues that prompt the reader to read against the grain or between the lines (as I will argue in the case of Xenophon's obituary of Cyrus). The clearest case of invalid reading is when the reader is ignorant of some basic factual background; for instance, if his or her reading is based on the belief that the Thracians were Greeks or that Athens had won the Peloponnesian War or that Xenophon was the first Greek writer to give a sympathetic treatment of a Persian.

It is a paradox that authors are both morally responsible for what they write and yet unable to control the uses to which their texts may be put. Rhetorical and literary strategies may, with varying degrees of success, shape and direct reader responses to a text, but they can never fully control them. Xenophon, however, may not necessarily have wanted his text, or particular parts of it, to support one specific reading or to contain a single meaning; a writer, for many different reasons, may actually encourage polyvalence and a multilayered range of meanings. But, however that may be, in the end it is the audience who determine which version of the past is accepted or rejected, and that acceptance or rejection may vary over time and across cultures and generations.

Although every reader sees a book through the filter of his or her own cultural and personal experiences, readers collectively may be said to comprise an "interpretative community," as defined by Stanley Fish. If we could reconstruct the interpretative community of the mid-fourth century BC, we might, in theory at least, be able to understand, or "read," the *Anabasis* as one of Xenophon's contemporary readers would have done. But two qualifications must be stated. First of all, readers from different parts of Greece, that is, Athenians, Spartans, and Greeks from Asia Minor, might have read the book differently inasmuch as their cultural milieux and collective experiences would have been different. Secondly, if the *Anabasis* is to have continuing power and significance as a work of literature, then it must speak to the concerns and experiences of the ever-changing "contemporary" reader. So in what follows I shall attempt to explicate what the *Anabasis* may have meant to Xenophon, to his contemporary Greek readers, and to readers ancient and modern of subsequent generations and, finally, what it may mean to us in the early twenty-first century.

Greeks and Barbarians

Walter Hill's movie *The Warriors* (a story of gang warfare loosely based on the *Anabasis*) was widely blamed for causing gang violence at theaters. The *Anabasis* similarly has been blamed for whipping up sentiment for a panhellenic war against the Persian Empire. The political ideology that modern scholars have termed "panhellenism" was the belief that the various Greek cities could solve their endemic political, social, and economic problems by uniting in common cause and conquering all or part of the Persian Empire. Although the origins of panhellenism lie in the fifth century BC, it was during the fourth century that it reached the high-water mark of its appeal.

Rhetorical calls for Greek unity in a war against barbarians begin with speeches delivered during the Olympic games. The sophist Gorgias (in 408 or 392) and the orator Lysias (in 388 or 384) both wrote speeches with the title *Olympic Oration* calling for such a war. The essayist Isocrates, however, was the most persistent and single-minded exponent of panhellenism. He pushed the idea in a series of political tracts and in letters to the great and powerful. In his *Panegyricus* oration of 380 BC (which he is said to have spent either five or ten years composing), Isocrates argued that Athens and Sparta together should share the hegemony over such an expedition; he later hoped that a single leader, such as Philip of Macedon, could first reconcile and then lead the united Greeks in the great crusade.

Isocrates famously asserted: "If someone is not merely making a rhetorical display but also wishes to accomplish something, it is necessary for him to seek out those arguments that will persuade these two cities [Athens and Sparta] to share equally with each other and to divide the hegemony and to exact from the barbarians those advantages that they now desire to obtain for themselves from the Greeks" (*Panegyricus* 17). Modern scholars have long debated whether the *Anabasis*, indirectly and by example, provides the types of arguments Isocrates had in mind.

To be sure, the exploits of Xenophon and the Ten Thousand, recounted so vividly in the *Anabasis*, seem to have impressed on the Greek imagination that the Persian Empire was weak and ripe for conquest. Two concrete examples appear in Xenophon's *Hellenica*, a work composed in the 350s and so written after the *Anabasis*. The Spartan Lysander (3.4.2) and the Thessalian dynast Jason of Pherae (6.1.12) reputedly believed that the march of the Ten Thousand had proved the weakness of Persia. The reception of Cyrus's expedition in another work by Xenophon should tell us something about both contemporary attitudes and Xenophon's own sentiments. Still, one needs to be cautious, since the shift of focalization to characters who had not been on the expedition requires a subtle analysis, as the following example illustrates. In another passage of the *Hellenica* (3.2.16–18), the Persian satrap Tissaphernes, who failed to destroy the Greeks in the *Anabasis*, comes to terms with the Spartan commander Dercylidas rather than fighting him in a pitched battle, because "he remembered how the army of Cyrus had fought with the Persians and he believed that all of the Greeks were like them." Tissaphernes, however, was making a false analogy, since we are also told in the same passage that Dercylidas's Greek allies from the Ionian cities and the islands either had deserted or were about to. So Tissaphernes may have been correct about the military excellence of the Ten Thousand but quite wrong to infer that all Greek hoplites were just as courageous and well trained as they were.

In his *Panegyricus* oration of 380 BC, Isocrates stresses the failure of the Persians to destroy the Ten Thousand after Cunaxa, even after resorting to treachery. "Although these men made an expedition against the king himself," he concludes, "they returned in greater security than those who go to him on an embassy concerning friendship" (145–149). Some thirty years later in his *Philippus* (90–100) of 346, an essay that attempts to convince King Philip of Macedon (the father of Alexander the Great) to lead a panhellenic army against the Persian Empire, Isocrates stresses instead the easy victory of the Greek forces over the Persians during the battle of Cunaxa itself. Isocrates's emphasis shifts with his rhetorical purpose in each of his writings. Two centuries later, the Hellenistic historian Polybius (3.6.9–13) argued that the ultimate cause of Alexander's invasion of the Persian Empire was the return march, without opposition, of the Greeks under Xenophon. Many centuries later still (in the late fourth or early fifth century AD), the sophist and historian Eunapius began his *Lives of the Philosophers and Sophists* with the proud claim that Alexander the Great would not have become "great," had it not been for Xenophon.

It is unclear whether Isocrates himself ever read Xenophon's account of the expedition, since he never mentions Xenophon. Alexander the Great almost certainly did. In fact, the historian Arrian relates (2.7.8–9) that Alexander encouraged his men before the battle of Issus (333 BC) by reminding them that "Xenophon and his Ten Thousand had routed the king with his whole power near Babylon itself." Some modern scholars, partly influenced by its reception in antiquity, have interpreted the *Anabasis* as a kind of "panhellenist manifesto." According to this view, Xenophon's "message" is that if his band of mercenaries could so easily defeat the forces of the king and then escape from the interior of Asia, a united Hellenic force under the leadership of a professional general, such as Xenophon himself, could not fail to conquer the Persian Empire.

In Xenophon's *Hellenica* and *Agesilaus*, especially in his treatment of his friend and patron King Agesilaus of Sparta, there would appear to be a strong strain of what George Cawkwell (1979: 193) has famously called "Panhellenist big talk." Indeed, Agesilaus, who was Xenophon's "perfectly good man" (*Agesilaus* 1.1), was compelled to end his campaign of 396–95 in Asia Minor, because (as asserted at *Hellenica* 3.5.1–2) the most powerful cities of mainland Greece, supported by Persian gold, had risen up against Spartan hegemony. Xenophon claims, somewhat implausibly, that Agesilaus's ambition was not restricted to liberating the Greeks of Asia from Persian rule but entailed nothing less than the complete destruction of the Persian Empire (*Hellenica* 3.5.1 and 4.1.41; *Agesilaus* 1.36). Xenophon, however, never states that Agesilaus would have been successful had he actually carried out his plan to march into the interior of Asia in the spring of 394.

Although it is always slippery to talk about authorial intent, it is not completely clear that Xenophon intended either the *Anabasis* or the *Hellenica* to be read in so uncomplicated a way as a simple endorsement of panhellenist ideology. Or, rather, his depiction of the Persians themselves, like Herodotus's, is highly nuanced. In other words, leaving aside what Xenophon intended, the text itself invites various alternative readings. There are indeed hints in the *Anabasis* as to how someone in the future might conquer the Persian Empire, but also reservations both about the practicality of the attempt and the consequences of success. A panhellenist reading is one way of looking at the text, indeed an obvious way in the light of Alexander the Great's reference to Xenophon, but it is not the only way, and certainly not the reading that might appeal to many readers in the twenty-first century AD. There are many different roads to Babylon and back again.

Most obviously, the highly eulogistic treatment of Cyrus, as well as of the courageous and well-disciplined Persian nobles who perished at his side, is at odds with any kind of jingoistic or triumphalist reading of the *Anabasis*. The reader can well imagine the world that could have been had Cyrus been victorious at the battle of Cunaxa. The Greek commanders who served the new king, including Xenophon himself, would have reaped huge rewards. Cyrus promised that if he was successful, he would give a gold crown to each of the generals and captains, and he even hinted that some of them would hold satrapies and other lucrative positions of honor (1.7.6–8). Even the common soldiers, Cyrus predicted, would prefer to stay with him rather than return to their homes (1.7.4). Cyrus, moreover, undoubtedly would have repaid Sparta's assistance with support of her hegemony in Greece. Indeed, the hint of that other world, one so different from the reality of internecine strife that was endemic in Greece, imparts a feeling of lost opportunity.

One way that scholars have squeezed strongly panhellenist sentiments out of Xenophon is by taking isolated passages out of their immediate context. One passage in book 1 especially lends itself to just that sort of treatment. The narrator has just explained that Cyrus is in a hurry, since he believes that there is a direct correlation between the speed of his own advance and the king's lack of preparation for battle. This statement about Cyrus's plans leads to a generalization about the past that has implications for the future (1.5.9): "And it was possible for one who considered the matter to see at a glance that the king's empire was strong in the extent of its territory and in the size of its population, but weak in the length of its roads and in the dispersal of its forces, if someone should make war upon it quickly." If this is intended to be a piece of well-intentioned advice for some would-be conqueror of the Persian Empire, it is ironic that Alexander the Great rejected it (choosing instead to reduce the coastal areas before striking inland), just as he apparently rejected another piece of embedded advice. Xenophon later says "that the barbarians feared that the Greeks might attack them at night; for a Persian army at night is a sorry thing," primarily owing to the difficulties involved in preparing cavalry for battle in the dark (3.4.34; repeated in similar terms at *Cyropaedia* 3.3.26–27). Nonetheless, Alexander firmly rejected the recommendation of his father's old general Parmenio that he attack Darius's army at Gaugamela (331 BC) during the night (Plutarch, *Alexander* 31.5–7; Arrian 3.10. 1–2; Curtius 4.13.3).

Yet, if this apparent advice about how best to invade Persia is viewed in the context of the two passages between which it is sandwiched, it is not so clear that the narrator is trying to say that conquest would be easy for someone who attacked quickly. In the earlier passage (1.5.7–8) the narrator gives an example of what he calls "good discipline." Cyrus orders a group of noble Persians to jump into the mud in order to extricate some stuck wagons, even though they are wearing costly tunics and embroidered trousers as well as bracelets and necklaces. The scene seems intended to undercut the popular Greek notion that equated fancy dress with effeminacy. Indeed, the narrator observes that as soon as Cyrus gives the order, "they immediately jumped into the mud dressed in this way, *and more quickly than one might have thought possible,* lifted the wagons onto high ground." The passage (1.5.11–17) that comes after the advice to attack quickly is one of my favorites. A quarrel breaks out in the Greek camp after one of Menon's soldiers throws an axe at Clearchus. This quickly escalates to the point where the respective armies of Menon and Clearchus are on the verge of fighting a pitched battle against each other. Cyrus intervenes just in the nick of time and reminds them of their immediate situation (1.5.16): "Clearchus and Proxenus and you other Greeks who are present, you do not know what you are doing. If you fight with each other, believe that on this very day I will be cut down and you not long after me." The obvious irony is that it takes a Persian to tell Greeks not to fight each other and to remind them of the consequences of internecine strife. What I am trying to suggest is that the "meaning" of the narrator's advice is affected by what comes before and after it, and that consequently the panhellenist message is undercut by these paradigmatic examples of Persian discipline on the one hand and Greek indiscipline and infighting on the other.

It was to the battle of Cunaxa itself, of course, that later Greeks (such as Isocrates) pointed as proving how easy it would be for a Greek army to destroy the forces of the Persian King. Does Xenophon, as the author of the *Anabasis*, deliberately describe the battle in such a way as to give that impression? This may be a case where the later reception of the text can help us to decide how best to read the narrative. The Greek army was stationed on the right wing next to the Euphrates River. Plutarch believed, probably incorrectly, that the battle was lost because Clearchus disobeyed Cyrus's last-minute order to lead the Greek contingent directly against the king himself (*Artaxerxes* 8). This would have entailed the highly danger-ous maneuver of marching at an angle across the field (since the king was stationed beyond the left wing of Cyrus's army) and exposing the Greeks to envelopment on both flanks (1.8.12–13). Xenophon's narrative leaves the degree of Clearchus's culpability ambiguous: "Clearchus did not wish to draw the right wing from the river, fearing that he might be encircled on both sides, and he responded to Cyrus that he was taking care that things went well." This slippery response was not very helpful, and Cyrus found himself in the position of having to charge the king's cavalry in order to keep the victorious Greeks, who had set out in pursuit of their fleeing opponents, from being attacked in the rear. But the narrative makes clear that Clearchus's disobedience and Cyrus's intervention to protect the Greeks were not the ultimate reason for Cyrus's death and defeat.

Isocrates twice asserts that the battle was lost because of Cyrus's "rashness," his *propeteia* (*Philippus* 90, *First letter to Philip* 8). And that is what the narrator of the *Anabasis* strongly implies, even if he does not state it as explicitly as Isocrates does. When Cyrus's six hundred cavalry put the six thousand cavalry of the king to flight, Cyrus, although having very few of his men about him, "did not control himself" (*ouk anesketo*) and charged at his brother (1.8.25–26). A few pages earlier, Cyrus's Greek generals, quite unrealistically and for selfish motives, had urged Cyrus not to join in the fight but to remain stationed behind them (1.7.9). The clear implication, as Isocrates realized, is that Cyrus would have won this battle if he had indeed controlled himself and not let hatred for his brother master him.

Xenophon's account of the battle is actually not very clear and has proved resistant to reconstruction by modern military historians. It is thematically complex as well. The way the battle narrative proper begins and ends underscores this complexity. The Greeks easily defeat the Persian forces arrayed opposite them (1.8.18–21): "Before an arrow reached its mark, the barbarians gave way and fled." This is followed by a very emphatic statement that only one Greek soldier, who was shot by an arrow, was either killed or wounded in the initial onslaught (although some others were killed when the Persians attacked the Greek camp). The battle narrative ends, however, with an equal emphasis on the valor of Cyrus's personal entourage, the eight best of whom die alongside him (1.8.28–29). The battle narrative is given closure by focusing on one of these Persians in particular:

It is said that Artapates, who was the most trustworthy of his scepter-bearers, when he saw that Cyrus had fallen, leapt from his horse and fell upon him. And some say that the king ordered someone to slay him upon Cyrus, but others say that, drawing his dagger, he slew himself upon him; for he had a golden one. He also wore a bracelet and necklaces and the other items that the best of the Persians wear. For he had been honored by Cyrus on account of his goodwill and trustworthiness.

Why does the narrative end with an image of luxuriously dressed Persians dying nobly? This description of how Persian nobles conduct themselves, despite their finery, certainly calls to mind the earlier one in which they leaped into the mud on Cyrus's orders. The message might be that Xenophon's contemporary Greek audience should not be fooled by outward appearances into thinking that the Persian elite are weak and cowardly. There is also an allusion here to another text. One of the most famous episodes in Herodotus's *Histories* (1.45) describes how Adrastus accidentally killed Croesus's son Atys during a boar hunt, and the narrative ends with the unforgettable image of Adrastus killing himself over the youth's tomb. Both Xenophon and Herodotus use nearly identical phrases to narrate the deaths of Artapates and Adrastus ("he slew himself upon": *heauton episphaxasthai* in the former and *epikatasphazei heōuton* in the latter). I find it hard to believe that this is a coincidence. The reason for the allusion is less clear, but it perhaps points to the ill fortune of otherwise good men in each historical moment.

Moving forward in the story, when the Ten Thousand reach western Armenia, they conclude a treaty with the Persian governor Tiribazus, only to discover later that he is intending to attack them as they pass through a narrow mountain pass (4.4.14–22). The Ten Thousand then make a surprise attack on the Persian camp, and the barbarians do not even await their onslaught, but immediately flee. The information that they seized Tiribazus's personal tent and found in it "couches with silver feet and drinking cups" has been considered an inducement to future conquest. To this reader, however, it seems just the opposite. Could it really be worth all of the hardships the army has suffered from heavy snow and frostbite just to be able to strip the silver off some couch legs? Moreover, if one pays very careful attention to the narrative of this incident, the failed ambush is absolutely not an example of treacherous, oath-breaking Persians once again being defeated by honest, pious Greeks. The treaty that the Greek generals concluded with Tiribazus specified that Tiribazus would not harm the Greeks, and the Greeks would take as many provisions as they needed but would not "burn the houses." Yet "out of reckless folly" some of them subsequently did burn the houses in which they had been quartered (4.4.14). The narrator does not need to say explicitly that Tiribazus decided to ambush the Greeks because they had violated the terms of the truce, since the narrative itself carries an implicit sequence of cause and effect. Again, were a few couch legs and cups worth the terrible conditions of the march and the impiety involved in breaking oaths? Hardly.

The purpose of this thematic complexity may have much less to do with persuading readers how easy it is for Greeks to defeat Persians in a set battle than with excusing the Ten Thousand both for joining Cyrus (he and his inner circle of Persian nobles were exceptionally brave) and then for not supporting him during the battle (Clearchus was fearful of being outflanked, and Cyrus failed to control himself). The text invites us to view Persians in many different ways, from the loyalty and self-sacrifice of Cyrus's elite followers to the treachery of the king and of Tissaphernes. So, too, in his *Hellenica*, the depiction of the Persian satrap Pharnabazus is highly favorable (1.1.6; 4.1.29–40) in contrast to Tissaphernes's treachery (3.4.5–6).

On the other hand, the three surviving members of Cyrus's elite inner circle, Ariaeus, Artaozus, and Mithradates, men who were "most trustworthy" to Cyrus (2.5.35), repeatedly attempt to trick the Greeks, once they have obtained their own pardon from the king. The king himself, apart from being an impious perjurer, is also, by implication, a coward. In the days following the battle "even the king, as it seems, was terrified by the approach of the Greek army"— a sentence Xenophon repeats for emphasis with a rare first person intervention: "The thing that I just wrote, that the king was terrified by their approach, was made clear in the following way, that although on the previous day he sent a message demanding that they surrender their weapons, now, at sunrise, he sent heralds to negotiate a truce" (2.2.18; 2.3.1). It is difficult to find in any of Xenophon's writings (except in the last chapter of the *Cyropaedia*) a generalized picture of plain-living, courageous, pious, and self-controlled Greeks in contrast to weak, extravagant, impious, and treacherous Persians—the sort of dichotomy that was so dear to the heart, or at least to the rhetoric, of Isocrates and that apparently appealed to many of Xenophon's contemporaries. Just as good and bad Greeks are depicted in his writings, so too are good and bad Persians, and in each case good and bad leaders set the example for others to follow.

Speeches in Context

Any modern reader (and one assumes this of ancient readers, too) must be struck by the tenor of Cyrus's prebattle speech to the assembled Greek generals and captains because of the way it manipulates ethnic stereotypes and biases with perfect pitch (1.7.3):

> Men of Greece, it is not because I lack barbarian men that I am bringing you as my allies; it is because I believe that you are better and stronger than many barbarians—that's why I have taken you along. Take care, then, to prove yourselves men who are worthy of the freedom that you possess and for which I count you fortunate. For know well that I would choose freedom instead of all the things that I possess and many other things besides.

Throughout the narrative Cyrus has been depicted as a very clever manipulator of Greeks, and it is in keeping with his characterization that he would use Greek perceptions of barbarians (that they are all slaves of the king and poor soldiers) as a means of encouraging his Greek mercenaries. There is no reason to assume that the narrator has included this speech primarily as a metatextual statement intended to encourage the external audience to attack barbarians.

The external audience has seen that Cyrus will say whatever he thinks is necessary to get his Greek mercenaries to do precisely what he wants them to do. Moreover, in the very next sentence Cyrus makes a prediction that turns out to be belied by the narrative—that the barbarians will attack with "much shouting," whereas in fact they advance in silence (1.8.11).

Traditional panhellenist sentiments are also repeatedly expressed in the speeches that the character Xenophon delivers during the emergency meetings at the beginning of book 3. Should we be surprised by this? If you were going to rally the dejected spirits of soldiers who had just been deceived and betrayed by the Persians, what would you say? In his first speech, the one addressed to Proxenus's captains, Xenophon stresses that the Greeks will have the gods as their allies because they have abided by their oaths, whereas the Persians have sworn falsely by the gods. He then throws in a stereotypical slur, one common in Greek thought from the time of Xerxes's invasion onward. "Moreover, we have bodies that are more capable than theirs of enduring cold, and heat, and toils; and we also have souls that, with the gods on our side, are more courageous than theirs" (3.1.23). But this theme of ethnic superiority is muted compared to the emphasis on Greek piety and Persian impiety.

It is in his third speech (3.2.7–32), the one before the entire army, that Xenophon presses panhellenist themes more openly. He begins by once again asserting that the gods will be opposed to the Persians and allies to the Greeks, but then he makes two new arguments. The first of these is a reworking of a traditional theme. He reminds his audience of the two Persian invasions of Greece (in 490 and 480–479 BC). After mentioning that the first invasion was repulsed by the Athenians alone, he then goes on to credit the victory over Xerxes's "innumerable army" to the ancestors of all of the Ten Thousand, thus making it a victory of the mainland Greeks in general over the barbarian horde. This is a bit of a rhetorical stretch, since the ancestors of some of them had probably fought on the side of Xerxes (since central Greece and most of Boeotia had joined the Persians). If we look at Xenophon's speech in context, he is saying what is appropriate, given the circumstances, to rally the men who are listening to him: "At that time our ancestors defeated the ancestors of these men both by land and by sea," and so his audience, too, should be able to defeat the Persians, just as they did a few days previously when they were fighting on behalf of Cyrus.

The big question, however, is whether this speech is aimed at two different audiences simultaneously, both the internal audience and an external one. The part of the speech dealing with the Persian invasions (3.2.11–13) begins with the words "I shall remind you of the dangers faced by our ancestors" and ends with "you were born of such ancestors." The "you" is especially ambiguous to someone hearing this text being spoken aloud, as would have been the case with many, or perhaps most, of Xenophon's contemporaries. It refers to the Ten Thousand, but it can also be addressing the external audience whose ancestors had also participated in the struggle against the Persian invaders. That external audience thus becomes part of the story as they relate this exhortation to themselves and their own situation. In this way Xenophon, as he speaks from the text, is creating a shared community of hearers who can respond to this speech in various ways.

The other new argument has proved to be rather difficult for modern readers to interpret. Xenophon goes on to say that the king would be even more alarmed if the Greeks decided to settle in his territory rather than attempt to escape. Instead of ending with that point, he adds (3.2.25–26):

> But what I really fear is that once we have learned to live in idleness and to pass our lives in abundance and to consort with the beautiful and stately wives and daughters of the Medes and Persians, just like the Lotus Eaters we may forget the journey home. It seems to me, therefore, to be reasonable and just first of all to attempt to return to Greece and to our families and to point out to the Greeks that they are voluntarily poor, since it is possible for them to convey here those who are now living in hardship there and to see them become rich. At any rate, men, it is clear that all these good things belong to those who conquer them.

There is something disquieting about the sentiments expressed here. What does Xenophon imply by "to consort with" (*homilein*)? Does he mean seizing these women as concubines or taking them as wives? And why send the poor of Greece? Does this imply (as stated elsewhere: 6.4.8) that the Ten Thousand were a better sort, and not the type who would need or want to leave Greece? And the reference to the Lotus Eaters can only have a negative connotation. In Book 9 of the *Odyssey* (lines 83–104), Odysseus relates how an adverse wind blew the Greeks off course. He sent three of his men to scout out the local people, and they came upon the Lotus Eaters, who gave them the lotus to eat, "and whoever ate its honey-sweet fruit no longer wished to report back again nor to return home, but they wanted to remain there munching lotus with the Lotus Eaters and to forget their journey home. Though they wept bitterly, I forced them back to the ships, and I tied them up and dragged them under the benches. Then I ordered the rest of my faithful companions to go on board the swift ships at once, for fear that others of them might eat the lotus and forget their return home."

This problematic passage of the *Anabasis*, with its explicit Homeric reference, resists any easy interpretation. But here again we can enrich our understanding of the *Anabasis* by reading it alongside the *Cyropaedia*. The older Cyrus, after conquering the whole of Asia with an army that oddly resembles Greek hoplites and Greek cavalry in its equipment and tactics, thinks that the Persians can maintain their old discipline and valor while appropriating the lifestyle and luxuries of the Medes and Babylonians. If one sees in the *Cyropaedia* (as I think one should) strong hints, which are confirmed in its epilogue (8.8), that the maintenance of traditional discipline is inherently impossible under such circumstances, then any would-be Greek conquerors of the Persian Empire would also find Eastern luxury to be corrosive of their traditional lifestyle, ethos, and values. This notion may explain Xenophon's assumption that the settling of the Ten Thousand in Mesopotamia would be equivalent to Odysseus's men remaining in the land of the Lotus Eaters.

One more speech, this one delivered in book 2, deserves to be discussed in connection with the themes of Xenophon's speeches in book 3. After the battle of Cunaxa, a Persian delegation that includes the Greek Phalinus attempts to persuade the Greeks to surrender their weapons (2.1.7–23). Proxenus, perhaps echoing Leonidas at Thermopylae, asks why the king does not come and take them. (Plutarch quotes Leonidas as telling Xerxes, when he demands his weapons, to "come and take them"; *Sayings of the Spartans* 225c.11). Another of the Greek officers, an otherwise unmentioned Athenian named Theopompus, points out that the Greeks have only two valuable possessions, their weapons and their valor (*aretē*), and one of these is useless without the other (2.1.12–14). He concludes by telling Phalinus, "Do not think that we shall hand over to you the only two good things that we have; rather, with them we shall fight to get hold of your good things too." In reaction to this, Phalinus laughs and says, "Young man, you sound like a philosopher and your words are not without charm. Know, however, that you are a fool if you think that your valor could prevail over the king's power." A curious thing is that the less reliable manuscripts of the *Anabasis* read "Xenophon" instead of "Theopompus" as the speaker of these bold words, and that has led some modern scholars to print "Xenophon" in their texts (as in the Teubner and Loeb editions). But which is more likely? That a copyist would have changed Xenophon's name to Theopompus for no apparent reason, or that "Xenophon" is a gloss on Theopompus? Surely the latter alternative is to be preferred.

The explanation, I think, is that some ancient editor or copyist rightly noted several peculiar things about this exchange: that in book 3 Xenophon is revealed to be both a student of Socrates and an elegant speaker, and that the sentiment expressed in this short speech is strongly panhellenist. He therefore assumed that the author Xenophon was putting his own views in the mouth of a pseudonym and then amended the text according to this assumption. There is indeed a striking correspondence between what Theopompus says here and what the character Xenophon later says in his speech to the captains of Proxenus. "All of these good things [the possessions of the Persians] now lie in the middle as prizes for whichever of the two of us [the Persians or the Ten Thousand] prove to be better men" (3.1.21). And Xenophon makes the same point again in his speech before the entire army (3.2.26, quoted earlier).

The claim that the possessions of the Persians were prizes for the taking would have had a special resonance for Xenophon's contemporary Greek audience. It is a commonplace in fourth-century rhetoric, repeatedly argued by Isocrates, that the economic problems of mainland Greece could be solved by settling the poor in parts of Asia Minor. Isocrates had argued that the poor and destitute, who wandered as exiles or sought employment as mercenaries, were a growing and imminent danger to Greece (*Letter 9, To Archidamus* 8–10; *Panegyricus* 168; *On the Peace* 24; *Philippus* 120–122). The solution he proposed to Philip of Macedon in 346 BC was to plant them in colonies on the fringes of the Greek world, where they would form a buffer zone (*Philippus* 120–122). Xenophon, too, speaks of sending the poor to Asia, as we saw above.

Once again, we face the problem of the two audiences, internal and external, and how this idea relates to each of them. One might say that the rest of the *Anabasis* demonstrates that settling the poor of Greece smack in the middle of the Persian Empire would actually not have been particularly easy. In fact, given how much difficulty Xenophon has with capturing a single Persian grandee at the very end of the work (see below), a reader might well conclude that "consorting with Persian and Median women" is a totally unrealistic fantasy.

Another pervasive stereotype in classical Greek culture is that fighting against Persian men was no different from fighting with women. The narrator manipulates this to comic effect in an amusing scene at the beginning of book 6. The Greek generals entertain some ambassadors sent by the king of the Paphlagonians. Various ethnic groups among the Ten Thousand perform dances with weapons, and this culminates with a dancing-girl performing a dance, while holding a shield, called the Pyrrhic (6.1.12–13). When she has finished, "there was much applause, and the Paphlagonians asked the Greeks if their women also fought alongside them. They responded that these were the very women who had driven the king out of their camp. Such was the end of that evening." The performance of this female dancer (she was owned by an Arcadian, but her own ethnicity is unstated) not only ends the evening festivities but is the final appearance of the army's female companions in the *Anabasis*. How should we interpret it?

In narrating this episode, Xenophon appears to be alluding to an incident during the battle of Cunaxa he recounted earlier. In an attempt to plunder the Greek camp, the king's forces captured two of Cyrus's concubines, one of whom managed to get away (1.10.2–3): "The concubine from Miletus, who was the younger of the two, although she too had been captured by the King's men, escaped, naked, to some Greeks who happened to be defending the camp." These Greeks then killed many of the Persians and saved their camp, though some of them were also killed in the engagement. The theme seems to be that even Greek concubines (dressed or otherwise) can rout Persian men. The Hellenistic writer Demetrius, in his treatise *On Style* (131), cites this passage from book 6 as an illustration that Xenophon (like Homer) can turn a pleasantry into a sarcasm: "This grim pleasantry clearly has a double point, implying in the first place that it was not mere women who accompanied them, but Amazons; and the other point is aimed at the Great King, that he was so weak as to be put to flight by women." The theme of Persians being vanquished by Greek women was picked up by the historians who wrote about Alexander the Great. The Athenian prostitute Thais, according to one tradition, incited Alexander and his companions to burn Persepolis, the ceremonial capital of the Persian Empire, by pointing out how fitting it would be for the burning of Athens to be avenged by a Greek woman (Plutarch, *Alexander* 38; Diodorus 17.72; Curtius 5.7.3). Whether Xenophon intended this "grim pleasantry" simply to be read in context as a means for the Ten Thousand to inspire fear in the Paphlagonians (you had better not mess with us when even our women can fight in pitched battles) or to serve as a timeless example of how simple it is for Greeks to defeat Persians, one can readily imagine why later Greek readers would have picked up on the latter implication.

The advocates of Greek conquest in Asia never quite came to terms with the problem of how to treat native peoples. The *Anabasis* gives no hint that Xenophon, like Aristotle or Isocrates, thought that they were only fit to be slaves or serfs. In his speech to Hecatonymus, an ambassador from Sinope, the character Xenophon points out that the Ten Thousand considered to be their friends any barbarians who willingly provided them with a market (5.5.16–18). The author Xenophon's ethnographic curiosity is similar to that of Herodotus. His lengthiest digression is on the habits of the Mossynoecians (5.4.32–34), whom the Ten Thousand considered "the most barbarous of the peoples whom they had encountered and the furthest removed from Greek customs." The description of their habits, the opposite of Greek ones, has an obvious affinity to Herodotus's description of the contrary practices of the Egyptians (2.35–45).

One passage, in particular, seems both paradigmatic and particularly Herodotean (7.4.22–24). The Thynians, a tribe of Thracians who have attacked Xenophon's camp at night in breach of a truce, sue for peace. But Seuthes says to Xenophon that he will not conclude a truce if Xenophon wishes to punish them for their attack (and we already have learned that Seuthes's idea of punishment is mass execution). Xenophon replies to this, "Well I for my part believe that they now have punishment enough, if these people are to be slaves instead of being free." The simple idea that freedom is better than slavery is one any modern reader can appreciate prima facie, but it takes on depth in light of the emphatic expression of this theme both in Xenophon and in other Greek writers. Both Xenophon's Cyrus the Younger (1.7.3) and Herodotus's Cyrus the Great (1.126.5; 9.122) point out that being free is preferable to being a slave. What is striking and noteworthy is that Xenophon implicitly acknowledges that barbarians are as much entitled to freedom as Greeks. One will search in vain for even the faintest hint of Aristotle's theory of "natural slavery" (*Politics* 1252b5–9) in the pages of the *Anabasis* or indeed in any of Xenophon's many and varied writings.

There is no tidy summing up of panhellenist themes at the end of the *Anabasis*, but the capture of the elite Persian Asidates both explains how Xenophon came to be rich in a socially acceptable way (that is, not as a mercenary receiving pay) and furnishes a demonstration (both a good and a bad one) of what Greeks working together can achieve in terms of self-enrichment at the expense of Persians. As Xenophon has earlier said, their poverty is voluntary. Furthermore, the conspicuous role of divination in the Asidates story might seem to suggest that the gods have helped the Greeks in the past and will help them again in the future, if they abide by their oaths and act in ways pleasing to them (see chapter 8).

Xenophon personally leads an expedition of some nine hundred men with the objective of capturing Asidates and his possessions. The assault on Asidates's fortified tower is a failure, and the Greeks are forced to retreat while under attack by Persian reinforcements. They are saved by the intervention of two Greeks of notable heritage, Gongylus and Procles, and apparently by a very thin margin. The former is a son of the Gongylus of Eretria who sided with the Persians in the aftermath of Xerxes's invasion of Greece (Thucydides 1.128), and the latter a descendant of the deposed Spartan king Demaratus, who accompanied Xerxes as his advisor (Herodotus 7.101). The narrator leaves it ambiguous just how much difference their intervention made. Despite their assistance, "Xenophon's soldiers crossed the Carcasus River with difficulty, nearly half of them being wounded." Nor are we told why Hellas opposed her son Gongylus's intervention. Does her unexplained attitude strike an ominous note for the future success of resistance to Persian control over Asia Minor? This passage both looks forward to Gongylus's and Procles's voluntary support of Thibron later in this year (*Hellenica* 3.1.6) and suggests that profit-making ventures against Persian grandees are not really all that easy and indeed very dangerous.

If nothing else, it should at least be obvious that the *Anabasis* is a panhellenist tract only on the most simple and unreflective of readings, one that looks for confirmation of stereotypes while ignoring nuance and context. To be sure, the *Anabasis* lays out the advantages of cooperation among Greeks, the terrible consequences of disunity and poor discipline, and the rich booty that can be seized through luck and careful planning. Sometimes, however, barbarian forces flee as soon as a battle begins, but at other times they put up a very stiff resistance, and heavy casualties can attend even divinely sanctioned expeditions. If there is an overarching lesson to be learned from all of this, perhaps it is simply that war is never easy or predictable.

Portrait of Cyrus

Xenophon's portrait of Cyrus is carefully drawn to serve several competing purposes. On the one hand, it justifies Xenophon's decision to join the expedition, despite Socrates's warning. Cyrus is portrayed as a charismatic leader, a man worthy to be king of Persia, a person who knew how to help his friends and hurt his enemies, and who could inspire other Persians to maintain a high level of discipline. On the other hand, in order to make his case that only Clearchus knew the expedition's true purpose, Xenophon needed to portray Cyrus as being a clever manipulator, someone who was sparing with the truth in order to achieve his goals. In sum, the portrait of Cyrus is multifaceted and nuanced. Praise predominates on the surface, but those who read carefully and critically may feel some disquiet. It is tempting to see in the description in the *Cyropaedia* of the elder Cyrus's interactions with his inner circle of friends and, in particular, in his bestowal of gifts and honors on them (for instance, during the banquet described at 8.4), a projection of how Xenophon himself and his fellow Greeks would have been treated by a victorious Cyrus the Younger. Indeed, before the battle of Cunaxa, Cyrus promises a golden crown to each of the Greek officers and hints at even greater rewards, even satrapies (1.7.6–7). At the same time, there are cues both in the narrative (Cyrus does not always tell the truth to the Greeks) and in the prince's obituary (as we shall see) that undercut an uncomplicated reading.

Some modern readers have considered this portrait of Cyrus defective because it fails to stress that Cyrus was a traitor and would-be fratricide who revolted against the legitimate monarch for purely personal reasons. Xenophon's treatment of Cyrus has been explained either as an attempt to excuse the fact that he supported Cyrus or as an effort to cast him in the role of the paradigmatic ideal ruler, the living embodiment of all of the virtues and abilities Xenophon also attributed to Cyrus the Elder. In his *Oeconomicus*, Xenophon even has Socrates deliberately conflate the two Cyruses (4.16–25), while saying of the younger one, "If Cyrus had lived, it seems that he would have proved to be an excellent ruler" (4.18)—which, it should be noted, is not quite the same as saying that he *had been* an excellent ruler. Does Xenophon really depict Cyrus the Younger as a perfect leader, the historical realization of all the qualities he attributed to the mythologized Cyrus the Great of his other work?

Although the narrator does not offer any explicit criticisms and proffers a great deal of praise, the narrative is interesting for what it does not say. In my view, the reader is meant to notice that Cyrus is an imperfect replica of his famous namesake. He lacks certain of his virtues, such as self-control, humanity, and, most noteworthy of all, piety. One passage in particular might give one pause (1.9.11–13):

> It was clear also that if someone conferred any benefit on Cyrus or did him any harm, he attempted to outdo him. Indeed, some people used to report a prayer of his that he might live long enough to outdo both those who benefited him and those who did wrong by him, returning like for like. . . . Nor would anyone be able to say this, that he permitted criminals and the unjust to laugh at him; on the contrary, he punished them most unsparingly of all. Along the well-traveled roads it was often possible to see people who had been deprived of their feet, hands, and eyes.

The narrator then says that as a consequence, it was possible for everyone, both Greeks and barbarians, to travel where they wanted without fear. But is he being ironic? One would search the entire *Cyropaedia* in vain for an example of such treatment of enemies or criminals. Cyrus the Younger helps friends and hurts enemies (which was typical enough of Greek morality), but Cyrus the Elder focused his attentions on helping his friends (8.2.13: "It is said to have been apparent that there was nothing in which he would have been more ashamed to be defeated than in service to his friends"). The contrast, however subtly implied, is unmistakable.

More important, the elder Cyrus, like Xenophon himself, is depicted as someone who puts the reverence due to the gods above all other considerations and who seeks their counsel through constant sacrifice (*Cyropaedia* 1.5.14). Although the younger Cyrus has his Greek seer perform the customary sacrifices before battle (1.7.18; 1.8.15), there is no indication of his personal piety. Lest it seem that I am unduly emphasizing the importance of piety in Xenophon's conception of the model leader, a look at his encomium of the Spartan king Agesilaus should leave no doubts. At the end of the *Agesilaus*, Xenophon summarizes the king's virtues in order that the praise may be easier for the reader to remember. He starts the list with examples of Agesilaus's piety and notes (11.2): "He never stopped repeating that he believed that the gods took no less pleasure in deeds that were pious than in sacrificial offerings that were pure."

In the first book of the *Cyropaedia*, the young Cyrus recalls his father's earlier instruction that those who ask for unlawful things from the gods will fail to obtain them (1.6.6). And in the last book of the *Cyropaedia*, the dying Cyrus enjoins his own sons, in the strongest possible terms and at considerable length, to honor and love each other. All the relevant parts of the elder Cyrus's speech cannot be quoted here, but one statement seems particularly germane to another major theme in the *Anabasis*. Along with piety, the importance of the leader being trusted by his subjects is a central theme in the *Anabasis* and is underscored in Xenophon's long speech to Seuthes at the end of the work. So it is striking when Cyrus tells his sons (8.7.23): "If you plan some unjust action against each other, you will throw away in the eyes of all men the right to be trusted." Telling the truth, and the trust that a reputation for truth-telling inspires, were important virtues for the Persians. As Herodotus informed his readers, Persians between the ages of five and twenty were taught to do three things only—"to ride a horse, to shoot a bow, and to tell the truth" (1.136).

How does the younger Cyrus measure up? In the obituary, the narrator emphasizes that both cities and individuals trusted Cyrus (1.9.7–8) because "he made it clear that he considered it of the greatest importance that if he made a treaty or compact with anyone, or promised something to someone, he should not be false to his word under any circumstances [mēden pseudesthai]." This assertion, however, is strongly at odds with the narrative of Cyrus's dealings with his Greek mercenaries. Their true objective is known only to Clearchus. To the others, both generals and soldiers alike, Cyrus tells a variety of stories (they are never called lies in the text, but the reader recognizes them as such): he claims at different times that the expedition is against the Pisidians (1.2.1; 3.1.9), Tissaphernes (1.1.11), and Abrocomas (1.3.20). Trusting Cyrus is not such a good idea after all.

Anyone who reads Cyrus the Great's deathbed speech at the end of the *Cyropaedia* and then turns to the beginning of the *Anabasis* should be immediately struck by the disjunction. In the *Anabasis*, Cyrus the Younger, because he feels dishonored, begins the conspiracy to become king instead of his brother. Of course, most readers of the *Cyropaedia* would have known (from their knowledge of Herodotus and Ctesias) that Cyrus the Great's elder son Cambyses, who became the next king, arranged for his younger brother's assassination. The fatal power struggle between them is indeed alluded to at *Cyropaedia* 8.8.2 (the so-called palinode): "As soon as Cyrus died, his sons immediately began to quarrel, cities and nations immediately began to revolt, and everything began to deteriorate." Nonetheless, there is also a timelessness to Cyrus's deathbed sermon on the proper relationship between royal siblings. And it is clearly Cyrus the Younger, not Artaxerxes, who has transgressed his advice. So, even though Cyrus the Younger's obituary begins on a very positive note, far too much has been read into it. When Xenophon writes that Cyrus "was the most king-like and the most worthy to rule of all the Persians born after Cyrus the Elder" (1.9.1), he is not saying that the younger Cyrus was the moral equivalent of his namesake. He is merely saying that he was the best potential king since then. But as we know from the *Cyropaedia*, after Cyrus the Great's death "everything began to deteriorate" (8.8.2), and that includes the personal and moral qualities of Persia's kings.

As I stated before, there is no mention at all of piety in Cyrus the Younger's obituary, and perhaps this is for a very good reason. Could piety conceivably be the virtue of a fratricide? Did Xenophon expect his readers to notice the omission and draw the appropriate inference? There seems to be a certain amount of conscious misdirection in the obituary. The first person voice of the narrator repeatedly intrudes to validate certain things that the reader might not be expected to believe (no one had a greater number of eager followers or received more gifts or was more solicitous of his friends than Cyrus), culminating in the overarching statement "I for my part judge, on the basis of what I hear, that no one has been loved by more people, either among Greeks or barbarians" (1.9.28). Both Cyruses may have been "loved" by their subjects and friends, and both may have had admirable traits, but they were certainly not equivalent models of good leadership. If they were, Cyrus would not have "lost control of himself" in a fit of brotherly hatred and died so needlessly at Cunaxa (1.8.26).

But if Xenophon's portrait is not, after all, unambiguously favorable, then why have so many modern readers been misled into thinking that it is? This is once again a result of Xenophon's subtlety and his penchant for omitting things he might expect his readers to have known. He could easily have inserted incidents that pointed up Cyrus's hubris and willingness to sacrifice family members in his quest for power. A very interesting passage was interpolated (that is, inserted by an ancient editor or copyist, probably from Ctesias) into the *Hellenica* (2.1.8–9), relating how Cyrus put to death his two first cousins because they failed to thrust their arms through their sleeves in his presence (an honor accorded to the king alone). Moreover, it is claimed in the same passage that this display of excessive hubris was the real reason Cyrus's father Darius summoned him to court in 405 BC, his illness being a mere pretext. Xenophon omits such tales, simply stating as a fact, emphatically, in the second sentence of the *Anabasis* that Darius summoned his two sons because he was sick and suspected that he would soon die. His own reticence aside, many of Xenophon's readers would have encountered this and other hostile tales in other texts, most notably Ctesias's *Persica*.

One might also be misled because the *Anabasis* begins with a partial defense of Cyrus's decision to usurp the throne, insofar as it offers a rationale (1.1.3–8): "Tissaphernes slandered Cyrus to the king on the grounds that he was plotting against him." The king then arrested Cyrus and would have put him to death, but for the intercession of their mother, Parysatis. When Cyrus returned to his province, "having been in danger and having been dishonored, he began planning how he would never again be in the power of his brother, but, if he should be able, would be king instead of him. His mother, Parysatis, supported Cyrus, since she loved him more than Artaxerxes, who was the king." The sting of dishonor and a mother's support is an explanation of behavior; it is less clear whether it is intended as exoneration. The narrator does not say that Artaxerxes still suspected Cyrus or would have punished him at a later date. Rather, he asserts that "the king did not perceive the plot against himself" (1.1.8). That might seem to put Artaxerxes on the moral high ground while shifting the blame to Tissaphernes's treachery and Cyrus's ambitious indignation.

As we have seen, what Xenophon omits is sometimes as essential to the meaning of his text as what he includes. He does, however, mention that Cyrus, just before he entered Cilicia, put to death two high-ranking Persians for conspiring against him (1.2.20). The later trial of the even more high-ranking Persian Orontas (a man related to the king) is told in considerable detail, even if at second hand; for Clearchus, who was present as an advisor to Cyrus, told his friends what had transpired (1.6). The narrator then suspends the forward movement of the story in order to linger (for three sentences) on the fact that no one ever discovered how Orontas had been killed or what had happened to his body (1.6.11). When read in the light of these executions, the statement in Cyrus's obituary that, while no one deserted from Cyrus to the king ("except that Orontas attempted to do so"), many deserted from the king to Cyrus takes on an eerie irony (1.9.29). The reader realizes that what the narrator really means is that no Persians *successfully* deserted; and perhaps the reader is expected to recall, even if the narrator himself here omits them, the two Persians who were executed before the trial of Orontas.

Sparta and Athens

At the beginning of book 4, Xenophon and Cheirisophus have a very rough start to their relationship as they enter the mountainous territory of the Carduchians. Xenophon blames Cheirisophus for pushing ahead and leaving the rear guard in serious difficulty, with the result, as he points out, that "two good men have died" and are left unburied (4.1.19). They soon settle their differences, however, and work together, with the van (under Cheirisophus's leadership) and rear guard (led by Xenophon) helping each other to get through the mountain passes guarded by the Carduchians. The narrative gives a strong impression of Xenophon and Cheirisophus working closely as a team, and indeed exercising a de facto joint command. At the end of the Carduchian episode, the narrator says that Xenophon and Cheirisophus would come to each other's assistance whenever the van or rear guard was being held up by the enemy, and underscores this consistent cooperation by asserting, "And they always aided each other in this way and assiduously took care of each other" (4.2.25–26).

On one level, by putting himself on an equal footing with Cheirisophus, Xenophon is obviously emphasizing, and perhaps embellishing, his own role in these events. But one could also read his initial incompatibility and difficulties with Cheirisophus, which are followed by their successful teamwork, as a metaphor for relations between Athens and Sparta generally. In other words, Xenophon may be concerned to provide both an example and a blueprint for cooperation between these two cities. If he and Cheirisophus could exercise leadership together over a band of Greeks from many different cities, then their respective homelands could do the same. Is it possible, then, that what we have here is not so much the promotion of Xenophon's reputation as a demonstration of what others could do if they put aside their parochial quarrels and mutual misunderstandings, and worked together for the benefit of all Greeks, most obviously by acting in unison against their common non-Greek enemies?

On the surface, Xenophon and Cheirisophus do seem to get on exceptionally well. They greet each other as friends (4.5.34); they tease each other about their respective national stereotypes (4.6.14–16: Spartan education teaches boys how to steal whatever the law does not forbid; Athenian education teaches politicians to steal the public funds); and they only have one "quarrel" (4.6.3). Yet that quarrel is a significant one, not so much for its consequences as for what it indicates about the difference between the Spartan and Athenian temperaments. When Cheirisophus hits and then fails to tie up the village chief who is acting as their guide in Armenia (and whom Xenophon has gone out of his way to treat with kindness), the narrator points out, "This ill-treatment and neglect of the guide was the only cause for dispute between Cheirisophus and Xenophon throughout the whole journey." Cheirisophus, very much like his fellow Spartan Clearchus (1.5.11; 2.3.11), is too ready to resort to corporal punishment and has difficulty controlling his anger. So while there is a remarkable amount of congenial cooperation between Cheirisophus and Xenophon, contemporary readers might well have been struck by the cultural and temperamental gulf between them. That gulf complicates any easy lessons about how Athenians and Spartans should, or could, cooperate in the future.

In later episodes, the picture is no less complicated. After an initial misunderstanding at Calpe Harbor, Xenophon concludes a formal tie of guest-friendship with Cleander, the Spartan governor of Byzantium, who is much impressed by the army's discipline (6.6.35). Yet this is subsequently counterbalanced by the schemes of Aristarchus, Cleander's replacement, to entrap and kill Xenophon. Cleander, moreover, ignores the order of the Spartan admiral Anaxibius to sell any of the Ten Thousand he finds remaining in Byzantium, and "out of pity" attends to those who were ill. When Aristarchus takes over as governor, he sells no fewer than four hundred of them into slavery (7.2.6). Not all high-ranking Spartans were as congenial as Cleander or as cooperative as Cheirisophus.

Trouble with Greeks

The seeming optimism of certain passages in books 1–3 on the ease of conquering the Persian Empire is undercut in book 4 by the hardships suffered by the troops as they march north to the sea. Moreover, books 5 and 6 bring to the surface another serious problem, as the Ten Thousand discover that the Greek cities along the coast of the Black Sea are reluctant hosts. The people of Sinope and Cotyora are so afraid of the Greeks that the orator Hecatonymus from Sinope threatens to form an alliance against them with the king of the Paphlagonians. Xenophon cleverly counters this by saying that the king would like to get his hands on Sinope and that they could deliver it to him. This makes the Sinopeans back down. Xenophon finds himself compelled to negotiate an awkward and dangerous situation that involves Greeks threatening to enlist barbarians in a war against other Greeks (5.5.7–25).

Other parts of the story highlight the ethnic tensions that exist among the Ten Thousand themselves just below the surface of their common Hellenic identity. These tensions can lead to disastrous results. Immediately after the supreme command is given to Cheirisophus, strife breaks out in the army (6.2.9–12). The trouble begins when Lycon, an Achaean captain, proposes that they demand a huge sum of money from the Greek city of Heracleia. Cheirisophus and Xenophon refuse to go as ambassadors to Heracleia (neither of them approves of using compulsion on a friendly Greek city). Subsequently, when the threats of Achaean and Arcadian ambassadors backfire, the generals are accused of sabotaging their plan. The captains Callimachus, an Arcadian, and Lycon, an Achaean, "said that it was shameful for an Athenian to be in command of Peloponnesians and Lacedaemonians, when he was not contributing any contingent to the army; and it was shameful that they (i.e., the Arcadians and Achaeans) did the work, while others got the profit, even though they were the ones who were responsible for the army's preservation." Callimachus and Lycon go on to argue that they should elect their own generals, continue the journey by themselves, and "attempt to get something good out of it." In other words, these Greeks are motivated by greed, just as was the case in the unsuccessful plan to exact money from Heracleia. The upshot was that Cheirisophus was stripped of the supreme command after only five or six days, and the army split into three divisions, one led by ten newly elected Arcadian and Achaean generals, one by Cheirisophus, and another by Xenophon.

Given the persistent theme in Greek literature that pride invariably leads to a fall, the sequel has probably not surprised many readers, either ancient or modern. The claim that Arcadians and Achaeans should not be commanded by an Athenian rebounds on their own heads when they get into serious trouble while plundering Thracian villages and face total annihilation. Although the Arcadians and Achaeans make up more than half the number of hoplites in the entire army, they cannot fight on their own against the highly mobile Bithynian Thracians because they lack archers, javelin men, and cavalry. To the reader, this might seem to prove the legitimacy of dual hegemony—that all Greeks would be better off under the joint command of Athenians and Spartans, sensible and honest men like Xenophon and Cheirisophus.

But so simple a reading is problematized by Cheirisophus's reaction to this turn of events (6.2.13–14). Xenophon is dissuaded by Neon, Cheirisophus's second-in command, from joining them on the march (because Neon thinks that the Spartan governor of Byzantium is intending to send ships to pick them up at Calpe Harbor and he does not want to share them with Xenophon's men). As for Cheirisophus, "he was so depressed by what had happened and so full of hatred for the army because of it, that he gave Xenophon permission to do whatever he wanted." He soon becomes ill (6.2.18), and not long after we hear that he is dead (6.4.11). The partner of Xenophon's toils since book 3 does not even warrant an obituary. Instead, the focus of the narrative is on how Xenophon saves the Arcadians and Achaeans. And there is another curious feature of the text. Given that Cheirisophus had just been voted the supreme command of the whole army, why did Callimachus and Lycon say that "it was shameful for an Athenian to be in command of Peloponnesians and Lacedaemonians"? The incongruity in this statement led one editor (Madvig) to emend the text so as to have it say "it was shameful for an Athenian and a Lacedaemonian to be in command of Peloponnesians." There is no support for this change in any of our manuscripts, and rather than making the text say what we think it logically should say, it is better to see this as yet another narrative strategy by which center stage is given to Xenophon as the major protagonist in this drama.

Xenophon stresses the negative consequences of excessive ethnic bias, but in the denouement, instead of blaming the Arcadians and Achaeans for failing to recognize his superior leadership, he instead attributes their failure to impiety. The gods are punishing their excessive pride (6.3.18). It is the narrative of the rescue itself, rather than any explicit commentary, that illustrates Xenophon's superior generalship. And when the reunited forces "greeted one another like brothers" (6.3.25) at Calpe Harbor, it was that very action, rather than any authorial sermonizing, that revealed the tangible benefits of inter-Greek cooperation.

Discipline and Its Discontents

If one focuses on the sections of the *Anabasis* (principally in books 1–4) that stress inter-Greek unity and cooperation on the one hand and the weakness and treachery of Persians and other non-Greeks on the other, one may inadvertently gain a false impression of the overall tendency of the work. For a pendent to the successes of the Ten Thousand is the tale of their weaknesses. Some weaknesses, such as a lack of cavalry, can be overcome through creative leadership. But there is another weakness that recurs again and again and that constantly threatens to undermine the army's cohesion and very survival, even when it is led by an able general such as Xenophon. The recurrence of this nearly fatal weakness is a major theme of books 5–7.

Xenophon as author has prepared the ground for this theme and alerted the reader to its importance in the speeches Xenophon the character delivers at the beginning of book 3. When addressing the surviving generals and captains, he observes: "Good discipline seems to provide safety, whereas indiscipline has already destroyed many" (3.1.38). Then in his subsequent speech to the entire army he saves "the most important point" for last: "the enemy believed that, after they had seized our commanders, we would be destroyed by anarchy and indiscipline" (3.2.29). The character Xenophon returns to the problem of indiscipline in his two speeches at the end of book 5. By then, indiscipline brought about by greed and aggravated by inter-Greek ethnic tensions threatens to disintegrate the army. Despite the emotional effectiveness of his warnings, even at the end of the work Xenophon comes very near to being lynched (or, more accurately, stoned) during an assembly of the army, on the grounds that he has stolen their pay and is enriching himself (7.6.8–10). So the question naturally arises, could any panhellenic force do better in the future? Is the *Anabasis* actually a warning against a future expedition of Greeks from many different cities working together under a unified command structure?

The breakdown of discipline begins as soon as the Greeks arrive at Trapezus (5.1.14–17). The men will not even countenance an overland trip home, and Dexippus, who is supposed to procure merchant ships, instead flees in the warship Trapezus provides. We are surely meant to notice that Dexippus, a Laconian, sails off in a coldhearted act of betrayal, whereas Polycrates, an Athenian (who does good service elsewhere in the *Anabasis*: 4.5.24; 7.6.41), takes another warship and proceeds to capture merchant vessels. Their contrasting behavior signals a breakdown of the Athenian-Spartan cooperation that was so delicately forged by Xenophon and Cheirisophus in book 4. To make matters worse, Cleaenetus, a captain, takes out two companies on an unofficial foraging expedition, during which he and many of his men are killed.

The infringements of discipline become more serious as the story progresses. In the first assault on the stronghold of the hostile Mossynoecians, a large group of the Greeks joins the allied Mossynoecians on their own initiative, because they are after plunder. These Greeks are routed, many of them are killed, and, adding insult to injury, the Mossynoecians display their severed heads while dancing and singing. The rest of the Ten Thousand are furious that these Greeks who were acting without orders, even though they were very numerous, fled from the enemy, "a thing that they had never done before during the expedition" (5.4.16–18). As Xenophon points out in his subsequent speech to the army, discipline is the secret to their success, and his words prove true in the sequel, when the Mossynoecians are defeated the next day and their stronghold and city are quickly captured (5.4.16–21). Notwithstanding the moral of this tale, lawlessness on the part of the soldiers continued to increase, to the extent that at the end of book 5 Xenophon is compelled to deliver a major speech on the problem of indiscipline, though he hardly solves it (5.7.5–33). Book 6 witnesses the temporary secession of the Arcadians and Achaeans as a separate army and Neon's disastrous decision at Calpe Harbor to lead out a sizeable body of troops on a foraging expedition despite unfavorable omens. More than five hundred men die as a result of Neon's private initiative (6.4.23–24), and the survivors are too ashamed to be left in camp with their general when the army marches out as a whole (6.4.4). The common soldiers, to be sure, repent after each disaster, and their reaction is to pass resolutions that threaten future instigators of either lawlessness (5.7.34) or secession (6.4.1) with death. Their subsequent deeds, however, never quite match their regrets.

In the final analysis, the problem of indiscipline is never solved. Despite Xenophon's repeated scolding and the army's resolutions to act better in future, the problem recurs during the last campaign narrated in the work, Xenophon's expedition to capture Asidates. Xenophon chooses those whom he wants to accompany him on the expedition, especially friends and supporters whom he wants to reward, but six hundred others force their own participation, even though the captains who have been selected by Xenophon try to drive them off (7.8.11). Hints of continued insubordination spill over into the *Hellenica* (3.2.6–7), when the Spartan authorities issue a stern warning to the Cyreans, who are now in Spartan service, not to do any harm to the Greek allies in Ionia. The *Anabasis* gives little reason to hope that Greeks from many different cities, who are fighting for private gain and are motivated by greed, will ever maintain a consistent obedience and discipline, even if an excellent (and patient) commander can rein them in temporarily.

Further Reading

My method of reading texts has been especially influenced by Iser (1978, 1989), Fish (1980), and Davis and Womack (2002). Davis and Womack, along with Levine (2007), attempt to bring together different schools of criticism. Gallagher and Greenblatt (2000) offer an interesting set of case studies in the school of literary theory called New Historicism (understanding a work through its historical context and its dynamic relationship with other cultural productions). For the *Anabasis* as a panhellenist political tract, see Körte (1922), Morr (1926–27), Robert (1950; who argues that Xenophon's purpose was to advertise himself as a suitable general for a panhellenic expedition), and Gauthier (1985). Dillery (1995: 41–62 and 2001: 24–31) offers a more nuanced reading of Xenophon's attitude to panhellenism. Rood (2004b) is a powerful rejoinder to the traditional view, arguing that Xenophon stresses the difficulty rather than the feasibility of a panhellenic expedition. On panhellenism as a political ideology, see Flower (2000a and 2000b) and Mitchell (2007). Mathieu (1925) is still an excellent treatment of the political views of Isocrates; the best short treatment of Isocrates is Cawkwell (1982). Higgins (1977) is especially good on Xenophon's treatment of Cyrus the Younger. On Xenophon's treatment of individuals generally, see Tuplin (2003) and Due (1989: 147–206). Hirsch (1985) stresses the themes of trust and deceit in the *Anabasis*, while Higgins (1977) believes that the major unifying theme is men's self-deception in life. The social and political organization of the Ten Thousand is the subject of a highly influential study by Nussbaum (1967), and his division of the *Anabasis* into four separate phases has been widely accepted (service under Cyrus; struggle for survival until the Ten Thousand reach the sea; march from Trapezus to Byzantium characterized by indiscipline and greed; the problem of reintegration into a Greek world dominated by Sparta). Dillery (1995) reads the *Anabasis* as the depiction of the evolution and decay of a model community of order and discipline. Ma (2004) believes that the *Anabasis* is not really a story about going home but rather about the difficulty or impossibility of return.

· δ ·

The Hand of God Artfully Placed

Xenophon was pious, fond of sacrificing, and competent to interpret the omens from sacrifice.
—*Diogenes Laertius,* Lives and Opinions of Eminent Philosophers *2.56*

A very distinguished scholar, G. L. Cawkwell, has written of
Xenophon's *Hellenica:* "The hand of God is an explanation
that dulls the quest for truth, but it is the explanation to which
Xenophon, so unlike Thucydides, readily had recourse" (1979: 45).
That is undeniably true on a superficial reading of Xenophon's
works. He generally does not provide the sort of explanations for
events that Thucydides does, which makes that historian so attractive to political theorists. But, as in the *Histories* of Herodotus, there
are different levels of motivation and explanation, levels that are
calculated to overlap and to enrich each other.

Whereas panhellenism has been the subject of much discussion,
the religious dimensions of the *Anabasis* have attracted less attention. This imbalance needs to be addressed since, as Paul Cartledge
has stated (2002: 184), "what is arguably the single most important
issue in all Classical Greek historiography is this: How did Herodotus, Thucydides, and Xenophon construct and construe the role of
religion in history? How far, that is, did they believe that it was the
gods (or god or the divine) who 'made the difference,' who 'caused'
human events and processes to turn out a certain way in the sense
that, but for their supernatural intervention, they would have turned

out otherwise, or not happened at all?" Modern readers, who have been brought up in a different religious system or in none, may not readily perceive the way divine intervention, especially through the rites of divination, works as a unifying theme throughout the *Anabasis* and as a means of validating Xenophon's own decisions. The religious landscape of the narrative can seem as much a foreign country as the physical terrain through which the army passes. Yet one must come to terms with this religious landscape in order to fully appreciate Xenophon's narrative strategies. Indeed, the interplay between human decision-making and divine guidance has been crafted with a skill matched only by that of Herodotus.

In any text we must deal with the author's construction of his own religious mentality. Xenophon as author has very carefully and deliberately constructed the religious mentality of Xenophon the character. Characters in works of literature can have religious attitudes and beliefs that they may or may not share with the author who has created them. It is easy and tempting to assume a correspondence, but highly problematic to do so. Yet, in the case of Xenophon, it must be significant that all of his works express, in quite strong terms, the same set of religious ideas. Nonetheless, even if we assume a correspondence between the religious views of author and character (as does Diogenes Laertius in the epigraph to this chapter), that still leaves open the question whether those views are sincerely held or are specious. Outward displays of piety can simultaneously be both calculated and sincere, both a reflection of genuine religious belief and a means of manipulating others. Those "others" include both the text's internal and external audiences. I would judge both Xenophon the author's and Xenophon the character's religious beliefs about the nature of the gods' interventions in human affairs to be sincerely held. At the same time, the inclusion of religion as a theme in the story is also a potent device for persuading the audience to accept a particular version of Xenophon's motives and actions.

The actions of Xenophon are repeatedly justified by recourse to divination, the various means by which mortals try to obtain a sign from the gods that indicates their wishes or advice. Many different methods of divination appear in the *Anabasis*: the interpretation of the movements, behavior, and cries of birds (augury), the interpretation of dreams and of portents and, most frequently, the examination of the entrails of a sacrificed animal. In warfare, two types of sacrificial divination were of immense importance: one was the campground sacrifice (called *hiera*), and the other was the battle-line sacrifice (called *sphagia*). Performing *hiera* entailed examining the victim's entrails, especially the liver (the "victim" was usually a sheep), whereas performing *sphagia* consisted of slitting the victim's throat (often a young she-goat) while observing its movements and the flow of blood. As we have already seen, when Xenophon was deciding various issues (whether to discuss the founding of a colony, whether to accept supreme command of the army, whether to return home to Athens, whether to lead the army to Seuthes, and whether to remain with Seuthes or to stick with the Ten Thousand), he made these difficult and perplexing decisions by sacrificing a victim to the gods and then examining its entrails. The rites of divination were usually performed by a professional seer (*mantis* in Greek), and several named seers appear in the narrative (Silanus, Arexion, Eucleides, and Basias). Although Xenophon was not himself a seer, the character Xenophon claims that he sacrificed frequently and knew a great deal about how to interpret the results (5.6.29). We also see him deciding on the meaning of dreams (3.1.11; 4.3.8) and signs (the sneeze at 3.2.9) by himself.

It is obvious that divination looms large as an explanatory device in the *Anabasis*. It is obvious as well that the repeated assertions in Xenophon's speeches in book 3 that the gods will punish the Persians as oath-breakers and fight as allies of the Greeks are an appeal to a normative Greek belief as a means of encouraging despondent troops. It is less clear, however, to what extent the gods should be understood as actually causing events to turn out in a particular way. We can see divine agency at work in a few places, such as in the dream that rouses Xenophon to action after the arrest of the generals (3.1.11) and in the spontaneous house-fire that saves the Greeks when they are trying to escape from the Drilae (5.2.24). The most explicit acknowledgement of divine intervention occurs when

Xenophon rallies his men to aid the Arcadians who are surrounded by Thracians and on the point of annihilation. He tells them that now is the time either to die nobly or to accomplish the fairest of deeds by saving so many fellow Greeks, and adds: "Perhaps the god is guiding events in this way, wishing to humble those proud boasters, with their presumed superior wisdom, and to make us, who begin with the gods, more honored than they are" (6.3.18). People who begin with the gods are those who trust in divination rather than in their own mere human wisdom. Is this just a rhetorical statement to allay the fears of his troops, or does it represent how Xenophon himself thinks that history works?

It is fair to infer from many other passages in various of his works that this assertion indeed reflects Xenophon's own view of history, that the gods intervene, often in invisible ways, to punish transgressors and to reward the pious. In his *Agesilaus*, Xenophon lays great stress on making the gods one's allies through proper conduct (such as not breaking one's oaths, plundering temples, or using force on suppliants). This is essential because "the gods are capable of quickly making the great small and of easily preserving the small, even if they are in difficulties, whenever they wish to do so" (*Anabasis* 3.2.10). The belief that the gods can indeed become one's allies in battle finds a concrete example in the *Hellenica* (4.4.12), where Xenophon describes a Spartan victory over their Argive enemies: "The Lacedaemonians were not at a loss as to whom to kill. For at that time the god granted them an exploit of a sort that they would never even have prayed for. . . . How could one not believe this to be divine [*theion*]?"

The most explicit statement of divine intervention on a grand scale is Xenophon's explanation (*Hellenica* 5.4.1) for the catastrophic military defeat of the Spartans at the battle of Leuctra in 371 BC: it was because the gods had punished them as oath-breakers for their impious and illegal seizure of the acropolis of Thebes, called the Cadmeia, in 382. When the Spartans were trying to decide whether or not to order King Cleombrotus to attach Thebes in 371, a Spartan by the name of Prothous advised the Spartan assembly not to attack Thebes immediately and to have King Cleombrotus disband his army. Xenophon indicates that this was sound advice, but it was rejected (6.4.3): "When the assembly heard these things, they decided that he was speaking nonsense. For already, as it seems, the divinity [*to daemonion*] was leading them on." It is surely significant that the same verb (*agō*, to lead or guide) is used both here and in the passage quoted above from the *Anabasis* (6.3.18) concerning Xenophon's rescue of the Arcadians.

In the *Anabasis*, however, divine intervention in human affairs takes place not so much on the macro-level of the rise and fall of hegemonies as on the micro-level of individual decision-making. In ancient Greece (to judge from the whole range of evidence available to us), divination not only provided answers to perplexing and difficult questions but also facilitated decisive action in cases where someone might otherwise have been at a loss to act. When individuals were faced with alternative courses of action, divination allowed them to bypass indecision and proceed confidently with a specific plan. The situation is depicted in these terms when Xenophon cannot decide whether to accept the supreme command of the Ten Thousand (6.1.22–24; see also chapter 6):

> Since Xenophon was at a loss what to decide, it seemed best to him to consult the gods. He placed two victims next to himself and proceeded to sacrifice to Zeus the King, the very god who had been prescribed to him by the oracle at Delphi. He believed that the dream had come from this god, the dream that he had seen at the time when he began to take joint charge of the army. He also remembered that at the time when he was setting out from Ephesus for the purpose of being introduced to Cyrus, an eagle was screeching on his right. The eagle was sitting, however, and the seer who was escorting him said that although it was a great omen, one that did not pertain to a private individual and indeed signified glory, it nevertheless indicated distress. For other birds especially attack the eagle when it is sitting. However, he said, the omen did not portend making money; for it is rather while the eagle is flying that it gets its provisions. And

so, when Xenophon sacrificed, the god indicated to him very clearly neither to ask for the command nor, if they elected him, to accept it.

Here Xenophon combines four different divinatory experiences that took place at different times in order to justify his decision not to take the command that was being offered to him. This passage also serves to remind the reader how solicitous the gods have been in sending signs to Xenophon at critical moments. In this case his decision was a good one, since Cheirisophus got into so much trouble with the army that he held the supreme command for only a few days.

When the troops would not accede to Xenophon's arguments as to why he was not the best choice, he addressed them again (6.1.31):

> Well, soldiers, in order that you may understand the matter fully, I swear to you by all the gods and goddesses, that when I perceived your intention, I sacrificed to find out whether it would be better for you to entrust this command to me and whether it would be better for me to undertake it. And the gods gave me such signs in the sacrifices that even a private person could recognize that it is necessary for me to keep away from this supreme command.

This new argument apparently put an end to the debate; for the narrator next says, "And so indeed they chose Cheirisophus." The narrator depicts the evidence of the sacrifices as decisively settling the issue of the command in the eyes of the troops. From the standpoint of the average Greek hoplite, the evidence of divination was far more authoritative than so-called rational arguments, insofar as Xenophon had already explained at length why it was not a good idea for the command to be given to an Athenian in preference to a Lacedaemonian. After the troops gave the command to Cheirisophus, Xenophon's fears and the god's recommendation were immediately confirmed (6.1.32). Cheirisophus says to the assembled army that they had benefited Xenophon by not choosing him, since the deserter

Dexippus was currently slandering Xenophon to the Spartan admiral Anaxibius.

Xenophon was again faced with a critical personal decision near the end of the *Anabasis* (7.6.43–44), and this time, unlike in the previous example, both alternatives were fraught with danger. Xenophon must choose whether to remain in Thrace as the possessor of fortresses on the coast that the Thracian prince Seuthes has promised to give him or to accompany the remainder of the Ten Thousand as they undertake military service for Sparta. On the one hand, Seuthes has failed to keep any of his promises in the past and there is therefore no good reason to trust him now. On the other hand, Xenophon has heard rumors, both from Seuthes himself and from other sources, that the new Spartan commander, Thibron, intends to execute him as soon as he gets him in his power. Faced with two uncertain futures, both of them full of danger and impossible to evaluate by human reason and knowledge alone, Xenophon turns to the gods for assistance. Accordingly, he "took two victims and sacrificed to Zeus the King to find out whether it was better and preferable for him to remain with Seuthes on the conditions that Seuthes had proposed, or to depart with the army. The god directed him to depart."

The reader, of course, can never be sure to what extent Xenophon, the historical actor, really let divination settle his future for him. An especially challenging example concerns the generals collectively (5.5.1–4). The narrator tells us that the generals (and this must include Xenophon) desire to attack the fortresses of the Tibarenians, which are less strong than those of the people whose territory they had just passed through, in order to "get some profit for the army," even though the Tibarenians are offering them gifts of hospitality. Nonetheless, "after many victims had been sacrificed, all of the seers finally declared the opinion that the gods in no way permitted war." The generals, consequently, accept gifts of hospitality, and the army proceeds through the territory of the Tibarenians without plundering it. If there is some "rational" explanation for this reading of the victims, it is not at all obvious. Perhaps Xenophon is attempting to suggest to the reader that he and his troops were not the brigands that some made them out to be, because even when they did want to do something bad, the gods would not let them and they obeyed.

Indeed, the success of Xenophon, as well as that of his fellow Greeks, is represented as being in large measure due to piety. Xenophon emerges as an effective leader of men because he sees himself as being led by the gods. When the army splits into three, Xenophon sacrifices to Heracles, consulting him as to whether it is better for him to sail away or to continue with the soldiers who remain under his command, and the god indicates to him through the omens from sacrifice to continue on the expedition (6.2.15). It would have been sufficiently honorable for him to bail out at this point, since the disillusioned Cheirisophus had just told him that he could do "whatever he wanted." The god's reason for advising Xenophon to stay is not revealed immediately, as was also the case in the consultation about the supreme command. Rather, the reader eventually can infer that Xenophon's continued participation was necessary to save the Arcadian and Achaean contingents from total destruction at the hands of the Thracians. So the gods are not just looking out for Xenophon personally but are also concerned for the well-being of his fellow soldiers.

The most discussed and seemingly problematic incident in which divination plays a key role surrounds the events that take place at Calpe Harbor. In this famous episode, the narrator represents the Ten Thousand as being restricted to their camp at Calpe for three days without provisions and in great hardship because the omens are not favorable for marching out (6.4.12–5.21). This leads to a rather tense situation in which Xenophon is the target of the soldiers' frustrations and they even accuse him of bribing the seer Arexion to say that the sacrifices are unfavorable for departure (6.4.14–22).

Despite the fact that the gods are unwilling to give their permission for the army to leave camp, Neon, who has replaced Cheirisophus as general, leads out two thousand men on his own initiative. Five hundred of them are cut down by a cavalry force that, unbeknownst to the Greeks, has been sent by the Persian satrap Pharnabazus. Xenophon performs the *sphagia* (battle-line sacrifice) and goes to the rescue. On the following day, the fourth day of this incident, the Greeks fortify a base camp on the Calpe peninsula, and a boat arrives bringing food and sacrificial victims. Now that the Greeks have a secure position to which to retreat in case of a defeat, know that a substantial force sent by Pharnabazus was supporting the local people, and have received provisions, the victims prove favorable on the very first attempt: "Xenophon rose early in the morning and sacrificed with a view to marching out, and the sacrifices were favorable with the first victim. When the sacrifices were just about over, Arexion the seer saw an auspicious eagle and he directed Xenophon to lead the way" (6.5.2). Xenophon himself, later that day, encourages his men to join battle with the enemy by pointing out that all three types of omen are favorable (6.5.21): "The omens from sacrifice [*hiera*] are favorable, the bird omens are auspicious, and the *sphagia* are excellent. Let us go against the enemy."

In the *Anabasis* Xenophon, as author, does not permit any skepticism about divination as a system to enter into his narrative, since that would undercut divination's role in validating the decisions of Xenophon the character. As mentioned above, every life-altering personal decision Xenophon makes throughout the *Anabasis* has divine approval: that he become one of the generals, that he not accept the supreme command of the army, that he not abandon the army and return to Athens, that he lead the army to Seuthes rather than to the Chersonese, and that he not remain with Seuthes permanently. Even though divination is a means whereby the gods give advice, not orders, the constant referral of these important decisions to divine arbitration does tend to mitigate Xenophon's personal responsibility for the consequences of his choices.

It should come as no surprise, therefore, that the role of divination is particularly emphatic at the end of the *Anabasis*, where it again serves to validate the narrator's construction of Xenophon's character and actions, while also helping the work to achieve some semblance of closure. In the preceding narrative Xenophon has delivered two lengthy speeches, one to the assembled troops and another to the Thracian prince Seuthes, refuting the charge of his own soldiers that he had received money and gifts from Seuthes, while his own men had not been paid in full for their services (7.7.37–47; discussed in chapter 6). On the level of rhetoric, with their emphasis on arguments based on plausibility, these speeches have made a detailed, if overly long, case for Xenophon's innocence. In this scene, Xenophon proves his innocence on yet another level by providing a divine confirmation of his claims (7.8.1–6):

> From there they sailed across to Lampsacus, and Xenophon was met by Eucleides, a seer from Phlius, whose father, Cleagoras, had painted the inner walls in the Lyceum. He was delighted that Xenophon had returned safe, and he asked him how much gold he had. But Xenophon told him on oath that he would not have sufficient travel money for the journey home if he did not sell his horse and his personal belongings. Eucleides did not believe him. But when the people of Lampsacus sent gifts of hospitality to Xenophon and he was sacrificing to Apollo, he made Eucleides stand next to him. When Eucleides saw the *hiera* (omens/entrails), he said that he was persuaded that he did not have any money. "But I know," he said, "that even if money is ever about to come your way, some obstacle always appears—if nothing else, your own self." Xenophon agreed with this. Then Eucleides said, "Zeus Meilichios is an obstacle to you," and he asked him if he had already sacrificed to him, "just as at home," he continued, "I was accustomed to sacrifice for you and offer whole victims." Xenophon replied that he had not sacrificed to this god from the time when he had left home. And so Eucleides advised him to sacrifice just as he used to and he said that it would turn out for the better. On the next day, upon arriving at Ophrynium, Xenophon sacrificed and burnt whole pigs in the way that was customary for his family, and he obtained favorable omens. And on this day Bion and Nausicleides arrived in order to give money to the army and they were entertained by Xenophon. They retrieved and gave back to him the horse that he had sold in Lampsacus for

50 darics, suspecting that he had sold it because of poverty, since they heard that he took pleasure in the horse. And they were not willing to be reimbursed for its price.

Eucleides had not seen Xenophon since he had set out on Cyrus's expedition, some two years earlier in 401. The seer had assumed, it seems, that Xenophon would have made a great deal of money in the course of his adventure, and at first he was incredulous that Xenophon was now so destitute that he would have to sell his horse and personal possessions in order to afford the trip home to Athens. If a seer and a personal friend found it hard to believe that Xenophon did not make any money on the expedition, why on earth should we his readers believe him? The narrator deals with this problem by mapping the reader's incredulity onto Eucleides and then having Eucleides, through the sacrifices, come to believe Xenophon. Contemporary readers, however, are no longer participants in the system of religious belief and knowledge that would have given this passage a persuasive power, and so it is difficult for us to fully imagine or appreciate that power.

Since Xenophon assumes that his readers are familiar with Greek religious practices, he understandably leaves it unsaid that Zeus Melichios was Zeus in his capacity as the gracious and gentle recipient of propitiatory sacrifices. That Eucleides had correctly diagnosed the cause of Xenophon's troubles was verified the very next day when he was able to retrieve what must have been his most valuable and prized possession, the horse he had been forced to sell for the fantastic sum of 50 gold darics (about 1,300 Athenian drachmas, at a time when a drachma per day was a standard wage). When Eucleides comes to realize, on the basis of the sacrifices, that Xenophon actually is destitute, he then needs to discover a correspondence between the problem (Xenophon's poverty) and something unusual in Xenophon's social environment. When I wrote about this passage elsewhere (Flower 2008: 196–198), I concluded that the correspondence that Eucleides hit upon was not between his poverty and some aspect of the circumstances of Xenophon's recent employment, but between his poverty and a ritual fault, that is, his failure to sacrifice to Zeus Melichios. There is, however, more to it than that. When Eucleides says of Xenophon's failure to make money "that some obstacle always appears—if nothing else, your own self," the reference is vague. It includes the ritual fault; but is it not also a nod to Xenophon's penchant for putting the welfare of his men before his own? As Seuthes observed, Xenophon's major character flaw, and the one that always hurt him, was that he was "a friend to the soldiers" (7.6.4, and see chapter 6).

Given the emphasis throughout the entire *Anabasis* on Xenophon the character's piety and trust in the gods, it is certainly not surprising that the author Xenophon chose to end his work with a narrative that is framed by divination (7.8.8–23). While at Pergamum, Xenophon is informed by Hellas, the wife of the famous Persian sympathizer Gongylus of Eretria, that if he attacks by night with three hundred men he can capture a wealthy Persian named Asidates with his family and his possessions. "Xenophon sacrificed, and Basias, the Elean seer who was present, said that the omens were extremely favorable [*kallista*, excellent, rather than the usual *kala*, good] for him and that the man was easy to capture." Xenophon, accordingly, does not take the whole army with him on this venture but only his favored captains and others who have proved themselves trustworthy "in order that he might do them a good turn," and some six hundred others who insisted on participating. There is an explanatory gap in the narrative here, and it seems that the reader is supposed to assume that Xenophon, trusting in those excellent omens and in Hellas's advice, did not feel that a larger force was necessary.

Nonetheless, the assault on Asidates's fortified tower proves a dismal failure, and nearly half of Xenophon's nine hundred troops are wounded on the journey back when they are attacked by Persian-led reinforcements. It is implied (the narrator does not assert this explicitly) that the Greeks are only saved from this extremely dangerous situation by the timely intervention of the local Greek dynasts Gongylus (Hellas's son) and Procles. But on the very next day, seemingly undeterred, Xenophon again sacrificed, and then this time led out the entire army, and "happened upon" Asidates, who had abandoned his tower because he "knew that Xenophon had again sacrificed with a view to attacking him." Thus Xenophon and his army captured

Asidates himself, his wife, his children, his horses, and all his possessions. The narrative leaves it unclear whether this outcome was primarily due to good generalship or good luck. In any case, the account
comes to an end with these simple words: "And this is how the earlier
omens turned out," referring back to the initial sacrifice made by the
seer Basias. If that was Xenophon's idea of "easily captured," I wonder how many of his readers have been convinced that the end result
was worth the high number of casualties.

The *Anabasis* itself, moreover, neatly ends with a statement that
brings the narrative full circle to Xenophon's initial encounter with
the seer Eucleides. After the army had returned to Pergamum, we
are told: "There Xenophon greeted the god [Zeus Meilichios]. For
the Spartans, the captains, the other generals, and the soldiers cooperated so that he could take the pick of the plunder—horses, and oxen,
and the other things. Consequently, he was now capable even of
assisting someone else." So what would appear to a modern reader as
a dangerous and nearly fatal adventure that turned out successfully,
despite heavy casualties, was for Xenophon the validation of the pre-
dictions of two different seers, a justification for his decision to have
undertaken a risky mission with relatively few men and a confirmation that the gods, Zeus Melichios in this case, do indeed care for
those individuals who pay them reverence. It is striking, even disquieting, however, how divination is used both to structure the Asidates
episode and simultaneously to justify Xenophon's own actions. The
interjection that "the omens turned out in this way" excuses Xenophon's miscalculations as a commander while at the same time signi-
fying that all had turned out in accordance with the will of the
gods. Today's leaders may invoke religion in varying degrees but, for
the most part, cannot so easily use it to whitewash their mistakes.

Further Reading

On religion in Xenophon, see Dürrbach (1893), who accuses
Xenophon of manipulating religion in the *Anabasis* as part of his
self-defense; Anderson (1974: 34–40); Dillery (1995: 179–94); Bowden

(2004); and especially the sophisticated treatment of the *Anabasis* by Parker (2004). Zucker (1900) focuses on the role of divination in the *Anabasis*. Flower (2008) is a detailed investigation of the role of the seer in Greek society, and many of the passages that are discussed come from the *Anabasis*. Pritchett (1979) contains a highly detailed study of divination in warfare. A good general treatment of Greek divination is Johnston (2008).

Prominent Persons

The following are some of the most frequently mentioned individuals in this book. All dates are BC.

Agasias of Stymphalus in Arcadia: Captain in the Greek army who receives a highly favorable treatment in the *Anabasis*.

Agesilaus: king of Sparta c. 400–360. One of the most powerful and influential men of his time, and Xenophon's patron from 396. Xenophon served under him in Asia Minor in 396–395, returned with him to Greece in 394, and wrote a eulogy of him after his death at age eighty-four.

Anaxibius: Spartan admiral who expelled the Ten Thousand from Byzantium and attempted to coerce them into serving under Spartan command in the Chersonese (the Gallipoli peninsula). He later changed his mind and persuaded Xenophon to lead them back into Asia, which Xenophon was unable to do.

Ariaeus: Persian who was Cyrus's second-in-command. After Cyrus's death he at first remained loyal to the Ten Thousand but then joined Tissaphernes.

Aristarchus: Spartan governor of Byzantium as successor to Cleander. He treated the Ten Thousand harshly, selling some four hundred of them into slavery, and plotted against Xenophon.

Artaxerxes II: King of Persia, 405–358. He succeeded his father, Darius II, as king, defeated his younger brother Cyrus at Cunaxa in 401, and had the longest reign of any Achaemenid Persian monarch.

Asidates: Wealthy Persian with an estate near Pergamum in Asia Minor. The last episode in the *Anabasis* is the capture of Asidates, his family, and his possessions by forces commanded by Xenophon.

Cheirisophus: Spartan who had been officially sent to aid Cyrus in his attempt to depose his brother. After the arrest of the other generals by Tissaphernes, he commanded the van of the Greek army and cooperated closely with Xenophon, who commanded the rear guard.

Cleander: Spartan governor of Byzantium, succeeded by Aristarchus. After an initial misunderstanding at Calpe Harbor, he became Xenophon's guest-friend and well disposed toward the Ten Thousand.

Clearchus: Spartan exile and the most prominent of the mercenary generals serving under Cyrus. After the latter's death, he de facto took over command of the Ten Thousand but was outwitted by Tissaphernes, who arrested him and sent him to King Artaxerxes for execution.

Ctesias of Cnidus: Greek doctor who tended King Artaxerxes at the battle of Cunaxa. He resided at the Persian court and wrote a history of Persia in twenty-three books. Ctesias is cited by Xenophon in his narrative of Cunaxa, but his history no longer survives.

Cyreans: Name given to the remnant of the Ten Thousand, who were then serving under Spartan commanders, by Xenophon in his *Hellenica*.

Cyrus the Elder (Cyrus the Great): King of Persia, 559–530, and founder of the Persian Empire. He is the subject of Xenophon's longest and generically most innovative work, the *Cyropaedia* ("The Education of Cyrus").

Cyrus the Younger (c. 424–401): Charismatic Persian prince who hired the Ten Thousand in an attempt to overthrow his older brother, King Artaxerxes. His death at the battle of Cunaxa left the Greeks stranded in the vicinity of Babylon.

Dercylidas: Spartan commander sent in 399 to succeed Thibron in Asia Minor. He was himself replaced by King Agesilaus in 396.

Dexippus: Lacedaemonian officer who deserted the Ten Thousand at Trapezus on the Black Sea and then slandered Xenophon to various Spartan commanders.

Heracleides: Greek from the city of Maronea (on the Aegean coast of Thrace) who acted as the personal agent and advisor of Seuthes. He was on bad terms with Xenophon and tried to turn Seuthes against him.

Lacedaemonian(s): Term that includes both Spartans (full citizens with voting rights) and *perioeci* (free-born inhabitants of Laconia who lacked voting rights and did not pass through the traditional Spartan education: the word literally means "those who dwell nearby").

Menon of Thessaly: One of Cyrus's generals who was suspected of collusion with the Persians after Cyrus's death. Despite being on good terms with prominent Persians, he was arrested with the other generals by Tissaphernes and later executed. He is depicted unfavorably in the *Anabasis* and is given a highly vituperative obituary.

Neon of Asine in Laconia: Lacedaemonian who replaced Cheirisophus as a general after the latter's death. Frequently at odds with Xenophon, he wanted to enlist the Ten Thousand in Spartan service during winter 399 rather than with the Thracian prince Seuthes.

Pharnabazus: Persian satrap of northwestern Asia Minor. He sent a cavalry force to attack the Ten Thousand when they were at Calpe Harbor, and he entered into agreements with the Spartans Anaxibius and Aristarchus to keep the Ten Thousand out of Asia.

Proxenus of Boeotia: General serving under Cyrus, who invited his guest-friend Xenophon to join him in Asia Minor. After his arrest by Tissaphernes, Xenophon was elected general as his replacement.

Seuthes: Thracian prince who hired the Ten Thousand during the winter of 399 to help him regain his ancestral kingdom (see under "Thracians"). Despite the success of these operations, he defrauded them of their pay.

Silanus: Greek seer employed and highly paid by Cyrus. He clashed with Xenophon over the founding of a colony on the coast of the Black Sea, and soon thereafter deserted the Ten Thousand, taking with him an enormous sum of money he had been awarded by Cyrus.

Sophaenetus of Stymphalus in Arcadia: The oldest of the Greek generals. He may have been the author of another *Anabasis* that did not give Xenophon a prominent role.

Thibron: Spartan commander sent to make war on the Persian satrap Tissaphernes. He hired the remnant of the Ten Thousand in the spring of 399.

Thracians: Group of non-Greek tribes inhabiting areas in southeastern Europe. The Odrysians were the most powerful of these, and Seuthes's (probable) grandfather, Teres, had created an Odrysian kingdom in the early fifth century. Seuthes's father had ruled a small semiautonomous part of this kingdom before the local Thracian tribes expelled him.

Timasion of Dardanus in the Troad: General in the Greek army who at first opposed Xenophon's leadership, especially over the issue of founding a colony on the Black Sea, but came to value him when the Ten Thousand were serving under Seuthes in Thrace.

Tiribazus: Persian governor of Western Armenia. The Ten Thousand seized and plundered his camp after they learned that he was planning to ambush them.

Tissaphernes: Highly influential Persian satrap who was assigned the task of leading the Ten Thousand out of Asia after the death of Cyrus. He lured the Greek generals to a conference, where they were arrested. He then harassed the Ten Thousand until they made their escape into the mountains of the Carduchians.

Bibliography

Abbott, H. P. 2008. *The Cambridge Introduction to Narrative*. 2nd ed. Cambridge.

Anderson, J. K. 1970. *Military Theory and Practice in the Age of Xenophon*. Berkeley.

Anderson, J. K. 1974. *Xenophon*. London.

Azoulay, V. 2004. "Exchange as Entrapment: Mercenary Xenophon?" In Lane Fox 2004b. 289–304.

Badian, E. 1993. "Thucydides and the Outbreak of the Peloponnesian War." In *From Plataea to Potidaea: Studies in the History and Historiography of the Pentekontaetia*. Baltimore. 125–162.

Badian, E. 2004. "Xenophon the Athenian." In Tuplin 2004c. 33–53.

Bal, M. 1997. *Narratology: Introduction to the Theory of Narrative*. 2nd ed. Toronto.

Baragwanath, E. 2008. *Motivation and Narrative in Herodotus*. Oxford.

Barchiesi, A. 2001. "The Crossing." In S. J. Harrison, ed., *Texts, Ideas, and the Classics: Scholarship, Theory and Classical Literature*. Oxford. 142–163.

Bassett, S. R. 1999. "The Death of Cyrus the Younger." *Classical Quarterly* n.s. 49: 473–483.

Bassett, S. R. 2002. "Innocent Victims or Perjurers Betrayed? The Arrest of the Generals in Xenophon's *Anabasis*." *Classical Quarterly* n.s. 52: 447–461.

Batstone, W. W. 2009. "Postmodern Historiographical Theory and the Roman Historians." In A. Feldherr, ed., *The Cambridge Companion to the Roman Historians.* Cambridge. 24–40.

Batstone, W. W., and C. Damon. 2006. *Caesar's Civil War.* Oxford.

Bigwood, J. M. 1983. "The Ancient Accounts of the Battle of Cunaxa." *American Journal of Philology* 104: 340–357.

Bloch, M. 1998. *How We Think They Think: Anthropological Approaches to Cognition, Memory, and Literacy.* Boulder, Colo.

Booth, W. 1983. *The Rhetoric of Fiction.* 2nd ed. Chicago. Originally published 1961.

Bowden, H. 2004. "Xenophon and the Scientific Study of Religion." In Tuplin 2004c. 229–246.

Bradley, P. J. 2001. "Irony and the Narrator in Xenophon's *Anabasis.*" In E. Tylawsky and C. Weiss, eds., *Essays in Honor of Gordon Williams: Twenty-Five Years at Yale.* New Haven. 59–84. Reprinted in Gray 2010. 520–552.

Braun, T. 2004. "Xenophon's Dangerous Liaisons." In Lane Fox 2004b. 97–130.

Breitenbach, H. R. 1967. "Xenophon von Athen." *Real-Encyclopädie der Classischen Altertumswissenschaft* IX A2, cols. 1567–1928.

Briant, P. 2000. *From Cyrus to Alexander: A History of the Persian Empire.* Trans. P. T. Daniels. Winona Lake, IN.

Burrough, B. 2004. *Public Enemies: America's Greatest Crime Wave and the Birth of the FBI, 1933–34.* New York.

Calvino, I. 1999. "Xenophon's *Anabasis.*" In *Why Read the Classics?* London. 19–23.

Carlier, P. 1978. "L'idée de monarchie impériale dans la *Cyropédie* de Xénophon." *Ktèma* 3: 133–163. Translated as "The Idea of Imperial Monarchy in Xenophon's *Cyropaedia*" in Gray 2010. 327–366.

Cartledge, P. A. 1987. *Agesilaos and the Crisis of Sparta.* Baltimore.

Cartledge, P. A. 2002. *The Greeks: A Portrait of Self and Others.* 2nd ed. Oxford.

Cawkwell, G. L. 1972. "Introduction." In *Xenophon: The Persian Expedition.* Trans. R. Warner. Harmondsworth. 9–48.

Cawkwell, G. 1976. "Agesilaus and Sparta." *Classical Quarterly* n.s. 26: 62–84.

Cawkwell, G. L. 1979. "Introduction." In *Xenophon: A History of My Times.* Trans. R. Warner. Harmondsworth. 7–46.

Cawkwell, G. L. 1982. "Isocrates." In T. James Luce, ed., *Ancient Writers: Greece and Rome.* Vol. 1. New York. 313–329.

Cawkwell, G. 2004. "When, How, and Why did Xenophon Write the *Anabasis?*" In Lane Fox 2004b. 47–67.

Cawkwell, G. L. 2005. *The Greek Wars: The Failure of Persia.* Oxford.

Cawkwell, G. L. 2011. *Cyrene to Chaeronea: Selected Essays on Ancient Greek History.* Oxford.

Cohn, D. 1999. *The Distinction of Fiction.* Baltimore.

Conte, G. B. 1994. *Genres and Readers.* Baltimore.

Culler, J. 1997. *Literary Theory: A Very Short Introduction.* Oxford.

Curthoys, A., and J. Docker. 2005. *Is History Fiction?* Ann Arbor.

Dalby, A. 1992. "Greeks Abroad: Social Organisation and Food among the Ten Thousand." *Journal of Hellenic Studies* 112: 16–30.

Davis, T. F., and K. Womack, eds. 2002. *Formalist Criticism and Reader-Response Theory.* New York.

Delebecque, É. 1946–47. "Xénophon, Athènes et Lacédémone: Notes sur la composition de l'*Anabase.*" *Revue des études grecques* 59–60: 71–138.

Delebecque, É. 1957. *Essai sur la vie de Xénophon.* Paris.

Dillery, J. 1995. *Xenophon and the History of His Times.* London.

Dillery, J., ed. 2001. *Xenophon, Anabasis.* (Reprinted with corrections.) Cambridge, Mass.

Dolezel, L. 2010. *Possible Worlds of Fiction and History: The Postmodern Stage.* Baltimore.

Dover, K. J. 1997. *The Evolution of Greek Prose Style.* Oxford.

Due, B., 1989. *The Cyropaedia: Xenophon's Aims and Methods.* Aarhus.

Dürrbach, F. 1893. "L'apologie de Xénophon dans l'*Anabase.*" *Revue des études grecques* 6: 343–386.

Eagleton, T. 1996. *Literary Theory: An Introduction.* 2nd ed. Minneapolis.

Evans, R. J. 1997. *In Defense of History.* New York.

Erbse, H. 1966. "Xenophons *Anabasis.*" *Gymnasium* 73: 485–505. Translated as "Xenophon's *Anabasis*" in Gray 2010. 476–501.

Fish, S. 1980. *Is There a Text in This Class? The Authority of Interpretive Communities.* Cambridge, Mass.

Flower, H. I. 1992. "Thucydides and the Pylos Debate (4.27-29)." *Historia* 41: 40-57.

Flower, M. A. 1994. *Theopompus of Chios. History and Rhetoric in the Fourth Century BC.* Oxford.

Flower, M. A. 2000a. "From Simonides to Isocrates: The Fifth-Century Origins of Fourth-Century Panhellenism." *Classical Antiquity* 19: 65–101.

Flower, M. A. 2000b. "Alexander the Great and Panhellenism." In A. B. Bosworth and E. Baynham, eds., *Alexander the Great in Fact and Fiction.* Oxford. 96–135.

Flower, M. A. 2008. *The Seer in Ancient Greece.* Berkeley.

Gallagher, C., and S. Greenblatt, eds. 2000. *Practicing New Historicism.* Chicago.

Gauthier, P. 1985. "Xénophon et l'odyssée des 'Dix-Mille.'" *L'Histoire* 79: 16–25.

Gautier, L. 1911. *La langue de Xénophon.* Geneva.

Genette, G. 1980. *Narrative Discourse.* Ithaca and London.

Genette, G. 1988. *Narrative Discourse Revisited.* Ithaca and London.

Gera, D. L. 1993. *Xenophon's Cyropaedia: Style, Genre, and Literary Technique.* Oxford.

Gordon, E. F. 2010. *Book of Days: Personal Essays.* New York.

Gray, V. 1989. *The Character of Xenophon's Hellenica.* Baltimore.

Gray, V. 1998. *The Framing of Socrates: Xenophon's Memorabilia and Its Literary Form.* Hermes Einzelschriften, Heft 79. Stuttgart.

Gray, V. 2003. "Interventions and Citations in Xenophon's *Hellenica* and *Anabasis.*" *Classical Quarterly* n.s. 53: 111–123. Reprinted in Gray 2010. 553–572.

Gray, V. 2004. "Xenophon." In Irene de Jong, R. Nünlist, and A. Bowie, eds., *Narrators, Narratees, and Narratives in Ancient Greek Literature: Studies in Ancient Greek Narrative.* Leiden. 129–146.

Gray, V., ed. 2010. *Xenophon.* Oxford Readings in Classical Studies. Oxford.

Grayson, C. H. 1975. "Did Xenophon Intend to Write History?" In B. Levick, ed., *The Ancient Historian and His Materials.* Farnborough, Hants. 31–43.

Green, P. 1994. "Text and Context in the Matter of Xenophon's Exile." In I. Worthington, ed., *Ventures Into Greek History.* Oxford. 215–227.

Herman, D. 2007. *The Cambridge Companion to Narrative.* Cambridge.

Herman, G. 1987. *Ritualised Friendship and the Greek City.* Cambridge.

Higgins, W. E. 1977. *Xenophon the Athenian: The Problem of the Individual and the Society of the Polis.* Albany, N.Y.

Hirsch, S. W. 1985. *The Friendship of the Barbarians: Xenophon and the Persian Empire.* Hanover.

Hölkeskamp, K.-J. 2006. "History and Collective Memory in the Middle Republic." In N. Rosenstein and R. Morstein-Marx, eds., *A Companion to the Roman Republic.* Malden, Mass., and Oxford. 478–495.

Horn, R. C. 1935. "The Last Three Books of Xenophon's *Anabasis.*" *Classical Weekly* 28: 156–159.

Hude, C., ed. 1972 (corrected by J. Peters). *Xenophon, Expeditio Cyri.* Teubner text. Leipzig.

Hutchinson, G. 2000. *Xenophon and the Art of Command.* London.

Iser, W. 1978. *The Act of Reading: A Theory of Aesthetic Response.* London.

Iser, W. 1989. *Prospecting: From Reader Response to Literary Anthropology.* Baltimore.

Jacoby, F., et al. 1923–58, 1994–. *Die Fragmente der griechischen Historiker (FGrH).* Berlin and Leiden.

Johnston, S. I. 2008. *Ancient Greek Divination.* Malden, Mass.

Kingsbury, A. 1956. "The Dramatic Techniques of Xenophon's *Anabasis.*" *Classical Weekly* 49: 161–164.

Körte, A. 1922. "Die Tendenz von Xenophons *Anabasis.*" *Neue Jahrbücher für Pädagogik* 25: 15–24.

Krentz, P., ed. 1994. *Xenophon: Hellenika II.3.11–IV.2.8.* Warminster.

LaForse, B. 2005. "Xenophon's *Anabasis*: The First War Memoir." *Syllecta Classica* 16: 1–30.

Lane Fox, R. 2004a. "Introduction." In Lane Fox 2004b. 1–46.

Lane Fox, R., ed. 2004b. *The Long March. Xenophon and the Ten Thousand.* New Haven.

Lee, J. 2004. "For There Were Many *Hetairai* in the Army: Women in Xenophon's *Anabasis.*" *Ancient World* 35: 145–165.

Lee, J. 2005. "Xenophon and the Origins of Military Autobiography." In A. Vernon, ed., *Arms and the Self: War, the Military, and Autobiographical Discourse.* Kent, Ohio. 141–160.

Lee, J. 2007. *A Greek Army on the March: Soldiers and Survival in Xenophon's Anabasis.* Cambridge.

Lendle, O. 1995. *Kommentar zu Xenophons Anabasis.* Darmstadt.

Lendon, J. E. 2009. "Historians without History: Against Roman Historiography." In A. Feldherr, ed., *The Cambridge Companion to the Roman Historians.* Cambridge. 41–62.

Lenfant, D., ed. 2004. *Ctésias de Cnide. La Perse. L'Inde. Autres fragments.* Paris.

Levine, C. 2007. "Strategic Formalism: Toward a New Method in Cultural Studies." *Victorian Studies* 48: 625–657.

Llewellyn-Jones, L., and J. Robson. 2010. *Ctesias' History of Persia: Tales of the Orient.* London.

Lossau, M. 1990. "Xenophons Odyssee." *Antike und Abendland* 36: 47–52.

Ma, J. 2004. "You Can't Go Home Again: Displacement and Identity in Xenophon's *Anabasis.*" In Lane Fox 2004b. 330–345.

MacLaren, M. 1934. "Xenophon and Themistogenes." *Transactions and Proceedings of the American Philological Association* 65: 240–247.

Marchant, E. C., ed. 1904. *Xenophontis, Expeditio Cyri.* Oxford.

Marincola, J. 1997. *Authority and Tradition in Ancient Historiography.* Cambridge.

Marincola, J. 1999. "Genre, Convention and Innovation in Greco-Roman Historiography." In C. S. Kraus, ed., *The Limits of Historiography: Genre and Narrative in Ancient Historical Texts.* Leiden. 281–324.

Marincola, J. 2001. *Greek Historians.* New Surveys in the Classics 31. Oxford.

Marincola, J. 2005. "Concluding Narratives: Looking to the End in Classical Historiography." *Papers of the Langford Latin Seminar* 12: 285–320.

Marincola, J. 2007. "Speeches in Classical Historiography." In Marincola, ed., *A Companion to Greek and Roman Historiography.* Vol. 1. Oxford and Malden, Mass. 118–132.

Marsh, B. 2009 (22 August). "Faked Photographs: Look, and Then Look Again." *New York Times.*

Mathieu, G. 1925. *Les idées politiques d'Isocrate.* Paris.

Meyers, J. 1977. "Xenophon and *Seven Pillars of Wisdom.*" *Classical Journal:* 72 142–143.

Mink, L. O. 1987. *Historical Understanding.* Ithaca.

Mitchell, L. G. 2007. *Panhellenism and the Barbarian in Archaic and Classical Greece.* Swansea.

Morr, J. 1926/27. "Xenophon und der Gedanke eines allgriechischen Eroberungszuges gegen Persien." *Wiener Studien* 45: 186–201.

Most, G. 1989. "The Stranger's Stratagem: Self-Disclosure and Self-Sufficiency in Greek Culture." *Journal of Hellenic Studies* 109: 114–133.

Nadon, C. 2001. *Xenophon's Prince: Republic and Empire in the Cyropaedia.* Berkeley.

Nall, G. H. 1903. *Xenophon's Anabasis Book 7.* Macmillan.

Nussbaum, G. B. 1967. *The Ten Thousand: A Study in Social Organization and Action in Xenophon's Anabasis.* Leiden.

Parker, R. 2004. "One Man's Piety: The Religious Dimension of the *Anabasis.*" In Lane Fox 2004b. 131–153.

Pelling, C. 2007. "Ion's Epidemiai and Plutarch's Ion." In V. Jennings and A. Katsaros, eds., *The World of Ion of Chios.* Leiden. 75–109.

Pernot, L. 1998. "Problèmes et méthodes de l'éloge de soi-même dans la tradition éthique et rhétorique gréco-romaine." *Revue des études grecques* 111: 101–124.

Pownall, F. 2004. *Lessons from the Past: The Moral Use of History in Fourth-Century Prose.* Ann Arbor.

Pritchett, W. K. 1979. *The Greek State at War.* Vol. 3. Berkeley.

Purves, A. C. 2010. *Space and Time in Ancient Greek Narrative.* Cambridge.

Rijksbaron, A. 2002. "The Xenophon Factory: One Hundred and Fifty Years of School Editions of Xenophon's *Anabasis.*" In R. K. Gibson and C. S. Kraus, eds., *The Classical Commentary: Histories, Practices, Theory.* Mnemosyne Supplement 232. Leiden. 235–267.

Robert, F. 1950. "Les intentions de Xénophon dans l'*Anabase.*" *L'Information littéraire* 2: 55–59.

Roberts, D. H., F. M. Dunn, and D. Fowler, eds. 1997. *Classical Closure: Reading the End in Greek and Latin Literature.* Princeton.

Rood, T. 2004a. *The Sea! The Sea! The Shout of the Ten Thousand in the Modern Imagination.* London.

Rood, T. 2004b. "Panhellenism and Self-Presentation: Xenophon's Speeches." In Lane Fox 2004b. 305–329.

Rood, T. 2006. "Advice and Advisers in Xenophon's *Anabasis.*" In D. Spencer and E. Theodorakopoulos, eds., *Advice and Its Rhetoric in Greece and Rome.* Bari. 47–61.

Rood, T. 2010a. "Xenophon's Parasangs." *Journal of Hellenic Studies* 130: 51–66.

Rood, T. 2010b. *American Anabasis: Xenophon and the Idea of America from the Mexican War to Iraq.* London.

Roy, J. 1967. "The Mercenaries of Cyrus." *Historia* 16: 292–323.

Roy, J. 1968a. "Xenophon's *Anabasis:* The Command of the Rearguard in Books 3 and 4." *Phoenix* 22: 158–159.

Roy, J. 1968b. "Xenophon's Evidence for the *Anabasis.*" *Athenaeum* 46: 37–46.

Roy, J. 2004. "The Ambitions of a Mercenary." In Lane Fox 2004b. 264–288.

Schwartz, E. 1889. "Quellenuntersuchungen zur griechischen Geschichte." *Rheinisches Museum* 44: 104–126, 161–193.

Stadter, P. A. 1991. "Fictional Narrative in the *Cyropaideia.*" *American Journal of Philology* 112: 461–491. Reprinted in Gray 2010. 367–400.

Stronk, J. P. 1995. *The Ten Thousand in Thrace: An Archaeological and Historical Commentary on Xenophon's Anabasis, Books VI, iii–vi–VIII.* Amsterdam.

Stylianou, P. J. 2004. "One *Anabasis* or Two?" In Lane Fox 2004b. 68–96.

Tatum, J. 1989. *Xenophon's Imperial Fiction.* Princeton.

Todorov, T. 1990. *Genres in Discourse.* Cambridge.

Trevelyan, G. O. 1876. *The Life and Letters of Lord Macaulay*. Vol. 1. London.

Tsagalis, C. C. 2009. "Names and Narrative Techniques in Xenophon's *Anabasis*." In J. Grethlein and A. Rengakos, eds., *Narratology and Interpretation: The Content of Narrative Form in Ancient Literature*. Berlin. 451–480.

Tucker, A. 2004. *Our Knowledge of the Past: A Philosophy of Historiography*. Cambridge.

Tuplin, C. J. 1993. *The Failings of Empire: A Reading of Xenophon Hellenica 2.3.11–7.5.27*. Historia Einzelschriften 76. Stuttgart.

Tuplin, C. J. 2003. "Heroes in Xenophon's *Anabasis*." In A. Barzanò, C. Bearzot, F. Landucci, L. Prandi, and G. Zecchini, eds., *Modelli eroici dall'antichità alla cultura europea*. Vol. 4. Rome. 115–156.

Tuplin, C. J. 2004a. "Doctoring the Persians: Ctesias of Cnidus, Physician and Historian." *Klio* 86: 305–347.

Tuplin, C. J. 2004b. "Xenophon, Artemis and Scillus." In T. J. Figueira, ed., *Spartan Society*. Swansea. 251–282.

Tuplin, C. J., ed. 2004c. *Xenophon and His World*. Historia Einzelschriften 172. Stuttgart.

Walbank, F. W. 1965. "Speeches in Greek Historians." Third J. L. Myres Memorial Lecture. Oxford. Reprinted in Walbank 1985. 242–261.

Walbank, F. W. 1985. *Selected Papers: Studies in Greek and Roman History and Historiography*. Cambridge.

Walker, A. D. 1993. "*Enargeia* and the Spectator in Greek Historiography." *Transactions of the American Philological Association* 123: 353–377.

Waterfield, R., ed. 2005. *Xenophon: The Expedition of Cyrus*. Oxford.

Waterfield, R. 2006. *Xenophon's Retreat: Greece, Persia and the End of the Golden Age*. Cambridge, Mass.

Westlake, H. D. 1987. "Diodorus and the Expedition of Cyrus." *Phoenix* 41: 241–255.

White, H. 1973. *Metahistory: The Historical Imagination in Nineteenth-Century Europe*. Baltimore.

White, H. 1978. *Tropics of Discourse: Essays in Cultural Criticism*. Baltimore.

White, H. 1987. *The Content of the Form: Narrative Discourse and Historical Representation*. Baltimore.

Zucker, A. 1900. *Xenophon und die Opfermantik in der Anabasis*. Nuremberg.

Index of Passages Cited

Index

Index | 239